THE AMERICAN EXPLORATION AND TRAVEL SERIES
(For a complete list, see page 234)

DOWN THE COLORADO

DOWN THE

ROBERT BREWSTER STANTON

COLORADO

EDITED AND WITH AN INTRO-
DUCTION BY DWIGHT L. SMITH

NORMAN   UNIVERSITY OF OKLAHOMA PRESS

LIBRARY OF CONGRESS CATALOG CARD NUMBER: 65–10109

COPYRIGHT 1965 BY THE UNIVERSITY OF OKLAHOMA PRESS,
PUBLISHING DIVISION OF THE UNIVERSITY.
COMPOSED AND PRINTED AT NORMAN, OKLAHOMA, U.S.A.
BY THE UNIVERSITY OF OKLAHOMA PRESS. FIRST EDITION.

FOR ANNE STANTON BURCHARD

ROBERT BREWSTER STANTON was reluctant to publicize his own Colorado River exploits unless it could be done in what he regarded the proper context. He believed his story should be presented as a part of the over-all history of the discovery and exploration of the river. Since such a work had not been written, he set about a self-assigned task of producing one.

He maintained in his preface that "of no other portion of our country—I may almost say of the world—is there so little accurately known, except by the few, as of this mysterious far Southwest and of the Great River which flows through it." His meticulous research resulted in an ably written 1,038 folio pages in two volumes. This manuscript contained his own account of his 1889–90 exploration survey of the Colorado River. Since his history of the river was never published, the story of his expedition has not been publicized much beyond contemporary newspapers and a report or so in professional engineering journals.

Because of the sustained interest of his family, especially of his daughter, Anne Stanton Burchard, the great bulk of Stanton's papers which survived a fire several years ago are now deposited (restricted) in the New York Public Library and the Miami University Library in Oxford, Ohio. Fortunately they include most of the Colorado River manuscripts and the sketches, snapshots, and official photographs which illustrate this volume.

It would not have been possible for me to have prepared Stanton's narrative account for publication without the interest and help of a number of individuals and institutions. Specifically, John D. Millett, formerly president, and Harris G. Warren, chairman, Department of History, Miami University, directed my attention to the Stanton manuscripts, and a grant from Miami University enabled me to conduct the research. The staffs of the New York Public Library, especially Robert W. Hill, keeper of manuscripts; the Engineering Societies Library of New York City, especially Ralph H. Phelps, director; the Lilly Library, Indiana University, especially Geneva Warner, curator of special collections; the Miami University Library, especially Leland S. Dutton, director of libraries; the Indiana University Library, especially E. Lingle Craig, reference librarian; and the Purdue University Library, especially Keith Dowden, head, Reference Services, freely made the manuscript holdings and collateral materials available to me. C. Gregory Crampton, professor of history, University of Utah, knowledgeable in Colorado River history and a collaborator with me on past studies in this field, gave me sage advice on the special methodological requirements of such an endeavor. The University of Oklahoma Press early recognized the merit of the Stanton account and made possible the publication of my efforts.

Throughout the whole project it has been my special privilege to work closely with Anne Stanton Burchard. It was she who called the attention of Miami University—her father's Alma Mater, of which her grandfather had been president—to the Stanton manuscripts; and she has been a constant source of firsthand information and inspiration.

Miss Patricia A. Ruhlman of Oxford, Ohio, prepared the original typed draft of my manuscript, and Mrs. Reba J. Smith of Bloomington, Indiana, typed the final draft. Both made constructive suggestions that measurably improved its appearance.

Finally, my wife, Jane D. Smith, spent countless hours collating and proofreading successive drafts and performed many other chores necessary for such a project.

Dwight L. Smith

Bloomington, Indiana
January 4, 1965

THE Spaniards became aware of the Colorado River country about half a century after the first landfall by Columbus. As early as 1539, Francisco de Ulloa was in the estuary waters of the river in the upper reaches of the Gulf of California. Within the next year Hernando de Alarcón navigated the lower river and Melchior Díaz followed a part of the same course. Also in 1540, García de Cárdenas, leading a detachment of Coronado's men, discovered the Grand Canyon.

Although there was some activity along the lower river and perhaps farther up, the next event of consequence in Colorado River history did not occur until 1776. In that year Francisco Domínguez and Francisco de Escalante led a trail-blazing expedition from Santa Fe westward. Crossing the Colorado River near present Una, Colorado, and the Green River near present Jensen, Utah, and moving westward to the Utah Lake area, they turned southward to reach the approximate latitude of Monterey, California, which they hoped to follow westward. Near present Cedar City, Utah, the lateness of the season forced them to head again for Santa Fe. The terrain of the country over which they moved eastward almost proved to be their undoing; but they eventually forded the Colorado at what is now known as the Crossing of the Fathers.

Not until the coming of the mountain men and fur trappers into the Colorado River basin about half a century later was any earnest effort made to explore the river system. And then, of course, it was in search of beaver and other furs. William H.

Ashley was prominent among these men. In 1825 he embarked on the Green River near the mouth of Big Sandy Creek in present southwestern Wyoming and traveled to a point some fifty miles beyond the mouth of the Duchesne River in present eastern Utah. Indians informed him that the river went on endlessly southward through mountain country.

Scattered hints in the records of the fur trade indicate that some activity continued on the river, but it is not possible to determine its extent. A few carved inscriptions on the canyon walls in southern Utah reveal that Denis Julien, a French-Canadian trapper and trader out of St. Louis, was there in 1836. River-running was not extensive or of any consequence before 1869, however, because through hard experience even the toughest and most rugged men learned to respect the canyon country. Although there was some government-sponsored activity in the 1850's, such as that of Joseph C. Ives in 1857–58, it added little to the general knowledge of the river.

It remained for John Wesley Powell to make the first important and substantial exploration of the Colorado River and to present his findings to the world. His memorable expeditions in 1869 from Green River Station in Wyoming Territory to the mouth of the Río Virgin in the present Lake Mead area of Nevada, and again in 1871–72 from the same point of departure to Kanab Wash in the lower part of the Grand Canyon, have become widely known through the publication of the personal accounts of the men who participated in the ventures and a number of books on the subject.

After Powell, other parties traversed considerable portions of the river. These are generally well known. Each year thousands of visitors to the South Rim of the Grand Canyon National Park attend Emory C. Kolb's lectures and movies and review much river history at his studio. What is not well known, however, is the story of the second great exploration of the Colorado River, by Robert Brewster Stanton in 1889–90. Although his exploration is equally well documented, circumstances have kept other than the barest outline of his exploits from the public notice they deserve. What little has been published is not readily accessible. But the story is as vivid and as exciting as that of any other exploration of the West. Its setting, interestingly enough, is a part of the railroad phase of the development of the trans-Mississippi frontier.

In 1889, chance brought a prospector and a real estate speculator together. While prospecting in northern Arizona and observing surveys of a transcontinental railway line pushing westward, S. S. Harper envisioned a railroad that would follow the Colorado River. His vaguely defined idea struck the fancy of Frank M. Brown, a prominent Denver businessman who was looking for a project for investment purposes. Powell's much-publicized expedition had caused others to conjecture about the possibilities of such a fantastic scheme, but it took the Harper-Brown combination to attempt to translate the dream into action. It seemed to these men and others that a water-level railroad along the river to the Gulf of California and on to the Pacific Coast at San Diego would be a good business venture. In the rapidly developing coast cities of California, coal was a much-needed commodity, but it was rather expensive because it had to be imported from other countries. Since coal was abundant in southwestern Colorado, why could it not be shipped by a Colorado River railway to California cheaper than it could be imported? Nor was it difficult to imagine other uses of the line —business that would accrue from mining, lumbering, cattle, irrigation, and tourist activities.

Was it feasible from an engineering standpoint? Could such a road be constructed? While, of course, there were skeptics and scoffers, some men whose opinions in such matters were valued believed it to be possible. But it needed to be proved. This called for an engineering survey. As an act of faith, or with a gambler's daring for the spectacular, Brown and several other men pledged money to defray the expenses of a survey. On March 25, 1889, a formal organization was effected for the Denver, Colorado

Canyon and Pacific Railroad. Frank M. Brown was elected president; H. B. Chamberlin, vice-president; John Hurlbert, second vice-president; J. C. Montgomery, treasurer; and E. A. Reynolds, secretary.

While still a student at Miami University, at Oxford, Ohio, Robert Brewster Stanton had read accounts of Powell's exploits on the Colorado River. He envisioned the Grand Canyon area as a vast plateau region of solid rock, cut through by a half-mile chasm whose walls were virtually vertical and whose depth was about a mile and a quarter. What a feat of engineering it would be to construct "a single-span railway bridge across that chasm"! Dreamer and scheme came together when on May 13, 1889, Stanton was appointed chief engineer for the Denver, Colorado Canyon and Pacific Railroad survey.

Robert Brewster Stanton (1846–1922), was born in Woodville, Mississippi. He was the son of a prominent Presbyterian minister who during Robert's childhood served churches in New Orleans and Chillicothe, Ohio, was president of Oakland College in Mississippi, and a professor at Danville Theological Seminary in Kentucky, and in 1866 became president of Miami University at Oxford, Ohio. Young Stanton took advantage of this opportunity to enroll in the university, being graduated in 1871 with a classical education. During a summer vacation when he worked with a railroad surveying party in Ohio, Stanton decided to become a civil engineer. Accordingly, he made the most of mathematics within the framework of his formal education and on the side picked up some practical experience in surveying. Finances did not permit him to continue with graduate work in mathematics and engineering as he had hoped.

Stanton's first employment came in 1871 as a levelman with a preliminary survey for the Atlantic and Pacific Railroad pushing westward through Indian Territory. During the next several years he gained surveying and construction experience on railway lines in Ohio, Kentucky, and Tennessee. His varied experiences gained him a reputation as a capable engineer. On leave of absence from his duties with the Kentucky Central in 1877, he assisted in a horseback reconnaissance for the Atlantic and Pacific in Indian Territory and Texas.

As a division engineer for the Union Pacific, 1880–84, Stanton built the famous Devil's Gate Viaduct, or Georgetown Loop, as it was more generally known, between Georgetown and Silver Plume in Colorado. Quitting the Union Pacific, he went into private practice as a consulting civil and mining engineer. Although not as extensively experienced in mining as in railroad engineering, he had done some mining work from time to time and was soon to gain creditable competence in that field also. He served, for example, as general manager of an Idaho Territory mine for two years. With this accumulated valuable experience and background, his next considerable venture was as chief engineer of the Denver, Colorado Canyon and Pacific Railroad survey. Before the survey was completed, circumstances thrust him into the position of leader of the expedition, and he became an explorer in his own right. His subsequent career took him to many parts of the world in civil and mining engineering work and to all parts of the United States as a lecturer. He regarded his western experiences, especially those on the Colorado River, as the highlights of his colorful life.

As chief engineer for the Denver, Colorado Canyon and Pacific Railroad survey of the Colorado River, Stanton was to determine the engineering feasibility (and incidentally to estimate the use-potential) of a railroad along its course. If the results of the survey were favorable, the company hoped to attract construction capital for the railroad. Although Powell had explored the river twenty years earlier, this survey was in a very real sense an exploration venture itself.

The actual survey began on March 28, 1889, at Grand Junction, Colorado, under the supervision of Frank C. Kendrick. While President Brown traveled to the East to make further arrangements, Kendrick ran the survey down the Grand River, the designation then given to the Colorado River to its junction

with the Green River in Utah Territory. This was history-
making in itself because the Kendrick party was the first to
navigate the canyons of the Grand River for any distance.

The main survey party under the direct supervision of President Brown, with Stanton as chief engineer, traveled by rail to
Green River Station in Utah Territory, where the Denver and
Rio Grande Railroad crossed the Green River. The party of
sixteen, with all its provisions and supplies loaded on six boats,
embarked on May 25, 1889, and traveled down the Green to
the junction of the Grand, the terminal point of Kendrick's
survey.

The accident-plagued expedition, although badly crippled by
loss of supplies and damaged boats, obtained relief supplies and
doggedly pushed on through the Cataract Canyon area, the
stretch of river known as Narrow Canyon, and then the Glen
Canyon portion. The party left Lees Ferry and plunged into the
Marble Canyon in northern Arizona Territory. Disaster lurked
in these rough waters. President Brown was drowned when his
boat upset. After two more men lost their lives in an accident,
the party decided to quit the river and return later more adequately prepared. Supplies and instruments were cached in a
cave, and the men climbed out of the gorge to return to Denver.

The company was reorganized, Stanton being elected to the
board of directors and charged with the responsibilities of raising more funds and of completing the survey. Although sufficient
money had not yet been secured, Stanton resumed the survey
because the season was getting late. With new supplies and better
equipment the twelve-man party, including only three members
of the previous expedition, re-entered the Colorado River in
early December, 1889, near the head of Glen Canyon. Christmas
was celebrated at Lees Ferry, and three days later the Stanton expedition plunged into the treacherous waters of Marble Canyon.

The photographer broke his leg and had to be carried out.
Another man left the party in the Grand Canyon. When a boat
was splintered beyond repair in a rapid in the Grand Canyon,

it was necessary to reduce the party by three more men. Without further mishap Stanton, with the remaining six men and a new cook, successfully completed the survey on April 26, 1890, when the group reached tidewater on the Gulf of California. Later Stanton made "field examinations" for a Yuma to San Diego route.

After the completion of the 1889–90 Brown-Stanton Colorado River expedition, Stanton was asked by a publishing house to write his experiences; but he did not immediately attempt anything more ambitious than an occasional newspaper letter and a few articles in popular magazines and professional journals.

In 1906, however, in his spare time he began to put his story together from the rather extensive records which he had kept while on the expedition. His firsthand knowledge of the river had in the meantime been increased by his placer gold-mining venture in the Glen Canyon area in the years at the turn of the century and by occasional visits after that time.

Because of the misinformation and misconceptions current about the Colorado River, Stanton became intrigued with the idea of correcting erroneous impressions and of compiling information to write a history of the river. He diligently perused every document and account he could find and assembled a considerable collection of material which enabled him to preface his own story with several hundred pages of narrative concerning those involved in river history before him.

By 1909 this project was nearly completed. Others had made attempts to run the river since his 1889–90 venture, and he decided to add their stories to his already voluminous account in order to bring his history of the river up to date.

Stanton's manuscript too far exceeded the normal size of an ordinary book to tempt any publisher seriously. His knowledge of the river increased, his acquaintance with river men widened and became more intimate, and he continued to add to his prodigious account by revisions and various appendices. Indeed, he became one of the foremost authorities on the history of the Colorado River.

The final and only extant complete revision of his manuscript is dated March, 1920, about two years before his death. Even this manuscript bears ample evidence of much painstaking revision and polishing. Stanton titled his 1,038 folio page manuscript:

THE RIVER AND THE CANYON
The Colorado River of the West,
and the
Exploration, Navigation, and Survey of its Canyons,
From the Standpoint of an Engineer.

It is unfortunate that "The River and the Canyon" was not published in its entirety when Stanton completed it. It would have become the standard treatise in the field, for it contains much on the history, the science, and the romance of an intriguing subject. Most of the history of the river has since been investigated, written, and published by others. Scientific data and observations are now much more complete. The published accounts of subsequent river runners are readily available.

With the exception of an occasional brief mention of his expedition, in which he is usually regarded as an "also ran" in the shadow of John Wesley Powell, the details of Stanton's accomplishments have up to now remained buried in his own records. With the publication of this volume, Stanton can assume his rightful place among the leading historians of the river and achieve well-deserved recognition as an explorer and chronicler of the Colorado River.

The first eleven chapters of the second volume of "The River and the Canyon," in which Stanton tells of the 1889–90 exploration, form a unit in themselves. They also reveal Stanton to have been as much a master of words as a respected explorer and skilled engineer. These chapters are the basis for the present volume. Stanton revised his final typewritten manuscript from time to time in different-colored inks and pencils, and it was subsequently edited by at least four other persons in various colored pencils. What is here presented is the manuscript as revised by Stanton himself, the later revisions by others having been disregarded.

Stanton's story is so complete that it requires a minimum of editorial aids. Controversial points and certain other matters, extraneous and not pertinent out of the context of the larger work, have been omitted without further notice than editorial ellipses. Minor obvious slips of the pen and typographical errors have been corrected silently. Quotations from Stanton and others have been corrected, without editorial notice, to conform to the original sources. Such deviations from sources usually represent inconsequential changes made by Stanton to meet different standards of punctuation and style. A few other editorial liberties have been taken, such as the standardization of time designations for the sake of clarity, the omission of Stanton's marginalia, and minor adjustments in punctuation. With these few emendations, the material that follows remains as Stanton wished it to appear.

CONTENTS

Preface   ix

Editor's Introduction   xi

I. Denver, Colorado Canyon and Pacific Railroad Survey   2

II. A Railroad Proposed Through the Canyons   13

III. The Survey Work   29

IV. Cataract Canyon   44

V. A Sad Interruption   70

VI. The Second Attempt   93

VII. Marble Canyon   110

VIII. The Grand Canyon of the Colorado   140

IX. The Grand Canyon, Continued   164

X. The Grand Canyon, Continued   189

XI. The Grand Canyon, Continued   211

Index   228

1. Profiles: Atcheson, Topeka, and Santa Fe Railroad
   system from Kansas City to the Pacific Coast;
   Denver, Colorado Canyon, and Pacific Railroad
   line from Omaha to San Diego   24

2. Inscription on end of sugar keg   58

3. Sketch of cross section of Cataract Canyon at Camp 20   63

4. "Map of [the Colorado] River cut in rock at mouth
   of Escalante Creek, Glen Canyon."   75

5. Sketch map of the river where President
   Brown was drowned   79

6. Sketch of cross section of Echo Canyon
   with high water mark indicated   82

7. Profile sketch of a rapid in the upper part
   of Marble Canyon   113

8. Sketch map of the mouth of the Nan-co-weap   133

9. Sketch map of Rapids 184 and 185   135

10. Sketch map "in first 14 Miles of Grand Canyon."   145

11. Sketch map of the mouth of Bright Angel Creek   157

12. Sketch map of section of the river
    just below Bright Angel Creek   160

13. Sketch map of Rapids 261 and 262   173

14. Sketch map of the mouth of Shinumo Creek   182

15. Sketch map of Rapid 326   186
16. Profile sketches of the canyon looking upstream
    and downstream a short distance above Rapid 350   199

Robert Brewster Stanton, 1907   *facing page*   6

Camp No. 3 on Green River   7

Camp No. 12 in Cataract Canyon   22

Robert Brewster Stanton   23

Portaging Supplies   38

The Whirlpools and Eddies of Cataract Canyon   39

Glen Canyon   54

Soap Creek Rapid in Marble Canyon   55

Marble Canyon   86

Below Marble Canyon   87

The new outfit at the head of Crescent Canyon   102

The first mile in the Grand Canyon   103

The Grand Canyon two miles
     below the Little Colorado   150

In the Grand Canyon below Cataract Creek   151

The Grand Canyon   166

The end of the expedition   167

Map of The Colorado River Region   page   17

DOWN THE COLORADO

Much of the success of any one in any kind of work, and especially in work subject to the peculiar difficulties of that we are considering, depends upon the spirit in which it is undertaken.

—ARTHUR M. WELLINGTON[1]

B

EFORE entering upon a description of the work in which I was particularly engaged upon the River during 1889 and '90, some little explanation may not be out of place. . . .

In reading the chapters that follow . . . a number of points must be borne in mind. . . . my connection with the Colorado River of the West and its canyons was only that of an engineer in the discharge of his ordinary and everyday duties. I do not claim the glory of discovery or the heroism of an explorer. We went to and down the River, for the purpose of making a railway survey *along its banks.* The River had been explored, surveyed, and mapped years before. It is true that for nearly twenty years no one had attempted to navigate the five hundred and more cataracts and rapids at the bottom of its canyons; and, as we believed at that time, only one party had ever before succeeded in doing so, even for a part of the distance. But it was not our purpose to explore the canyons, or to dash through the rapids, for the glory of its accomplishment. In the serious undertaking of a perilous railroad survey, however, it is also true that those same mysterious influences that infect the air one breathes, still hung in those same peculiar veilings of pink, lilac, and pale yellow over the upper walls of the great canyons, and the dark blue shadows in the inner gorge were as depressing, and at the same time as awe-inspiring, as ever before, and I would defy anyone,

1 Arthur M. Wellington, *The Economic Theory of the Location of Railways: An Analysis of the Conditions Controlling the Laying Out of Railways to Effect the Most Judicious Expenditure of Capital* (6th ed.; New York, 1898), 8.

even at this late day, whatever his object may be, to make a journey by boat of twelve hundred miles through those still, weird chasms, and down that yet mysterious River, and not be brought under their influence. If he did, he would be a man without nerves, devoid of all poetic sentiment—a mere bag of bones.

I am free to acknowledge that I was influenced, and, on occasion, let my imagination run riot with my thoughts—especially as at night I lay wrapped in my blanket, on a bit of sand or upon the soft side of a granite ledge, but a few feet from the everlasting roar of a mighty rapid, and looked up [at] the moonlight, streaming in over the rugged edge of the highest cliffs, as it lit up one wall of the canyon with such a curious, unreal glow, while the other was blacker than night itself. It is then that one sees those "Vertical" walls *rise up,* thousands of feet above his head, and *feels them draw* in close at the top and *hang over him,* ready to fall and crush him to atoms.

But with all this, I had one check to my imagination, perhaps different from any which guided others who have gone through the same experiences. When Mr. E. H. Harriman, of railroad fame, was once asked if he thought a railroad would be built through the Grand Canyon, he replied: "You never can tell what some damned fool may do." When we were making the survey, we hoped to find a syndicate of that particular variety of fools who would build the railroad, and hence, whenever I allowed myself to be temporarily influenced by the strangeness of my surroundings, I was suddenly brought back to the *reality of my work* by remembering that the notes I was taking, and the impressions I was recording, were to be put into a report and upon maps, which would be inspected by engineers and contractors; that thousands, in a short time, while the road was being built and after, would be where I was, see what I had been seeing, know what I had been doing, and measure my statements with another transit, level, and chain. I was, therefore, debarred from feeling that no one could later dispute my conclusions. That even such a fact, in such a country, could keep all the virus of

4

that pernicious air from getting into my brain is, perhaps, more than could be expected; still, it had a very restraining influence.

THE CONCEPTION OF A CANYON

The impression the great canyons make upon anyone depends upon his view-point, and his mental make-up, and upon, perhaps, his previous conception of what a canyon should be. "The common notion of a canyon is that of a deep, narrow gash in the earth, with nearly vertical walls, like a great and neatly cut trench. . . . It is perhaps in some respects unfortunate that the stupendous pathway of the Colorado River through the Kaibabs was ever called a canyon, for the name identifies it with the baser conception. But the name presents as wide a range of signification as the word house. . . . Yet the contrast between Saint Marc's and the rude dwelling of the frontiersman is not greater than that between the chasm of the Colorado and the trenches in the rocks which answer to the ordinary conception of a Canyon.

"There are in the world valleys which are longer and a few which are deeper. There are valleys flanked by summits loftier than the palisades of the Kaibab. Still the Grand Canyon is the sublimest thing on earth. It is so not alone by virtue of its magnitudes, but by virtue of the whole—its *ensemble*."[2]

I once sat with a tourist on the upper rim of the Grand Canyon, opposite the Bright Angel. He was entirely disappointed. There was nothing to it—no beauty, no grandeur, nothing to inspire admiration. It was a trench in a mass of rock—all barrenness and desolation, all solitude and loneliness, all worthless, empty and unreal. I pitied him. He had wasted his time and money in coming to see "the sublimest thing on earth."

[2] Clarence E. Dutton, *Tertiary History of the Grand Canyon District with Atlas* (Department of the Interior, *Monographs* of the United States Geological Survey, Vol. II [Washington, 1882]), 142–43. Stanton reverses the paragraphs in this quotation from Dutton.

To me the great canyons had a double meaning. First, I looked upon them all, particularly the Grand Canyon, from the standpoint of an engineer as a place to build a railroad—on the same principle that a tailor would sponge his coat in Niagara. With this in view, I studied them foot by foot and mile by mile. In criticizing my views on this phase of the subject—that is, the feasibility of the route (not the commercial question—will it pay?) I think there is but one proper rule to be employed, that is, the two-foot rule of twenty-four inches. Even scientific men forget this simple rule at times.

Nothing is so misleading as the manner in which one sometimes looks at a mountain, and particularly at a canyon wall. Major Powell . . . [in] his famous report, writes:

As the twilight deepens, the rocks grow dark and somber; the threatening roar of the water is loud and constant, and I lie awake with thoughts of the morrow and the canyons to come, interrupted now and then by characteristics of the scenery that attract my attention. And here I make a discovery. On looking at the mountain directly in front, the steepness of the slope is greatly exaggerated, while the distance to its summit and its true altitude are correspondingly diminished. I have heretofore found that to properly judge of the slope of a mountain side, you must see it in profile. In coming down the river this afternoon, I observed the slope of a particular part of the wall, and made an estimate of its altitude. While at supper, I noticed the same cliff from a position facing it, and it seemed steeper, but not half as high. Now lying on my side and looking at it, the true proportions appear. This seems a wonder, and I rise up to take a view of it standing. It is the same cliff as at supper time. Lying down again, it is the cliff as seen in profile, with a long slope and distant summit. Musing on this, I forget "the morrow and the canyons to come." I find a way to estimate the altitude and slope of an inclination as I can judge of distance along the horizon. The reason is simple. A reference to the stereoscope will suggest it. The distance between the eyes forms a base-line for optical triangulation.[3]

[3] John Wesley Powell, *Exploration of the Colorado River of the West and Its*

ROBERT BREWSTER STANTON, 1907

CAMP NO. 3 ON GREEN RIVER

"The Boats were of thin, brittle cedar, entirely unfit for swift rapids
and cataracts."

And, he might have added, is frequently used, when desired, for optical illusions. . . .

Even cameras, like figures, may be made to misrepresent facts, if in the hands of a good manipulator. It was my endeavor to take my photographs to show the true physical conditions of the lower portion of the canyon walls, with reference to the actual construction of a railroad, and where the walls were really Vertical, or nearly so, to show them as such, in profile. . . . it is almost impossible for the camera to give a true idea of the immensity of the Grand Canyon; in almost every case it belittles the dimensions.

Secondly: I saw, or at least thought I saw, the canyons in their beauty, in their grandeur, in their sublimity. I lived among them for nearly a year on my first visit and came under the spell of the depression, as well as the exhilaration, of such a life among the rapids of a river flowing through the bowels of the earth, and at times gave myself up to their mysterious influences. Under such a power, I have no apologies to make for my thoughts of prehistoric times, or the realities, or unrealities, of the storms which I experienced in the canyon, nor for the sunrises or sunsets, and the forms and colors of the great canyon walls, as I saw them. Of such matters one has a right to claim *"De gustibus non est disputandum,"*[4] and at the same time grant that the impressions of others are as true and just as his own.

THE SUGGESTION OF A RAILROAD

The idea of a railroad down the Colorado, which led to its survey, originated with Mr. S. S. Harper, now of Philadelphia. It was enthusiastically taken up by the Hon. Frank Mason

Tributaries. Explored in 1869, 1870, 1871, and 1872, under the Direction of the Secretary of the Smithsonian Institution (43 Cong., 1 sess., *House Misc. Doc. 300* [Washington, 1875]), 15–16.

4 "There is no disputing about tastes," or "Everyone to his liking."

Brown, who became president of the corporation. To President Brown belongs all the credit of putting the undertaking into a practicable shape. He was a man of great ability—an optimist par excellence. He never saw an obstacle in his way, and, with all, he had an energy and determination that knew no bounds, and he never shirked a duty. Mr. Louis Kingman, C.E., in discussing my paper before the American Society of Civil Engineers, writes: "It is not often that an engineer is accompanied on an exploring expedition by the President of the company, he is usually sent with the best wishes of the higher officials. We have heard of proposed laws requiring the President to ride on the cow-catcher to insure the safety of his trains; but in this instance a railroad president volunteers to go to the front on a most hazardous expedition and loses his life. I think President Brown should have a monument as high as the walls of the Grand Canyon to commemorate, among men, an act so rare."[5]

During the first few weeks of the survey, up to July 10th., 1889, the whole work was under the personal charge and direction of President Brown, I acting as chief engineer under his orders. On the death of President Brown, the direct charge of the work fell to me, until I reported to the company at Denver, July 29th., after leaving the river in the middle of Marble Canyon. No one else being willing at that time to assume the responsibility for the completion of the survey, I voluntarily undertook to raise the money and complete the work, on my personal responsibility. This was done for good and sufficient reasons, as it seemed to me and to a number of my friends, but whether this determination was wise or otherwise, each individual has a right to his own opinion. I succeeded in raising about one-half of the funds necessary, and then—again wisely or unwisely, it being necessary to do it then or never—I signed a contract to complete the survey, and took upon myself the entire burden,

[5] Robert Brewster Stanton, "Availability of the Canyons of the Colorado River of the West for Railway Purposes," *Transactions* of the American Society of Civil Engineers, Vol. XXVI (1892), 351–52.

which cost me financially, at least, more than I had a right to expend.

To those who assisted me I have in the proper place given credit and acknowledgment. But I owe a special debt of gratitude to my wife for the burdens she assumed, both financial and otherwise, in order that I might not leave half-done a work in which she had as great a pride as myself.

The one man to whom I owe most, for the final successful accomplishment of the enterprise, was my first assistant, John Hislop, C.E. His loyal support, his brave and manly character, his determination and untiring energy, all of which he put into the work from the beginning to the end, left me a debt which I freely acknowledge, but which I was never able to repay, and his untimely death was a blow and a sorrow from which I have never recovered.

To all the other men, from first to last, who were with me on the Colorado, I am most grateful for their untiring service, and the faithful manner in which they fulfilled their duties as they saw them, and, as occasion requires, in my story which follows, I have given each his due meed of praise. Every man selected for such an expedition could not be a Hislop; if so, it would mean that the millennium had arrived.

To those who have never been placed in a position, either as a subordinate or commander, where the very nature of the work in which you are engaged—whether in the arctic regions, or the inhospitable depths of the great chasms of the earth—requires discipline and obedience, without the power to enforce either, it is almost impossible to understand what patience, tact, and self-sacrifice, on the part of everyone, are needed to successfully conduct an expedition through a country where the work may bring death at any moment, and at times starvation stares you in the face. An unkind word, a flippant remark, means vastly

9

more under such circumstances, when men's nerves are strung to the highest pitch, than in the affairs of ordinary and every-day life.

In all my work upon the River, I can now recall but two instances in which I spoke a harsh word to any one of my men. In both cases, after all these years of reflection, I still believe, that for the good of the whole party, I was right. On the other hand, more pleasant to relate, I cannot remember one cross word that was spoken to me by any man while on the River. I speak freely of this for this reason: On the completion of the survey as far as Diamond Creek, one of the Denver newspapers published a story, entitled the "Czar of the Colorado." The whole story, as written, emanated from the brain of the newspaper reporter. The statements were flatly denied, at the time, by the men who had returned from the party at Diamond Creek,[6] so that, when I saw the article months later, it required no notice from me. Trivial circumstances can be turned to good or bad account, in the story of a journey filled with danger, hard labor and privation which would never occur or be of the least importance at home. The most curious charge ever lodged against me as to the conduct of the Colorado River expedition, that I ever heard of, was by one of the men, who told me seriously, a year afterwards, that he thought I treated him harshly and unfairly, because, at the time when food was scarce and we were on less than half rations, I gave each man exactly the same amount. He thought, and so stated, that, because he had the greater appetite and capacity for food, he should have had more than the rest!

The one man who left the party in the Grand Canyon did so of his own free will. There was never a word of dispute or disagreement between us. His grievance was against some of the other men, whose lack of skill placed more burdens upon his shoulders, as detailed later on.

6 The "Czar" article appeared in the *Rocky Mountain News* (Denver), March 23, 1890. James S. Hogue and A. B. Twining made effective denials of the charges in the *Republican* (Denver), March 24 and 25, 1890.

One other point needs explanation in advance. As has been said, our work was that of a railroad survey. As such—a preliminary angle line survey—it began and was carried on with continuous transit line and careful levels and contour topography—with the addition of a series of photographs, which show almost a complete panorama of the route from the head to the mouth of the Colorado. When the work was renewed, after the death of President Brown, it was not possible, on account of lack of funds, to carry such a complete survey through to the Gulf. From that time on, the work was that of an "Instrumental Reconnaissance," with the addition of the complete set of photographs. Transit and level lines were only run, and topography sketched, at difficult points, and full descriptive notes taken of the whole line. Where the alignment of the river and slopes of the walls were of such a nature, that no question could arise except what would be clearly answered by the photographs and descriptive notes, the instrumental work was left undone.

A most curious criticism of our work has been made, simply because the critic seems not to have had the least idea of what we were there for. He writes of us, as we were in the heart of Cataract Canyon:

> They seldom attempted to cross the river, working down along one side and never entering the boats at all except where absolutely necessary. Thus they were greatly hampered in their movements. With our boats [Powell's second expedition] we never gave the crossing of the river a thought, and were in them continually, except where a portage was demanded. We could therefore always choose our course with as much freedom as is possible.[7]

It is such criticism of one's work, without use of the afore-

[7] Frederick S. Dellenbaugh, *The Romance of the Colorado River: The Story of Its Discovery in 1540, with an Account of the Later Explorations, and with Special Reference to the Voyages of Powell through the Line of the Great Canyons* (New York, 1904), 351. Brackets by Stanton.

mentioned essential two-foot rule, that makes an engineer weary.

We were running a transit line, for the construction of a rail-road (it was hoped), driving stakes every two hundred feet, and taking levels upon them, on the river bank, not in the water, and we were "working down along one side" to find, if possible, a railroad line there, to save even the very expensive *thought* of crossing the River with steel bridges, and, if we had remained in our boats "continually," we might, it is true, have "chosen our course" with even more freedom and ease, but it would have been of little value for a railroad survey. But the truth is, we did use our boats in Cataract Canyon many times to assist the survey whenever possible—in crossing the River, in taking the transitman in and running him through a rapid ahead to save time, and bringing up the back flagman and running him through a rapid—to save his legs. But the survey was kept down on one side, where it should be, though we occasionally had to triangulate the cliffs on that side, from the opposite bank.

In the account of our work which follows, I have added to the story of our journey down the River by boat some little discussion of the railroad route, which I hope may be of interest to some at least. One point I wish to make clear in advance. This story is not simply "my diary written on the spot." In my various note books there are many, many things recorded that are not given here, and there are a number of facts, real facts, about our expedition included in these pages which were not written in my note books at the time. . . . Certain former errors have been explained and corrected. While still others may yet be found, it has been my endeavor, however, as already stated, to be min-utely accurate as far as it is humanly possible.

CHAPTER TWO

It is an undertaking fraught with difficulties of great magnitude; *in fact, it is impracticable. . . .*[1] No railroad can run along the rocks at the top of the canyon, because the whole region is a labyrinth of stupendous lateral gorges from half a mile to a mile deep, . . . and no engineering known to man can bridge them. In the main canyon the water often rises 40 to 60 feet *so that the roadbed would have to hang upon the sides of the cliff, which much of the way is perpendicular.*

—JOHN WESLEY POWELL[2]

He [Powell] did not and could not see it with the eye of an engineer, for he is not one . . . we hold it to be quite impossible for any one not an engineer to form even a valuable impression of the practicability of a canyon route like this for a railway.

—ARTHUR M. WELLINGTON[3]

I

T has generally been the impression that it was a wild, visionary, and impracticable scheme to attempt to build a railroad down the Colorado River; that is from a physical and engineering standpoint. The commercial side of the question has seldom been discussed, for the physical difficulties, to the ordinary mind, have seemed so great that it was not necessary to go farther. This impression came about from two causes. First, from the seeming immensity of the undertaking, and second, from the very erroneous [ideas] . . . of the physical nature of the Canyons. . . .

When . . . I was engaged in preparing for our second work on the River, [I wrote] an article, with photographic illustrations, that appeared in the *Engineering News* of New York . . . .[4] This article [was commented upon] . . . by the Editor, the late Arthur M. Wellington, C.E., an engineer of world wide reputation, and author of the standard work upon The Economic Theory of Railway Location. . . . The comments of Mr. Wellington are worthy of careful study by doubters. Only one or two points require mentioning here. The immensity of the under-

[1] Powell to [Frank M. Brown?], April 9, 1889, as quoted in Stanton, "The Denver, Colorado Canyon & Pacific Railroad Project," *Engineering News and American Railway Journal* (hereafter referred to as *Engineering News*), Vol. XXII (September 21, 1889), 270. Italics by Stanton.

[2] Powell, *Tribune* (New York), August 18, 1889, as quoted in *ibid.*, 269. Italics by Stanton.

[3] Wellington, "The Colorado Canyon Survey," *Engineering News*, Vol. XXIV (October 18, 1890), 349.

[4] Stanton, "The Denver, Colorado Canyon & Pacific Railroad Project," *Engineering News*, Vol. XXII (September 21, 1889), 269–72.

taking, that is, the false idea of it, comes largely from the immensity of the chasm, which in places has a depth of a mile and a quarter, and a width on top of from six to twelve or thirteen miles, but which dimmensions, in fact, have nothing whatever to do with the problem, yet they naturally impress the mind.

The most expert observer in such a region can hardly bring himself to believe what is of course the fact, that the difficulty of constructing a railway through a gorge is not a whit enhanced by its enormous depth, but that on the contrary it is only the lower hundred feet or two which counts at all; or, to speak more exactly, which counts unfavorably. The vast heights above lend grandeur and impressiveness to the route, but they do not affect one way or the other the mere details of construction, except as blocks may be liable to fall from above, an occasional, but not in the aggregate, very important, contingency.

To see this more clearly: Imagine all the upper 5,000 ft. or so of the depth of the Colorado canyon to be sheared off for several miles back, leaving the lower 200 ft. precisely as it now is. The mystery and impressiveness of the canyon would then disappear, but the only way in which this would really affect the problem of constructing a railway there would be in diminishing the rapidity and volume of discharge from the lateral streams, which we will assume to be unaffected. Yet what sane engineer could then be made to believe that the bed of a large river, having the general characteristics shown in the lowest 200 ft. in height of our photographs (which are precisely what might be anticipated from the general character of the valley) was then "impracticable"?[5]

When the statement is made . . . that "the roadbed would have to hang upon the sides of the cliff, *which much of the way is perpendicular*,"[6] one would suppose there is some shadow of truth in it. The Grand Canyon was always considered the most difficult portion of the route, and the railway survey has shown that, in its 220½ miles, there is not one mile of vertical cliff,

[5] Wellington, "Canyons and Railway Lines," *Engineering News,* Vol. XXII (September 21, 1889), 813–14.
[6] See note 2 above.

that would require half tunneling, or would in any way seriously affect the construction or operation of a railroad. There are, on the other hand, about 100 miles of *sloping* granite walls, but no more difficult than hundreds of miles of such walls on other railway lines. The really true Vertical walls of Glen Canyon, where they would affect a railway, would be avoided almost entirely by the necessary tunneling at the sharp bends of the River. It is not intended to enter into a lengthy description of the practicability of a railway route through the Canyons of the Colorado, either from an engineering or commercial standpoint. Those who care to go more fully into this phase of the subject can find my presentation of the case, as it appeared on the completion of the Survey in 1890, in the *Transactions* of the American Society of Civil Engineers, with discussions pro and con by other engineers.[7]

So much, however, has been published on the subject by persons who know absolutely nothing about the facts . . . that it may be pardonable to give this short account of the project, with a few illustrations and comparisons with canyon railroads that have been in actual operation for the past forty-five to sixty years, so that the reader—though not an engineer—can, to some extent, understand the real conditions. This is also necessary to enable one to appreciate the difference in the work of our expedition, of 1889 and '90—a technical railway survey—and the first exploration of the River in 1869, or the later flights through the Canyons. . . .

OTHER CANYON RAILROADS

There are in operation today, through canyons in the Rocky Mountain region, hundreds, if not a thousand, miles of railroads that were as difficult to construct, and are as difficult to maintain

[7] Stanton, "Availability of the Canyons of the Colorado River of the West for Railway Purposes," *Transactions* of the American Society of Civil Engineers, Vol. XXVI (1892).

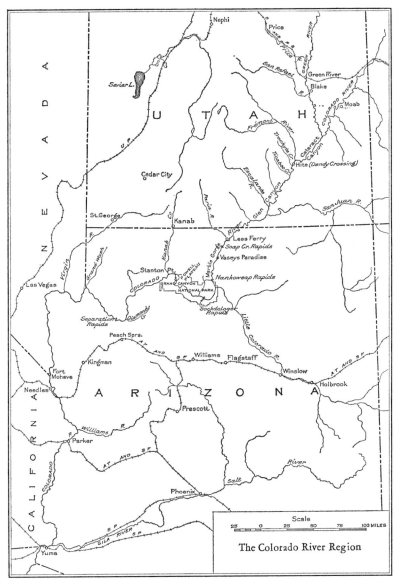

C. H. Birdseye, U.S. Dept. of Interior, modified by Prof. Malcolm A. Murray, Miami University.

and operate, as the line that was proposed down the Colorado, and, in more than one instance, where there are any at all, have more and higher *Vertical cliffs*, towering above and frowning down upon their roadbeds, than can be found in the whole of the Grand Canyon, that would in any way affect a railway. Trains are operated over these roads night and day, without a question as to their "practicability," and, at this day, with hardly a comment, except the *ah*'s! and *oh*'s! of the tenderfoot tourist on his first journey across the continent. . . . I have frequently been amused, when lecturing on my journey through the Canyons and telling something of the railway possibilities, to find how easily an audience can be caught by a little trick. After showing some lantern slides of the worst portions of the Grand Canyon, and explaining the difficulties of the route, I have said, now I will show a picture of the railroad completed, so the audience can see it will not be such a difficult task to build it, and, when there has been thrown upon the screen a view of the Denver and Rio Grande Ry. in the Canyon of the Grand River, above Glenwood Springs, with walls and Vertical cliffs as high and as formidable looking as any in the inner gorge of the Grand Canyon, there is always sure to be some person in the audience who speaks out and says: "Oh! but that is only on paper; the road has never been built." When they are told what the picture really is, and that hundreds and thousands of people, perhaps they themselves, ride over it every year in safety and luxurious Pullman cars, there is not a word said in reply.

If critics of the proposed railway had only considered the miles upon miles of successfully operated railroads, in Clear Creek Canyon, the Royal Gorge of the Arkansas, the Black Canyon of the Gunnison, the Canyon of the Grand River, and other portions of the Rocky Mountains in Colorado, and such roads as the Canadian Pacific in its crossing of the Rockies, and its line through the Canyon of the Frazier [Fraser] River, in British Columbia, where the conditions are the same in many respects, and, in some instances, worse than those on the Grand and Colorado, they would have clearly seen that the only difference is one of length in miles. An inspection of [Table 1 page 226] . . . will show what this means. It is true, as so often urged, that there is danger from the crumbling of the slopes and benches of the upper walls, but it is also true that "pieces of scenery" occasionally roll on to the roadbeds of existing roads, in other rocky canyons, but in no case do I know of a line being abandoned, or any of the hundreds of thousands of yearly passengers refusing to ride over them on this account. If, then, some thousand miles of such roads . . . are, comparatively speaking, cheaply and easily built, and safely and successfully operated through other canyons, and one hundred miles built and operated through the canyons of the Grand River, what are the physical, engineering, or other reasons, why the same railroad could not be as easily *extended* one hundred and forty miles farther down the canyons of the *same Grand River,* and 500 miles on through the Canyons of the Colorado?

That this distance is not all *in canyons proper,* from a railroad construction standpoint, can be seen by referring to [Table 1]. . . .

The commercial question—the value of the whole proposition in 1890, or at the present time, that is, will it pay?—is not within the scope of this work. Conditions have changed materially since 1890, as regards all transcontinental transportation problems, and the question (will it pay?) has new aspects, some against, and many in favor of, the proposition—but they can not be considered here. That the proposed road is feasible and practicable, and at a reasonable amount of cost, is beyond question, but for the present the history of its conception and actual survey will, it is hoped, be more interesting.

MY FIRST KNOWLEDGE OF THE RIVER

It was in the fall of 1869 and the spring of 1870, while I was a

Junior in College, that the first accounts were published of Major J. W. Powell's explorations of the Colorado River of the West, made in 1869, and his description of the Grand Canyon given to the public at that time, and reiterated in his famous "Report" to Congress, made an impression upon my mind that lasted for twenty years, and, at the same time, created in me the first ambition of my engineering life.

The impression made at that time was the same that was made upon almost everyone who later read the "Report," and the same, in a way, that almost everyone gets who reads even his last published work on the Canyons of the Colorado.[8] . . . The first impression made, on me at least, was of a vast plateau extending over the western slope of the continent, through it a winding river that by corrasion had cut its way down into the solid rock, to a depth of a mile and a quarter, *forming a canyon with practically vertical walls from the water's edge to the level of the plateau.* The chasm in width, at the surface, a quarter, perhaps a half of a mile!

The ambition raised in my youthful engineering mind was that I should some day throw a single span railway bridge across that chasm![9]

When in 1871, having graduated from the University, I received, through the kind assistance of Judge Jesse L. Williams, of Indiana, Government Director of the Union Pacific Railroad,

[8] John Wesley Powell, *Canyons of the Colorado* (Meadville, Pennsylvania, 1895).—Stanton.

[9] "This idea of bridging the Grand Canyon would seem to be a rather wild conception, but I learned later that it had been entertained by a very distinguished Engineer years before. Gen. Wm. J. Palmer . . . wrote . . . 'In this connection it may also be repeated, that if the Grand Canyon of the Colorado, which Ives found at points to be not over 50 yards wide at the bottom, with very precipitous walls, should be ascertained to be narrow enough at the top to be spanned by a suspension bridge at any point on the Colorado Plateau, in Arizona, that can be reached from the vicinity of the "White Mesa Line," Aubrey Valley, of the Yampa, the temptation of a possible saving of 5,000 feet of rise and fall would warrant a reconnaissance westward in California, to ascertain if this point of crossing could be favorably connected with Tehachapa Pass.' "—Stanton.

an appointment as levelman upon the surveys of the Atlantic and Pacific Railroad, I started for my first experience in the far west.

Thus my youthful "ambition" received its first forward impulse, for I was assigned to the special corps, that was attached to the "Overland Party" of the Chief Engineer, Mr. Jacob Blickensderfer, Jr., as he was then known. This overland party, with the Chief Engineer at its head, was to make an exploration, or more accurately speaking, an instrumental reconnaissance, of the whole proposed route, from the then terminus of the *original* Atlantic and Pacific Railroad (afterward the St. Louis and San Francisco), at Pierce City, Missouri, to its intended Pacific Coast terminus on the Bay of San Diego, California.

The Chief Engineer and the Division Engineer were to inspect and select the route, take notes, with astronomical, barometrical and other instrumental observations, while our regularly organized corps was not intended to make a complete survey of the whole route, (there were many other parties in the field) but was to be on hand to make accurate instrumental surveys of river crossings, difficult canyon lines, and over mountain passes, so as to supply the Chief Engineer with detailed data upon the most difficult features of the route for his forthcoming report, and thus we were to push as rapidly as possible across the whole continent, over the entire proposed line, to what we hoped would prove a well earned rest on the beautiful harbor of the Bay of San Diego.

A TRIBUTE TO MY CHIEF

It may be pardonable, just here, to pause a moment and pay a tribute of respect to the first Superior Officer under whom I ever served. To the experiences of this first journey through the West, and to the after years of service under, and association with, my good friend Jacob Blickensderfer, I owe much of the success, and some of the failures of my life. From the very first,

I liked his gruff, quick, and sometimes tyrannical way of giving orders and executing work, and learned in after years to greatly admire him, for behind it all was a kind and loving heart, as tender as that of a woman, full of sympathy and kindness for any one in need, be it man or beast, and, when not in a temper, absolutely just. If, in his more excitable and warmer moments, the slightest word of injustice had been spoken, he was the first to recall it, and his earnest and sincere (even to the humblest chainman in the party): "I beg your pardon, Sir, I beg your pardon," wiped out forever all possible feelings of resentment. A noble man, a thorough and distinguished Engineer, it was an honor to serve under him, as I did, on four different railroads, and, in less than five years after our first acquaintance, to be appointed to succeed him as Chief Engineer of one, on his personal, unsolicited recommendation.

I did not leave his service finally until 1884, after making a second horseback reconnaissance with him, in 1877, of some 1,300 miles in the southwest, and later, relocating and building the now somewhat famous "Georgetown Loop," in Clear Creek Canyon, Colorado, which Mr. Blickensderfer had first located several years before.

The training under such a man during my first experience in the wild Southwest—for it was still *wild* in those days—served me well in years of future pioneer work throughout the whole western part of our Continent, from British Columbia to Mexico, as well as, later on, in the jungles of the Far East, on the Islands of Java and Sumatra, in the Dutch East Indies, and it is with feelings of pleasure and profound respect that I here record a tribute to the memory of my first Chief, and express my gratitude for the help he gave me in the younger days of my professional life.

MY FIRST WESTERN JOURNEY

As we pushed on farther west with the Atlantic and Pacific

CAMP NO. 12 IN CATARACT CANYON

"We chose a narrow sand bar for our camp."

ROBERT BREWSTER STANTON

"The Cook snaps me resting and enjoying my pipe."

reconnaissance, my earliest formed "ambition" grew apace. In the long evenings around the campfire, I dreamed of the time that I felt was sure to come, when I should build that single span bridge over the deep but narrow chasm of the Colorado River. I longed for the day when our survey should cross its unfathomable depths—how, I did not know—and I pictured to myself the care with which I would select the site for my future mid-air structure. My ambition was to receive a severe setback. In December, a courier brought instructions to the Chief Engineer to abandon all work, disband the parties, and return to St. Louis, and much to my sorrow and regret, we never reached that bridge site!

Man may be, to some extent, the Architect of his own fortunes, but seldom is he his own Engineer. "Fate and circumstance so change the stream in devious courses"—the Company goes into bankruptcy, and he goes broke, and, at once, has to seek another "job." It was not till some eighteen years after, in 1889, that my young "ambition," carefully laid away so long in the secret recesses of my brain, had an opportunity to be taken out and aired.

It is necessary at this time to go back a few years, and trace the origin of the idea of building a railroad through the Canyons of the Colorado, which led to the actual survey here recorded.

ORIGIN OF THE RAILROAD IDEA

In the summer, during those years, Mr. S. S. Harper was a prospector seeking mineral wealth in the northern part of Arizona, in the country east of the San Francisco Mountains. When bacon and flour got low in Harper's pack, as it often did, he became a cowpuncher, or turned a hand to anything that would bring him a grub stake, so that he could go back to prospecting.

During this time, the earlier surveys were being made through New Mexico and Arizona, for the Atlantic and Pacific Railroad,

23

that portion of the road which is now the Western Division of the Santa Fe Railway System. Harper, in his prospecting journeys, was familiar with the country through which the surveys were made, and, being of a mechanical and engineering turn of mind, criticized the route chosen, on account of the many mountain ranges which it crossed, not only to himself, but to his friends. I submit here a condensed profile of the Santa Fe line from Kansas City to the Pacific Coast as it was built. Since then many extensive and expensive changes have been made to reduce the grades and avoid the high mountain passes, but Harper only saw the line as it was being located, and as he sat on the summit of the high mountain passes, resting his weary bronco, he would trace out the survey lines up and down the mountains, of what was to be the "saw-tooth route" as he designated it.

There is also given for comparison a profile, on the same scale, of the survey of the Colorado River route.

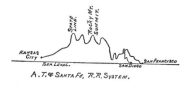

A.T.& SANTA FE, R.R. SYSTEM.

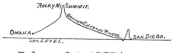

D. COLORADO CAÑON & P. R.R. LINE.

1. Profiles: Atcheson, Topeka, and Santa Fe Railroad system from Kansas City to the Pacific Coast

Denver, Colorado Canyon, and Pacific Railroad line from Omaha to San Diego

In the quiet of his lonely evenings around a prospector's camp fire, Harper, in some unaccountable and mysterious way, conceived the idea of building a railroad, from the western slope of the Rocky Mountains to the Pacific, with a water grade by way of the Colorado River, and through its many Canyons. At that time, Harper knew absolutely nothing about the Colorado River or its Canyons, except what was given in Lieut. Ives's *Report* published in 1861.[10] Nor had he ever heard, in 1870, of Major Powell and his exploration of the year previous. In the fall of that year, the supply of Harper's flour and bacon getting down uncomfortably near zero, he came across a party of cattlemen who were driving a small band of cattle north, and they offered him work, and also offered him an interest in their *business* if he would join them. He accepted the work and took the other matter under consideration. The party started with their cattle, and Harper noticed that each day they added a steer or two to the band, and that many of the steers were differently branded, and none of them "vented." This set him to thinking. Finally they reached the Colorado River. Harper can not locate the point where they came to the River; but, from his general descriptions of the country, I think it must have been opposite the point where was afterwards located Lee's Ferry. By this time, Harper was convinced that he had, unwittingly, joined a band of "Rustlers," who were "gathering" stray cattle and horses, to drive them across the Colorado, to sell to the Mormon settlers farther north. It now became his determination to quit the band, for he was not that kind of a cowpuncher, nor had he ever had any intention of engaging in such business enterprises, and he cast about for an excuse for leaving, that should not excite the enmity of the rest of the men. During the night, some of the cattle of their little band wandered off, going back towards their own ranges. The men were for leaving them and pushing ahead; Harper objected, stating that if the stray cattle returned, their owners would follow the back track and overtake the band of rustlers, which in those days meant death to every man in the outfit. So he offered to go back, round up the cattle that had strayed away, and bring them to the River, while the other men were crossing the River with those they had. This being agreed

10 Joseph C. Ives, *Report upon the Colorado River of the West, Explored in 1857 and 1858* (36 Cong., 1 sess., *House Exec. Doc. 90* [Washington, 1861]).

25

to, Harper mounted his bronco, and rode south, away from the River, just as fast and as far as that trusty bronco could carry him without stopping, never looking right nor left for stray, or any other kind of cattle, and he has never seen the "rustlers," *or the Colorado River from that day to this*. However, he had spent part of a day and one night on the great River. He had looked upon and drunk of its waters, and had had a glimpse, both up and down, of its canyon walls. It is true he had camped on the bank of the River where it is as easy to build a railroad as on the plains of Illinois, and he had not been in a single River Canyon, nor had he seen those "perpendicular walls that rise from the water's edge," still, he had seen the River, and had pictured to himself again his water grade railroad to the Pacific.

YEARS LATER IN COLORADO

Years after, in the latter seventies, Harper found himself in Leadville, and Denver, Colorado, and, as occasion offered, talked to his friends and others of his pet railroad scheme. Most of them thought him beside himself, so that for some time he never said a word upon the subject, for fear of the consequences. It may be remarked here, that to others, even at that time, it did not seem so wild a notion as Harper feared. Ever since the publication of the first accounts, and especially after Major Powell's report to Congress was made, in 1875, the subject, of the possibility of a railroad to the coast by way of the Colorado River, had been discussed seriously by eminent engineers in Colorado, notably among them the late Gen. John Pierce of Denver, who, notwithstanding Major Powell's descriptions, believed the route to be entirely practicable.

At some time during his residence in Colorado, Harper became acquainted with the Hon. Frank M. Brown, who was engaged in the Real Estate business in Denver. In January 1889, he went to Brown to interest him in a mining venture at Leadville. Brown would not invest, stating that he considered both the mining and real estate business to be overdone, but he remarked: "Now Harper, if you could give me a good railroad scheme, I would go into it. A first-class railroad proposition would just suit me, I would give up my other business, and put all my means and all my energies into it."

Harper replied that he had just such a proposition, and that he would tell him all about it, if he would not laugh him out of court. He then laid the scheme before him, and Brown immediately became interested. They got Lieut. Ives's and Major Powell's reports, and all the information possible on the subject. They talked with Gen. John Pierce and other engineers, and with their friends in Denver. The outcome of all of which was the organization of the Denver, Colorado Canyon and Pacific Railroad Company, with Mr. Brown as its President. Funds were raised, which were thought to be sufficient, to make a complete survey of the proposed railway route and President Brown set to work, with his usual energy, to prepare for the expedition.

President Brown's former connection with such matters had been that of a promoter and builder of several irrigation enterprises, both in California and Colorado, but he had never undertaken the building of a railroad. He was eminently fitted, however, with just such energy, push, and determination as is necessary to originate and start going such an undertaking, but his abilities were particularly those of a conscientious promoter, straightforward, frank, and honest.

From January to the latter part of May, President Brown made two trips to the eastern states. He laid his scheme before engineers, financiers, and others, and discussed his whole plans with the Hon. James G. Blaine, then Secretary of State, for President Brown was also from Maine. Nearly all these gentlemen, as he related his experience to me, especially the Secretary of State, gave him great encouragement. He several times told me he had made, in New York, conditional arrangements for financing the road in its first stages dependent upon a favorable report from a competent Engineer. He also called upon Major Powell in Washington and talked his plans over with him. The details of this interview, or interviews, he related to me several times before and after the expedition started. These were the beginnings that led to the actual survey of the water grade route, from the western base of the Rocky Mountains to the Pacific Ocean.

CHAPTER THREE

Using the proverb frequently in their mouths who enter upon dangerous and bold attempts, "The die is cast," he took the river.

—PLUTARCH[1]

O N May 13th., 1889, I was appointed Chief Engineer
of the Railroad Company for the purpose of making the survey
from the head of the Colorado, at the junction of the Green and
Grand, down the Colorado to the Gulf of California, and across
to the Bay of San Diego. The road was to start from Grand Junction, Colorado, the point where the Denver and Rio Grande
Railroad crosses the Grand River, and follow down the Grand
to its junction with the Green, and thence down the Colorado.
In March, President Brown had organized a preliminary party
of engineers to make a hurried survey down the Grand, and, on
March 27th., left Denver with the party to witness himself the
driving of the first stake.

The surveying party consisted of Frank C. Kendrick, Engineer
in charge, and T. P. Rigney, his assistant, and, to show that no
time was lost in inaugurating the enterprise, it is recorded that
they, with President Brown, arrived at Grand Junction March
28th., at 3:45 P.M., and, at 3:47 P.M., the first stake was driven
for what he confidently believed would prove to be the greatest
of transcontinental railroads.

After purchasing a boat, an ordinary flat-bottomed dory, fifteen feet in length, made of pine and ribbed with oak, and provisions for the party, President Brown returned to Denver, in
order to go East for the purpose of making arrangements for the
larger expedition down the Colorado. Kendrick employed men

1 *Life of Caesar.*

for the survey, and a special boatman to have charge of the boat while the party was at the survey work on land, and to follow along where the water was smooth. A careful and complete survey was made to the mouth of the Grand River, a distance of $160\frac{8}{10}$ miles, by the survey, reaching that point May 4th.

The navigation of the Grand was a simple matter for the first twenty-four miles, the water being swift but smooth. At that point began a short canyon with rugged walls and lively rapids. These were all navigated and the survey carried on. Forty-three miles from Grand Junction, the survey left the bank of the river and cut off a long bend. For some distance the fall of the river is steeper and there are a number of heavy rapids, but the party was not "forced to make a portage for twelve miles," as has been stated,[2] on account of the rapids, but, as the survey for twelve miles was to cross the big bend and be nearly all the time six miles away from the river till they reached the Cisco Pump House, the whole outfit was transported overland, as the one boatman could not handle the boat alone. The party was not organized for adventure, but for a railway survey, and chose the simplest and most economical methods of doing the work. At the end of one hundred miles, the line crosses the Little Grand Valley, a most fertile agricultural valley some two or three miles wide by twelve to fifteen long, in which is situated the Mormon settlement of Moab.

From Moab to the junction of the Green, for sixty miles, no difficulties were encountered, for the river has but little fall, and the water is smooth, though in places swift, and with one small rapid near its mouth. As to the railway possibilities of this one hundred and sixty miles of the proposed route, it is only necessary to remark, that the Denver and Rio Grande Railroad Company had for a quarter of a century, and more, operated its railway for one hundred miles on the banks of this same river, through its canyons, with cliffs as high as any of those that

2 Dellenbaugh, *The Romance of the Colorado River*, 346.

frowned down on Kendrick and his men, and said nothing particularly about it except to call attention to the beautiful scenery. That there should be more tunneling, and more rock work, on the one hundred and sixty miles, is only a matter of multiplication or division by the number of miles.

Engineer Kendrick had been instructed to deliver his boat at Green River Station, Utah, one hundred and twenty miles or so up the Green, and, as his provisions were getting low, he started at once, and, although reduced to half rations, he pushed on, as such men generally do, determined to carry out his trust to the letter. Eight and a half days they toiled on, towing the boat against the stream, under a broiling sun with the thermometer varying around one hundred. After traveling some ninety-five miles, they had but one meal left, and that only a half one, when they reached Wheeler Bros. Cattle ranch, near the mouth of the San Rafael River, and there the cattlemen supplied them cheerfully with bacon, beans and such other luxuries as abound in cow camps. If the cattlemen had all been away, and the boys had forced open the cabin, cooked and eaten all they wished, taken enough food to carry them the remaining distance, *washed the dishes and left everything clean,* leaving a note stating who they were, and why they had done it, they would have been just as welcome, according to my own experiences in that country, as they were when the men were at home. But if they had gone away leaving the *dishes unwashed* and the pots on the fire uncleaned, then woe betide them if they ever came back to that ranch hungry again.

Kendrick and his men reached Green River Station two days later, on May 14th, and he returned to Denver to work up his notes. Kendrick deserves all praise, for his work was well done, just as thousands of miles of railway surveys have been made in other as rough and difficult portions of the Rocky Mountains, but he has another credit; his party was the first, on record at least, to successfully navigate for any considerable distance the canyons of the Grand River, excepting, of course, the engineers who located and built the D. and R.G.R.R. along the upper Grand.[3]

PREPARATIONS FOR THE FINAL SURVEY

Preparations were now going on for the larger expedition to continue the survey, and, as stated, I took charge, May 13th, of the engineering work. Before this time, Pres. Brown had bought at Waukegan, Ill., five new boats for the expedition, and they had been shipped to Utah, and he had made all arrangements of every kind before I was engaged for the work; except selecting the men for the engineering parties and buying the provisions. The first instructions, given me, were to prepare a list of men needed for the railroad party, and a bill of supplies. The organization and supplying of such parties was an old story to me, and it was soon done. In order to more rapidly push on the work of the survey I provided for a double party, two transitmen, two levelmen, etc., but reducing the number of men to the lowest possible limit to carry on the work. As I have written elsewhere, while I had no appreciation at that time of the dangers and hardships to be encountered in a journey by boat down such a river, especially with an outfit such as had been provided, still I had carefully re-read Major Powell's report of his river experiences and thought that I understood the situation fairly well and knew something of the needs of such an expedition, and, hence, I had added to my list of men, four experienced boatmen, who, with the cook and his helper, were to handle the boats on the smooth portions of the River, while the rest of the men were making the survey on land. I did this for two reasons:—first, to

3 "It is not claimed that Kendrick navigated, with his boat, the whole of the lower Grand. For the reasons given above, he went across the bend to the Cisco pump house."—Stanton.

expedite the work, and, second, to have some good boatmen for the River-work, for my men were for the survey primarily, and only secondarily to be used as boatmen.

Every arrangement had to be submitted to President Brown, and when I turned over my list to him, he struck out all the boatmen, saying: "I, with Reynolds and Hughes, who are to be *guests* of the expedition, will take their places and keep the boats up with the survey." I was thunderstruck. "Guests"! on such an expedition! And they, two charming and genial young lawyers and clubmen of Denver, to handle the boats down the River that Major Powell's sturdy frontiersmen had found such a task! An engineer soon learns, especially if he has had his early training under a Blickensderfer, to either obey orders or quit the service. The latter I did not wish to do.

THE PRESIDENT OF THE COMPANY

Frank Mason Brown was born at Bluehill, Maine, June 9th., 1845. His boyhood days were spent with his parents in Washington City. He attended Bowdoin College, Brunswick, Maine, for two years or more, in the class of 1870, but left before completing his course, and became assistant Special Agent for Alaska for the U.S. Treasury Department, 1869–70. He was General Manager of the Amador Canal and Mining Company of California, 1873–79. During this time, he was elected to the California Legislature, serving as State Senator, 1877–78. He moved to Colorado, and was manager of the Farwell Consolidated Mining Company, at Leadville, in 1882. From there he went to reside in Denver, and engaged in the real estate business. In 1879, he married Mary, second daughter of Judge and Mrs. W. S. Ward of Denver. They had two sons, one nine years and the other an infant, in 1889.

Personally, Mr. Brown was a most genial and lovable gentleman, and a successful business man. His disposition [was] so happy and cheerful that he never saw any difficulties in anything he undertook, approaching everything with a smile, and yet with a candor and assurance that was convincing to most men, thus making him an ideal promoter, with his other qualities of honesty and frankness.

Such a character was just such an one as to be utterly incapable of appreciating the nature of the undertaking he was going into, or the dangers to be encountered, and, especially so, to scoff at the idea of any danger to himself.

Finding my plans for special boatmen were rejected, I began to inquire into the character of the outfit that had been ordered, and particularly as to the things that had not been provided for at all. I could not help criticising the boats, when President Brown told me they were built of thin red cedar, as being of too brittle a wood for the work to be done on the River. He answered that he had them built thus light in order to be easily handled when it was necessary to make portages, that he did not wish the expedition held back by cumbersome boats. He called my attention to the fact that while Major Powell had the heavy oak boats twenty-one feet long, the "Emma Dean," the one the Major himself rode in, was "made of pine, very light, but sixteen feet in length, with a sharp cut-water, and in every way built for fast rowing."[4] This I could not deny.

A MISTAKE OF JUDGMENT

Then came up that much vexed question of life preservers. I urged President Brown to provide them for all the men. . . . I could make no impression upon Brown, and called in my friend S. S. Harper, the real father of the enterprise, to help me. We both urged more caution and better preparation for the journey.

4 Powell, *Exploration of the Colorado River*, 8.—Stanton.

It was no use, even though the air grew blue as Harper tried to convince Brown that he was going into dangers that he knew nothing about. Harper and my other friends urged me to take a life preserver for myself, because . . . in my early childhood, I had had a battle with my Irish nurse, and, I suppose, getting the better of her while in her arms, she dropped me upon the pavement and so smashed up my left arm that it has been of little use to me since; hence . . . I could not swim a stroke, especially in the whirlpools of the Colorado. No life preservers were gotten for anyone. . . .

THE FIRST OUTFIT, 1889

Preparations having all been made and the men selected, President Brown and his men started from Denver on the evening of May 22nd, 1889, and arrived at the town of Blake, or Green River Station, Utah, the next night. The party consisted of Frank M. Brown, President of the company; myself, as Chief Engineer; Wm. H. Bush and John Hislop, Transitmen; G. E. Howard and Edward Coe, Levelmen; F. A. Nims, Photographer; with C. W. Potter, Geo. A. Sutherland, T. P. Rigney, E. W. Terry, Peter M. Hansbrough, Henry C. Richards and Geo. W. Gibson the Cook, (the last two being Negroes) besides, *as guests* of the President, Messrs. E. A. Reynolds and J. N. Hughes.

Friday morning before breakfast, I went to the railroad yard and opened the box-car to see our boats. As soon as I looked upon them my heart sank within me, not on account of their size, their build, or manner of fitting, but on account of the material —thin, light, red cedar—with which they were planked. The handling they had received in transportation had split two of of them almost from end to end. I recorded in my note book that day my impressions as to the boats, and also my determination to go with them whatever might be the consequences. Much criticism has been heaped upon the boats, upon President Brown for selecting them, and upon myself for starting or continuing in them. As to President Brown it was a mistake of judgment, caused by the fact that he was incapable of appreciating the work they were intended to do upon such a river. As for myself, I was then only a subordinate; I had already protested, but I had never yet put my hand to the plow and turned back.

Of the boats themselves there is something to be said. They were five in number, fifteen feet long, forty inches wide, and about eighteen inches deep, sharp at both ends, clinker built, and planked with thin, red cedar. Pres. Brown had selected them for the reasons already given. He had had them strengthened, with extra ribs and braces, decked over at both ends and along the sides, thus giving them stiffness, and perfect strength for the material of which they were built, and they were provided with large air-tight compartments in both ends. Their one defect was the material—thin, red cedar—with which they were planked, and the way it was put on, "clinker built," which made them more difficult to repair. These boats were well fitted in form for the water, even the rough waters of the Colorado, but the delicate cedar of their sides and bottoms could not stand the bumping on the rocks of the River, and not be split at every contact. . . .

THE JOURNEY ON GREEN RIVER

To return to my story. On May 25th., we began our descent of the Green River, after a most charming breakfast of mountain trout, strawberries and cream, and other things more substantial, furnished by our good friend, Mrs. M. H. Beardsley. President Brown had named our boats the "Ward," the "Mason," after his two sons, and the "Mary," after his wife, and the remaining two the "Denver," and the "Colorado." In addition to the five new boats, we had the old boat that Kendrick used on his survey on the Grand River. This was used as the cook's boat, carrying the pots, pans, and other tin dishes, and Gibson named it the "Brown Betty." Each boat was supplied with a duplicate set of oars and two hundred feet of rope to be used in lining them down the rapids. The supplies were all separated and divided so that each boat should contain some of all kinds of food, in case of accident to any of them. The men were only allowed *ten pounds of clothing* besides what they had on, and *fifteen pounds of blankets*. President Brown had provided for each new boat, instead of rubber bags, a square box, fitted in the center of each boat, lined with zinc and made water and air-tight by the covers being bolted down on rubber gaskets. It was found that with the bulky amount of instruments, transits, levels, etc., in their boxes, it was impossible to stow away all of our supplies and men in the six boats; hence it was ordered that the zinc lined boxes be taken out and lashed together in the form of a raft. Being air-tight and water-tight, they had been packed with the most valuable supplies—food stuffs—to protect them from the water, and in this form they made a perfect "flotilla" to transport our supplies to the mouth of the Green. It was never intended to transport them in this way any farther than that point; such a plan would have been absurd, but, for what it was intended, the arrangement was proper and successful.

In the . . . criticisms . . . on this and our subsequent work in Cataract Canyon, the fact is entirely ignored that our expedition was not intended for rapid exploration or a dash through the Canyons, but for the purpose of a detailed and laborious railway survey on the banks of the River, which would require many months, and it was necessary to take all the food supplies possible to the head of the Colorado, where our real work was to begin. We knew the nature of the Green, where any kind of a raft could easily be floated the whole one hundred and twenty—or so—miles to its mouth in perfect safety.

Arriving at the head of Cataract Canyon where our survey was to be taken up—the boats being relieved of all heavy instru-

PORTAGING SUPPLIES

"We always ran the rapids when possible because portaging was long hard work and took time away from our survey."

THE WHIRLPOOLS AND EDDIES OF CATARACT CANYON

"This is the section of the river where Hislop had his narrow escape."

ments, and the men engaged in the survey proper—it was intended to reload the boats with the air-tight boxes before going further. That this was not done was something I had no control over, but the transportation of the supplies by the raft, to the mouth of the Green, was perfectly, dryly, and successfully done, without any hindrance, accident, or delay.

The work of loading the boats and preparing the raft occupied the whole of the morning of May 25th., and, by that time everything being packed, we lunched on cold bread and river water, and ten minutes before one pulled out from shore. The whole population of Green River, both male and female, were on the river bank to bid us farewell. The postmaster took photographs of our fleet as we floated away, and everyone gave us several rousing cheers as we rowed down on the quiet water below the railroad bridge.

The boats were loaded down to their utmost capacity. The new boats, after being repaired, were entirely tight, but the cook boat, the "Brown Betty," with her heavy load, sank so deep into the water that she leaked near the top through a sun crack in the planking. After a short run, we stopped, unloaded her, hauled her out, and caulked up the overlooked crack.

About five miles below the railroad crossing was a light rapid, very broad and shallow, for the river had hardly begun its spring raise [sic]. This was known locally, by those who had never seen a real rapid, as the "Whirlpool" or "Devil's Anger." There was no difficulty here except the shallowness of the water. The boats being so heavily loaded, the "Denver" struck several times on the gravel bottom and stove three holes in her cedar planking. This caused another delay, but repairs were soon made, and by five o'clock we went into our Camp No. 2.

Although the line of the proposed railroad was not down the Green River, I took a continuous set of notes from the very beginning, descriptive of such a possibility, without doing any instrumental work. We had with us a transcript of Major Pow-

39

ell's report of his '69 journey, and each day noted the points and camps which he described.

A SUMMER PICNIC

The next day, our journey was uneventful as we floated down the quiet, peaceful stream. About noon we passed the mouth of the San Rafael, and soon entered the upper end of Labyrinth Canyon, with its low sandstone walls, which gradually grew higher as we proceeded. Later in the afternoon, we passed, without stopping, a noted point where three side canyons come together at their mouth, which, in 1871, Major Powell's men named Trin Alcove.[5] Just opposite here on the flat we started up three deer. Two of them jumped into the river and swam across. Our boat caught up with them, just as they reached shore, and Howard killed one with his revolver. So . . . our sudden change from lamb chops, strawberries and cream, to bacon and beans, was tapered off by a day's supply of fine venison, and we soon went into camp to enjoy our good fortune, at a point about forty-five miles below the town of Blake.

Our progress for the next three days was very slow, on account of the sluggish stream through Labyrinth and Stillwater Canyons. It took us more than two hours to row around BowKnot Bend, over which we could have walked in thirty minutes. The incidents of these three days made our journey one of peace, pleasure, and plenty, described by the men as "a perfect summer picnic." Gibson, the cook, shot geese and ducks, and at the mouth of the Grand we caught our first fish, and fine ones they were. Our larder was full. Later on, when we needed it, no game of any kind could be found, but that is the way of the world.

We reached the junction of the Rivers, at the head of the Colorado, at 3:30 in the afternoon of May 29th., and camped on

[5] Frederick S. Dellenbaugh, *A Canyon Voyage: The Narrative of the Second Powell Expedition down the Green-Colorado River from Wyoming, and the Explorations on Land, in the Years 1871 and 1872* (New Haven, 1926), 107. It is called "Trin-Alcove Bend" in Powell, *Exploration of the Colorado River*, 53.

the exact spot where the exploration party of '69 rested for three days.[6]

LABYRINTH AND STILLWATER CANYONS

From the town of Blake to the head of Labyrinth Canyon, at the mouth of the San Rafael River, is, by water, twenty-two and a half miles, through an open valley the greater part of the way. Labyrinth Canyon, fifty-nine, and Stillwater Canyon, thirty-six miles in length, make up the total of one hundred and seventeen and a half miles of the Green River, from Blake to its junction with the Grand.[7]

After passing the San Rafael, the upper country above the canyon is one of utter barrenness, the River having cut its way down through massive beds of sandstone, and the action of the water and wind having left little soil and less vegetation. The original drainage system being laid out in softer material, on a surface with very little fall, and although its course was in general south, it at once began to swing east and west, in places almost back upon itself, and as it cut its way down into harder strata has, with few exceptions, kept the same course, so that today Green River, winding its tortuous way, flows at some time towards every point of the compass, at one place making almost a perfect figure 8, some fifteen miles in length, and only two miles across the two bends, named by Major Powell, "Bow Knot Bend," on his second journey in 1871.[8]

At the upper end of Labyrinth Canyon, the walls and terraces rise 600 feet above the River, gradually increasing to 1,300 feet. Before reaching Stillwater Canyon, the upper terraces fall back, and the cliffs, next to the River, are not so high, but at the junc-

6 Powell, *Exploration of the Colorado River,* 57–60.

7 "These latest figures are from the U.S. Geological Survey's instrumental measurements of 1913 & 1914."—Stanton.

8 "Nearly all the local names on the Green and the Colorado were given by Powell, or his men."—Stanton. For the naming of Bow Knot Bend, see Dellenbaugh, *Canyon Voyage,* 108.

tion of the Grand and Green the cliffs, especially to the south, again rise to 1,300 feet. The fall of the Green, in 117½ miles is 176 feet, an average of 1.498 feet per mile;[9] but some stretches have a fall of no more than six inches to the mile.

The massive beds of sandstone, of orange, yellow and pink, in places, stand in vertical walls from the River's edge, though seldom, if ever, to the full height of the cliffs, and are cut in great alcoves and amphitheatres which form beautiful and impressive scenes, and with every sound send back from their arches most wonderful echoes. In other sections, where the rock strata are not so hard and massive, great stretches of talus skirt the bends, and, in the wider turns, beautiful flats, covered with bunch grass and greasewood and skirted next the water by willows, with the different shades of green of their foliage, make most charming pictures, as seen from the River against the orange colored cliffs. Between the Labyrinth and Stillwater Canyons, an easy ascent is made to the upper country—"the country of the standing rocks"[10]—where the massive rock strata have been eroded, and portions left standing in every imaginable form. "The landscape everywhere, away from the river, is of rock—cliffs of rock; tables of rock; plateaus of rock; terraces of rock; crags of rock—ten thousand strangely carved forms . . . cathedral shaped buttes, towering hundreds or thousands of feet; cliffs that cannot be scaled, and [upper] canyon walls that shrink the river [canyon] into insignificance, with vast, hollow domes, and tall pinnacles, and shafts . . . and all . . . colored— [yellow,] buff, gray, red, brown, and chocolate. . . ."[11]

To appreciate a country like this, it must be seen at sunrise, or just before sunset, when it is far more charmingly deceptive than the grandest mirage that ever loomed upon the desert. One

9 "Figures from U.S. Geological Survey's instrumental measurements of 1913 & 1914."—Stanton.

10 The designation of the "Land of Standing Rock" is, according to Powell, an approximate translation of the Indian designation for the area. *Exploration of the Colorado River*, 54.

11 *Ibid.*, 55.—Stanton. Brackets by Stanton.

section of this same country, to the west of this part of the River, on the road approaching the Valley of the Dirty Devil from the south, always held me in wondrous admiration whenever I looked upon it. In after years, coming from the River, we timed our journey so as to stop in Graves's Valley over night, and thus we approached it in the evening. Looking across from the south-west to the terraces beyond, just before the twilight, there is laid out, against the pale amethyst sky, a city of immense proportions, with streets and avenues, parks and pleasure grounds, cathedrals with towering domes and spires, palaces and halls, battlements and towers, monuments and minarets. And as the sun begins to sink behind the western hills, the bright rosy red rays, flashing back from the polished ledges of rock, bring out more clearly into view, first one and then another, the great carved palaces, with their windows all aglow; while the domes of majestic cathedrals burst forth in one ruby mass, and the towers upon the battlements one by one raise their beacons of flashing fire. Then, gradually, and sometimes suddenly, each light is extinguished, and the evening shades, in veilings of pink and lilac, are drawn over the seemingly perfect, yet weird metropolis, blotting out the scene and leaving but a single, rugged, and regretful mountain sky line.

CHAPTER FOUR

So weary with disasters, tugg'd with fortune,
That I would set my life on any chance,
To mend it or be rid on 't.

—MACBETH[1]

CATARACT CANYON FROM THE
JUNCTION OF THE GREEN AND GRAND
TO DANDY CROSSING

A FTER establishing a true meridian, adjusting all instruments, and locating by triangulation the junction of the three rivers, we took up Kendrick's line, on the afternoon of May 30th., and carried it down about a mile on the left bank of the Colorado, into the head of Cataract Canyon, and walked leisurely up the River and crossed in our boats to camp. The next morning, leaving one of my men with the cook and his helper, for President Brown and his two guests to bring on the boats and camp outfit, and make camp for us below, we continued down the River bank, some four miles, with the survey, until 4:30 P. M., when, although we could have run a mile or two further, we turned back to find our boats before it became dark. We found them some distance up, at the head of the first bad rapid, and camp made on the opposite side of the River. Why over there I never found out, for, as Reynolds says in his published article: "We . . . had difficulty in finding room among the rocks sufficient to spread our blankets,"[2] while, on the survey side of the River—the left bank—there were, perhaps, one hundred acres of good, level land, and smooth water between.

It would be a great relief, if it were possible, for me to blot

---

1 Act III, scene 1.

2 Ethan A. Reynolds, "In the Whirlpools of the Grand Canyon of the Colorado," *The Cosmopolitan,* Vol. VIII (November, 1889), 29. "None of the first railway party ever saw the Grand Canyon, and Reynolds left the party at Lee's Ferry, sixty-five miles above the head of the Grand Canyon."—Stanton.

out all remembrance of the two weeks following this evening of
May 31st.... [but] I feel it my duty to put on record this account,
taken from my note book written each day as the work progressed.

Our survey work had been all day on a broad almost level talus
flat, and although we had seen the boats start from camp in the
morning, and pass us about 11:30, we had not seen them again,
and only learned of their troubles when, returning up River,
we crossed to the new made camp on the right bank.

It was intended to reload the boats at the head of Cataract
Canyon and no longer use our raft, but for some reason, after
I left camp in the morning, this was not done. Feeling, as I did,
a particular interest in the two Negro boys, Gibson and Richards,
who had for years been servants in my family and nursed my
children, I had told them from the very start, as they were towing
the raft of zinc lined boxes, which would be a very difficult craft
to handle in rough water, if they got into swift water, to pull to
the nearest shore, tie up, and wait for assistance. On reaching
camp that evening, I found that this was just what they had done
when they first came down the River—had tied up the raft and
their own boat, to the left bank in the eddy at the head of the
rapid. They were then ordered from the camp, on the opposite
side, to bring the raft across the River. Gibson had served fifteen
years in the regular army, and knew the nature of an order. They
started to obey, and were being drawn down towards the rapid,
when, the River being shallow, they both jumped out into the
water and struggled hard to save the raft, but the current was too
strong, and finding they would be carried through the rapid—a
very powerful one—they cut the rope to the raft and let it go. By
quick and hard work they saved themselves from going over,
and, getting in their boat, pulled to camp. No blame whatever
could be attached to the men. We thought we had lost a large
part of our food supplies. This proved, however, not to be the
case, for we picked up the greater number of the boxes, later
on, in the eddies below in perfect condition.

THE STEEP FALL OF CATARACT CANYON

The next day, June 1st., we began our descent of that eighteen and a half mile stretch of raging, tumbling, foaming waters, that so appropriately have given their name to Cataract Canyon. Standing at the head of the first rapid of all, and looking over the tops of the high waves breaking among the angular boulders that filled the channel everywhere, I was forcibly reminded of the character of our brittle cedar boats. We were cautious at first. The survey work was dropped, and all hands spent the day getting our boats and supplies past the first three rapids. We portaged all supplies over the rocky talus and lined the boats down along the shore. All was successfully done, with but one or two exciting moments. As boat No. 3, "The Mary" was being lined down, with Hislop in it to ward it off the rocks, it was caught by a powerful wave, Hislop was carried into a whirlpool, and he and the boat were spun around like a top for several minutes, when suddenly, for no apparent reason, the River having shown what it could do, the boat was lifted up out of the vortex of the whirlpool, and shot into the eddy below, without the least damage. Hislop had lost his oars, which were recovered later, but Coe and Howard went out in another boat and brought him in. Tired out by our day's work we went into camp for our Sunday's rest.

Monday morning, we had our first experience in running real rapids on the Colorado. Having formed my opinion of the unsuitableness of the cedar boats, I can well remember my feelings, as I took my seat in boat No. 2, when, in a moment we were tumbling over the first fall and rolling over the great waves of Rapid No. 4, and on into Rapid No. 5. I tried to calculate how brittle cedar was, and how hard and sharp limestone boulders could be. The two rapids, however, were free from rocks, and the little fleet of six boats danced lightly over and through the waves, with no trouble except a good ducking for all of us.

In Cataract Canyon, which by river is forty-four and two-tenths miles long, this eighteen and a half mile stretch has a fall of 304 feet,[3] divided into fifty-seven rapids and roaring cataracts. It is almost one continuous rapid, being one of the three steepest portions of the Green and Colorado.

The three greatest descents on the two Rivers are as follows:

Lodore Canyon, 16 miles, 425 feet fall, average 26.56 ft. per mile. From Government Reports—and maps, and private data of 1912.

Cataract Canyon, 18½ miles, 304 ft. fall, average 16.43 ft. per mile, with a maximum fall of 55 ft. in two miles. From D.C.C. and P.R.R. Survey, 1889.

Grand Canyon, 10 miles, 165 ft. fall, average 16½ ft. per mile. From Government Maps of 1906, 1907 and 1908. Corrected in 1915.

As to which of these three is the most difficult to navigate with a boat is a matter of opinion, depending also upon the stage of water, and the time of year when it is undertaken. Major Powell had his greatest disaster in the Lodore,[4] we had ours in Cataract, and so did Best in 1891[5] with his heavy oak boats, but, later, [other] parties went through all three without any real disaster at all. When we were going through Cataract, the River was rising, though it had not gotten to its full high water stage, and that year, 1889, the rise did not reach its average height, so that most of the rapids were full of rocks above the water, and their sharp edges played havoc with our *thin cedar* boats. It was not any individual rapid, but the eighteen and a half miles of continuous boiling, tumbling waters among the rocks that wore them out, and so severely tried our powers of endurance.

To do no injustice to the events of this trying time, there would seem to be but one way, that is, by quoting, as far as possible, the record from my note books as written each day, and

---

3 "By the D.C.C. & P. Railroad levels."—Stanton.

4 One of Powell's boats was completely wrecked. Powell, *Exploration of the Colorado River*, 23–25.

5 A river-running venture under the leadership of James S. Best and under the auspices of the Colorado Grand Canyon Mining and Improvement Company. Stanton, "The River and the Canyon" (manuscript in the New York Public Library), II, 739–43. This manuscript is described in the Introduction.

then giving such explanations as are necessary to make them clear.[6]

"Monday, June 3. Loaded up all boats and all hands got aboard & ran the rapid just below camp [No. 8] and in fine style landing on left bank—I then took Bush, Hislop, Potter, Nims, Coe, Rigney & Terry & picked up [our survey] line. . . . Mr. Brown took rest of men to move boats down to next camp/ About noon we came up to [the] boats, & found Boat No. 5 'Colo.' had run against a rock & sunk . . . been under water one hour. Reynolds had Swam out and saved the boat, but almost every thing [in it] was lost. . . . Saved 2 Sax flour, black bag & medicine chest & some dried fruit. . . . [All hands] helped with boats till 2 P.M. [and then we resumed the survey, running two miles and] Quit work at 4 P.M. [to go up the River to find Camp. As no better progress had been made, it was decided that the next day the whole party should remain to portage the boats and supplies by the heavy rapids.] . . .

"Tuesday, June 4. . . . while we were finishing loading up Cook boat Brown Hughes & Reynolds [the two guests] start off in advance to run the rapid/ After going about ½ m their boat (No. 1 Ward) was Capsized in heaviest [part of the] rapid and all thrown out. They clung to boat & went down some half m. [farther] when they righted her—full of water—Still clung on [the air tight compartments keeping them up] & and were carried down about ½ mile when the eddy took them against [the]

6 Entries for June 3–6, 1889, Field Notes, Book A (manuscript in the New York Public Library). In this, as in subsequent quotations from his Field Notes, Stanton freely edits without notice; hence it is necessary to introduce editorial ellipses for the omissions he makes and brackets for the additions. Usually the words or passages in brackets represent a rearrangement or a different selection of words by Stanton, but they do not substantially change the meaning of the passages quoted from the Field Notes.

Also, in copying, Stanton supplies punctuation marks which are frequently lacking in his Field Notes. For the sake of accuracy these additions are deleted. For the sake of preserving the flavor of his original passages but at the same time increasing their readability, editorial virgules or slanting lines are introduced to supply needed punctuation.

right bank at cliff. They scrambled out & stayed on rocks, all day
—drying out clothes . . . [and remained there all night as they
could not get up the River that day].

"Soon after this in swinging boat 5 [the 'Colorado'] around
point—line broke. Sutherland in her & she was Swept about
a mile down stream thro same rapid as above but went thro
safely, shipped very little water & landed on Left shore. Sutherland quite frightened, but kept his head pulled in the loose line
& only lost one oar. One Portage nearly all day/ In rapid No. 10
we swing around all the small boats safely (except 5) when the
line of our Cook boat the Brown Betty, being swung round [a
point] in the same manner . . . caught on rock under water &
held her before she got into rapid. She was swinging into shore
nicely when the line as mysteriously let go as it had caught,
and let her down into the worst part of the rapid next the shore,
and against a huge rock. She did not break at once but soon filled
with water. Rigney tied a line around his body [while the men
held the line,] & jumped into the boat & unloaded her as far
as possible—Hislop also went over & helped. We saved a part
of the Cooks outfit, but lost all but seven of our plates, all
spoons, . . . two camp kettles, the buckets, pans &c &c—Saved
the three bake ovens, but only one Cover, the frying pans &
cups & a few Sauce pans &c. Lost nearly all our grub in Cook's
boat—Tried every way to save the boat but [jammed in under
the rock with the whole powerful current beating against it,]
she broke all up & was a total loss. After this accident we went
into camp (No. 10) just 3,000 ft beyond Camp No. 9, tired and
worn out. Having all of us been in the water some up to their
necks *all day* Nearly every thing was wet . . . so we spread out our
Supplies to dry & found many of them *Spoilt* by being wet & in
the sun. Dried peaches Spoiling/ Hominy so bad we had to throw
it away & everything in very bad shape—The matter of Supplies till we get to the Dandy Crossing begins to look serious.
Had a talk this evening with Hislop & Bush & proposed that
Brown & his crew [the guests] take Terry & push on & get sup-

plies at Dandy Crossing. They both said this met their approval & that they thought we would get along much better & faster if these men were out of camp. Talked to Several of the men & find a good deal of dissatisfaction among them as to the way Mr. Brown is managing the expedition & the way Hughes & Reynolds try to boss the handling of the boats. . . .

"Wednesday, June 5. . . . moved down river about a mile & camped . . . about center of large flat, one mile long by 1,000 ft wide at mouth of Side canyon coming in from East. . . . [Rapids] not so bad. . . . [The 'Mary' had bow badly broken—but all repaired on] reaching Camp—By the boats leaking *all* our provisions got wet again & I . . . Spread every thing out . . . & took stock . . . have still left about

> 4 weeks supply of flour,
> 3 weeks supply of bacon,
> 1 weeks supply of sugar
> 6 weeks supply of dried fruit &
> 6 to 8 weeks supply of coffee.
> With enough Salt, pepper &c . . .

"As we started with 75 days supplies of everything this looks rather serious. I . . . went to Mr. Brown [who had come across the River from their stay under the cliff] & proposed that he . . . [and his men, with Terry,] go in advance to Dandy Crossing & get supplies ready for us. And we would push on as rapidly as possible [with the survey]. Telling him that the men were getting alarmed about our grub & I feared that when the men Saw their supplies were getting so low they would abandon the Survey —take what was left & go down river. He said he would think of it over night. . . .

"Thursday, June 6. Mr. Brown told me this morning he could not go down river with one boat, but proposed to divide the party & go down with Seven men to Dandy Crossing—get supplies for us & start new survey there, & leave us to catch up. I told him this would gain nothing except get supplies & would cripple the party and in my opinion would be unwise . . . [and the discussion ended.] Resumed Ry Survey at 6:30 [(a mile and a half above camp No. 11)]/ . . . Ran today over 5 miles. . . . stopped at 4:30 to go back to find boats/"

Just here it may be well to explain, that it would have been possible to make the survey through the Cataract and Narrow Canyons in ten days, if we had had a means of keeping our camp up with the work. For the greater part of the way the survey was a simple matter, over the broad flats and sloping talus, as shown in many of our photographs. In a few places, the cliffs rising up vertically from the water to some height, though not to the top of the canyon, cut off easy progress on foot; but, with a boat to cross the River in smooth water, it is possible to walk at low water time, dry shod, the whole length by crossing from side to side. It is true that in doing this one would have to leave the River in a number of places, and go along the ledges a hundred or so feet above the water, and, in one place at least, three hundred feet up, but the whole distance could be traveled in that manner.

It would not be possible while making such a survey to transport on the men's backs the necessary supplies for subsistence, but, in a final location survey, trails could be cheaply built so as to transport by burros all necessary supplies.[7] . . . easily good wagon roads can be built, through some of the difficult portions of Glen Canyon . . . we built some years later. I refer to this, at this time, to show why our survey work went by fits and starts, and how the handling of the brittle cedar boats was so slow and disastrous, without special, experienced boatmen to handle them, while we were on the survey work.

June 6th (continued). We found the boats "about 2 miles back & 2 m. below last camp [No. 12]. Water had been good to this point & they had come down without accident—except

7 Stanton, "Availability of the Canyons of the Colorado River," *Transactions of the American Society of Civil Engineers*, Vol. XXVI (1892), 318-19.—Stanton.

boats leak—more provisions—and cook's bedding thoroughly wet. . . .

"Friday, June 7. Resumed Survey. . . . [two miles below camp, and] Ran about 2½ miles. . . . 2:15 Hansbrough comes up with a bucket of bread, corn bread & bacon all worked into a mush by being under the river for an hour. We each took a hand full of this mixture & 'sopped' it up & Started back to camp which we found 2½ miles back at the point where we Started line this A.M. We learn that, while Bush & Hislop came down from Camp 12 to this point safely early this A.M., when rest of party came down, the cook boat was upset—lost *all* plates & . . . Reynolds [and Hughes had their boat] . . . sucked down . . . in whirlpool [which Reynolds described later in these words:]

Just as we passed a jutting pinnacle of rock, we were unaccountably swept into a small but vicious whirlpool which was just behind it. Around and around we spun, and although I rowed with all my might, we drew steadily nearer the vortex. Finally my end of the boat began to sink, and Hughes's end to rise in the air. Finding we were going down, I let go of the oars, and hung on to the seat of the boat. I saw Hughes twirled around once or twice, and then the boat *seemed* to end straight up, and I went clean under the water together with half of the boat. I suppose that I was under but half a minute, though I found myself getting short for breath. The sensation was very queer, but there was a pleasant relief from the roar of the water. Suddenly, the vortex being choked, it released its grip, and the boat shot into the air. As I came up Hughes called to me to hold on. I called back, asking him if I was not holding on, and shook the water from my eyes just in time to see a huge wave roll over Hughes and give him a beautiful ducking. The boat did not capsize, and although we had lost an oar, we managed to paddle into the current, and soon reached shore. . . .[8]

". . . Sunday, June 9. . . . Mr. Brown's & Gibson's [the Cook's]

[8] Reynolds, "In the Whirlpools of the Grand Canyon of the Colorado," *The Cosmopolitan*, Vol. VIII (November, 1889), 30–32. Italics by Stanton.

Birthday/ [Gibson was much chagrined that his stores would not permit him to make a birthday cake for Pres. Brown.]

"Monday, June 10. . . . [To-day we made] *one* long & *two* Short Port[ages, and lined down our boats a distance of one and one-quarter miles, over some very heavy rapids, without serious accident and] . . . Went into camp . . . [tired out] at 4:30/

"Just before this Brown & Hughes . . . attempted to push on over rapid No. 31—Line got caught in oar lock, swung boat No. 1 ["The Ward"] into Current. They could not hold her—& so she went down [over the rapid. In it was a new] . . . transit, 2 sax flour 1 keg Vinegar, 3 sax fruit, 1 sax beans &c, &c. Brown & Potter followed boat . . . [on shore] for 3 miles, but saw nothing of it. [It was found four days later practically uninjured.]

"On the way [they] found *one* of the *five* floats [zinc boxes of the raft], which were lost June 1st. It was buried in sand in eddy . . . & contained 2 sax flour, 2 cans tomatoes, soap 2 sax fruit, 1 sax meal, & some tobacco all in pretty good condition. . . .

"Tuesday, June 11. . . . Brown, Reynolds & Hughes [the two guests] Stayed in camp—all forenoon/ Made in all *five* portages today two very long & 3 Short. . . . [Only two slight accidents to the brittle cedar planking of our boats.]

"Wednesday, June 12. (Reynolds) & Hughes start [up side Canyon] after resin for boats. All hands moving still further down river—but every one is so stiff and sore that but little progress can be made. . . . [Worked until noon, and then] went back to last camp for lunch because cook had *bean Soup* for us. . . . [In the afternoon the "Mary," No. 3, damaged] against a rock . . . losing our last coffee pot, all but nine cups, all our dried peaches and one sack of beans. . . . [We thought our cook would be in a bad humor with no coffee pot, but, with his characteristic cheerfulness, he simply said: 'Never mind sir; leave me a tomato can and a frying pan, and I'll get you a good supper,' and he did. Later, Howard and his men had a similar accident with Boat No. 5, 'Colorado,' losing the last of our meat, some more fruit and beans;] Rather a bad disaster to wind up the day

GLEN CANYON

"Three miles above Lee's Ferry near Paria Creek."

SOAP CREEK RAPID IN MARBLE CANYON

One of the party looks downstream toward Soap Creek Rapid near where President Brown was drowned.

... [at camp No. 17, but] Potter ... reports finding two more 'floats' intact ... [containing] 2 sax flour, coffee, Syrup, 2 kegs pickles, 12 cans cond. milk. A [very] good find.

"Thursday, June 13. ... Breakfast on Flap Jacks, Syrup & coffee/ [the engineer party walked back two miles and resumed the survey.] ... Line today is the heaviest work we have yet encountered.... [Made camp, two miles, by 3:00 P.M., and, from 4:30 to 6:15, one and one-quarter miles farther. It is also the heaviest fall in the river, put down in the Government reports as] '75 ft fall in ¾ mile' ... [but our levels show] only about 55 ft in *two miles* ... [as the greatest fall in any mile distance.]"[9]

OTHER DANGERS BESIDE RAPIDS

One personal incident, in Cataract Canyon, I will relate, as one time when, I am free to acknowledge, I was completely unnerved. Going over the rough rocky talus, stepping from boulder to boulder, I slipped and my right foot went down between two rocks. My foot was jammed in tight, and I lost my balance sideways, so that my whole weight was thrown against the strength of the bones of my right leg, resting against the top edge of the rock about one-quarter way below the knee. It was only a few seconds, but it seemed an hour while I was waiting to hear those bones snap. In that short time, I realized the whole situation; where we were, the height of the limestone cliffs, the distance to outside assistance, the heat of the summer, and that when those bones gave way—the end. Not a sudden blotting out of existence, that was not what I feared, but with a mangled leg, a sure, but lingering, death in that hot desolate canyon. I was utterly astonished that the bones could resist such a sudden strain, but they did not break. I regained my balance, and, extricating my foot, stood up, but then came the reaction and I fell limp upon the ground. In after months, we dashed in our boats at least one

9 Entries for June 6–7, 9–13, 1889, Field Notes, Book A.

hundred times into the head of a rapid, with no certainty that we would be alive at its foot; that never affected me, but the memory of the moments, which seemed hours, of waiting for those bones to snap, and contemplating that *lingering death,* makes me shudder, even to this day.

Such work as we had in Cataract Canyon, with our frail boats, being thrown into the water bodily every day, and working in water almost up to ones arm pits for days at a time, guiding boats through the whirlpools and eddies, and, when not thus engaged, carrying sacks of flour and greasy bacon on ones back, over boulders half as high as a house, is not the most pleasant class of engineering work to contemplate—except as a "backsight."

Hislop and I had another experience, at our Camp No. 17, which we never told of at the time, but which afterwards leaked out. Our instruments had had some pretty severe knocking about over the rocks, and after adjusting them, we decided to take that night another observation on the North Star, for a true meridian, to test the transit work. We were camped on a broad flat, cut by many small gulches, and in order not to carry the instrument out in the night, we set it up over a permanent hub in a little cove on the side of one of the gullies, before dark, and went to bed to wait for the proper time for our observation towards morning. We were up before 2:00 A.M., in plenty of time, and, with a lantern, wandered up and down that flat for an hour and a half, searched in and out of every gulch we could find, looked behind every rock—but nowhere could we find a transit.

The North Star had other business to attend to, and paid no attention to our misfortunes, but went on its way and was soon in a position to be of no service to us that night. The next morning, we slipped out and said nothing, to find where that transit had gone, and we discovered it, encircled by our footmarks in the sand where we had walked around it a half-dozen times—within twenty feet of it. We had lost a half night's sleep; lost our tempers as well, and had gotten no observation. We attempted to account for this by the peculiar shape of a bush near by, and seeing them together we thought the transit part of the bush—for we did not admit, even to ourselves, that we could not find it. The boys found us out later, and it was our treat, so we invited them all down to the (sand) bar and gave them a cup of River water at our expense.

In my note book I find:

"Thursday, June 13. . . . While in camp (17) at dinner I . . . took stock of all provision . . .

> No meat
> 5# dried fruit
> [150#] . . . flour . . .
> 2 weeks [supply] coffee
> 12 Cans Cond. milk
> 10# beans
> 6 cans Tomatoes
> 30# lard
> 2# baking powder
> Salt, pepper &c.

. . . Sutherland found [to-day in a drift pile] ½ barrel ½ full white *lump sugar*.

This is pretty slim for sixteen men & will not last even with *short* allowance for Six days. Mr. Brown does not seem to grasp the Situation . . . but goes on as if we had two months Supplies in camp. He seemed much Surprised when I started out after dinner (4:30) to run more line & was thunderstruck when I suggested that he and the rest of the men [in camp] . . . bring down . . . [the rest of the boats. Nothing was done except our survey work,] but at dark all howled for Supper. This making *four* meals for . . . [our guests] today. . . . After supper . . . I took Brown aside and explained the Situation that we did not have Six days provisions in Camp, and if we went on as we were . . . we would all be hungry before we got . . . [to] Dandy Crossing. . . . I told him I would take 5 men . . . our share of the [grub and go ahead with the survey,] . . . and leave him 10 men to repair boats and overtake us. . . . [He consented,] & said if . . . I was able to go on & do as I thought best, . . . I then went to the [men, and] . . . will take Hislop, Coe, Rigney, Potter & Hansbrough.

"Friday, June 14. . . . At 9:00 A.M. . . . [we were ready to separate. My party] had 10 cakes of [light] bread . . . 12 inch in diam. & 1½ in. thick/ . . . [which] gave 1⅔ cakes to each man [in a cotton sack, some coffee and canned milk]. . . . We each stopped as we passed and took in our sacks some of the government Sugar . . . The keg was marked [on its end] thus, [the three dotted lines being so blurred that they could not be read:]

2. Inscription on end of sugar keg

[We] Ran 3 miles . . . & camped [without blankets] in broad [open flat]. . . . Our rations being very short we lunched today on *three lumps sugar* and *plenty* of river water. For supper . . . [one-tenth of the amount of bread we had,] with a cup of hot water & Condensed milk. . . .

"Saturday, June 15. . . . Breakfast consisted of ⅙ of loaf bread 2 cups of coffee & one lump of sugar. . . . [With] 2 lumps sugar & *plenty* of water for lunch. . . . [With this we ran three and one-quarter miles, when we came to] an *almost* perpendicular cliff rising out of the water with a very swift rapid running at its base. . . . [Having no boat to cross the river, three of us started over to get a sight ahead. Made it easily, on a bench 300 ft. up. In a cove in the limestone, found a beautiful clear spring, with bright green shrubbery of many kinds growing around it. This was most refreshing, as we had not had a drink for many hours. We had gone farther than we supposed, and, on account of a bend in the cliff, could not see the instrument men. It being now 7 o'clock we could not return.]

"Sunday, June 16. . . . make another attempt to get along [under] the cliff . . . where the transitman can see us, but . . . [it could not be done] without a boat. . . . [and so we go] back over the cliff to join the other boys. . . . and go back to [get boat No. 1, the "Ward," the one lost six days ago, and which we had found.] . . . about 1 m. back [up the River, from the cliff we had crossed], met Howard & saw various things—bags blankets &c floating down river. Howard told us the whole party were about 2 ms up river, . . . that Bush and Hughes had lost the boat "Denver" . . . [in which] was Bush's transit, . . . [two sacks of flour, etc.] Meet whole party . . . about noon. They had come down from Camp # 17 [four miles, over some of the worst of the rapids,] in the last day & a half, . . . making five portages on Saturday and three today. [To get material to repair the boats,] They had torn up [the most damaged one—] the "Mary" . . . This affected Brown very much [and brought tears to his eyes,] as the boat was named for his wife. . . . The men went over river & got Boat Ward No. 1 [lost June 10th]. Found it little damaged [so we still have four boats. All the party being together again we made camp No. 19.]"[10]

PROMPT ACTION NECESSARY

I had a long talk with my old household servant, Gibson, who told me the real condition of affairs. There had been great grumbling. The men [were] threatening to take the boats and leave down the River for grub. It seemed to me that it was time for some vigorous action, and, without consultation with anyone,

[10] Entries for June 13–16, 1889, Field Notes, Book A.

I took the responsibility upon myself. I ordered Gibson to cook at once everything there was in camp, and then sat down for a rest. We had supper on a large fish Hislop had caught. After supper, the cook and I divided all the food into sixteen equal parts, putting it in separate piles on a log. Each pile consisted of one and one-half cakes of bread, twelve inches in diameter and one inch thick, without baking powder or salt, one can of condensed milk, a little coffee, and hand full of beans. I then called President Brown and all the men up to the log, and told them there was all there was left, that each man must take his share and care for it himself. That I had determined to remain with that amount of food, and finish the survey out of the canyon (twenty-seven miles) with as many men as would stay with me. This seemed to stagger most of the men. President Brown was particular to say he would not ask me to remain, nor would he ask any one to stay and work without enough to eat, but, if we did stay, he would hurry back supplies to us even if he had to carry a sack of flour on his shoulders up the River. It was arranged that he should go ahead, with one boat and a few men, and send back supplies from Dandy Crossing, some thirty seven miles down the River.

SEPARATION OF THE PARTY

The next morning, I learned from Hislop that the men had had a conference, and nearly all had determined to go out at once to try to induce all the men to leave, so as to prevent me from staying, in order to place upon me the responsibility of quitting the survey. I was determined to remain, knowing that if we abandoned the survey then, we could not return to it, and feeling sure we could carry on the work to Dandy Crossing with what food we had. I did not intend to leave without an effort to complete the work if men enough would remain to assist me.

At such times, men's real characters come to the surface. I

said to Hislop: "Well, Hislop, what are you going to do?" Straightening up his six feet two, and stiffening his Scottish backbone, he said: "Mr. Stanton, I came down here as your assistant engineer, to obey your orders. I am here, sir!" I spoke to the two Negro men, Gibson and Richards. They both said they would stay with me, and then C. W. Potter came without my asking and volunteered to remain.

The other men tried in every way to persuade Potter to go. It had no effect, for Potter was one of the most faithful, plucky, and determined little men I ever knew. They then attacked Gibson, thinking they could reach me through my personal servant. They tried to frighten him, by telling him we would all starve, and Gibson answered, with that true loyalty which I had known so long: "No, sir! If Mr. Stanton stays here and starves to death, I stay and starve to death with him." They also sent Hansbrough, my old foreman from Idaho, to plead with me not to stay. His effort was on account of his personal feeling for me, and he proved it by demanding later that he be one of the crew to bring us back food, which came the next week.

Of all the men who left me at that time, I have felt most kindly towards Hansbrough, for his efforts to save me from what he felt was sure destruction in the rapids, or, worse than that, starvation. It was not a pleasant prospect, for not far below where we were camped we had found, that day, a human skeleton, among the timbers of a drift pile—ghastly suggestion of what might be our fate. It was but a month after, when, not I, but Hansbrough himself sank beneath the muddy waters in Marble Canyon never to rise again. Six months later, as I helped to bury his bleached bones in the sands beside a marble cliff, I thought of his kind and earnest efforts to save me from such a last resting place.

On the morning of June 17th., we separated, the eleven men taking three boats, and leaving us one. In the first rapid, they had a slight accident and lost the "grub sacks" of three of the men, and then they threw everything away—blankets, clothes, and everything else, except their remaining grub. This was the last rapid, No. 57, of the 18½ mile tumble of Cataract Canyon. They soon turned a bend in the River, and we saw them no more for days to come.

Just how long it took President Brown and his men to reach Dandy Crossing, I do not know, but they arrived pretty well starved out. This incident was related to me afterwards. The Hites, with true frontier hospitality, at once set to work cooking dinner. The table in the little cabin, . . . was too small for the whole party to sit at, at one time. Part of them ate at the first table, among whom was the hungriest one of the outfit, the one man I had known as such, all the way from Green River. This man ate as long, and as fast, as the rest, and, when the second table was ready, went in again and ate as long as the second meal lasted. When the third batch was called, he tried it for the third time, but here he failed and gave himself away.

Food for a hungry man is common property in such a barren country, and I may relate here how one man invited himself to dinner, at my cabin on the Colorado, in 1897. We were camped at Tickaboo. We had just finished our dinner, when a stranger rode up and, without even saying "Howdy," exclaimed, as he alighted: "I'm good and damned hungry!" That was all. We soon filled him up, though there was a large cavity to fill, for he had been without food for two days, and I did not blame him for his emphatic language. This man became one of my best friends, in Utah, for the next four years.

THE WORK OF OUR PARTY OF FIVE

Our small party, with the one boat, triangulated around the cliff, and camped (No. 20) on the opposite bank of the River, at the foot of rapid No. 57. This cliff was the first Vertical one, more than forty or fifty feet high, that we had seen. It was perhaps 500 feet high, and *seemed* perpendicular from the water, but in reality had small benches along it, one of which, 300 feet up, we had traveled over twice in the last two days; and, above the 500 feet height, the walls benched back in easy benches to the top.

This is the only point where any such height of vertical walls is found in Cataract Canyon, and this is not one-half mile long nor is it straight. A sketch made in my note book at the time shows the cross section of the canyon at this point, as it appeared from Camp No. 20.

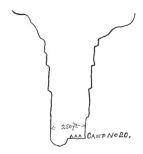

3. Sketch of cross section of Cataract Canyon at Camp 20

On this part of the survey we had no photograph instruments with us. . . .

Even with this form, it is remarkable what an effect such a narrow gorge has upon one in looking up through it, especially when lying in bed. At first it is perfectly natural in shape, but, as you look, the walls seem to close in upon you, especially from the top, and, if one will let his imagination run riot with his thoughts, he can easily *feel* the cliffs closing in upon him and hanging over his head. It was of this section, at a point a little farther down, that Major Powell wrote . . . "the canyon is very tortuous, so that we can see but a few hundred feet ahead; the walls tower over us, often overhanging *so as to almost shut out the light.*"[11] The rock of this part of the Canyon is hard flinty limestone.

11 Powell, *Exploration of the Colorado River,* 67.—Stanton. Italics by Stanton.

I find in my topography book the following notes, made during the survey, of the section just below the cliff at Camp No. 20, in short distances covering about three miles. "Over hanging cliffs both sides, water fills canyon, *with benches above* beginning from 40 to 100 ft. above River, and continuing to top," "Over hanging cliff, 40 to 50 ft. high, with talus slope below." "Second bench, 40 to 50 ft. wide, extends for three quarters mile, 40 to 100 feet above the River," the narrowest part from wall to wall being from 250 to 300 ft. wide, at the bottom. With these notes, and the evidence of the U.S. Geological Survey maps, made in after years, made largely, if not entirely, from the notes of the work of 1871 and '72, I rewrite what I stated in 1889—There is not a stretch of the River, one-half mile in length, where the direct rays of the sun do not shine on the water, at some time of the day, during some season of the year. And in this part of the Canyon, the cliffs do not over hang more than 10 to 30 feet and that only in points, and are only 50, 100, or 300 feet high, (the latter in one place) where they approach the vertical, and then bench back, by narrow and broader benches, to the top. The Canyon is about 1,800 feet deep, and the walls at the top are from *3,500 feet to one mile apart.* Rather a difficult place, I should think, *to "shut out the light!"*

Making our survey, with only one boat, in the narrow part of the Canyon, where the walls in points were vertical next to the river—even if only for fifty or one hundred feet up—was a risky operation. At one point, with the transit on a little sand pile at the mouth of a small side canyon, with vertical walls above and below us, the three boys went ahead in the boat to set a point a half-mile beyond, expecting to return for us, while Hislop and I remained to take the sight. The water was smooth, but, when the boys below tried to row upstream to us, they found the current was so strong in the narrow, confined channel, that they could make no progress. Hislop and I climbed up the little side gulch, and along the cliff on a bench a hundred feet above the River, and, after a hard scramble down, finally reached the boat.

We were now below all but one of the rapids of Cataract Canyon, and the water was much less powerful, having much less fall. We made good progress with our survey, except being hindered by having only one boat. At one point it was necessary to triangulate a cliff, about one hundred feet high, where the water filled the canyon from wall to wall. With five men, instruments, etc. in our boat, it was a very dangerous operation. We were fearful we would have to give up the work. It being late, we ran the rapid at that point to find a camping place. Everyone was sad with the possible prospect of having to abandon the survey. Drifting down about half a mile, we came to a good camping ground, and, at the same time rounding a point, we saw what seemed to be open country ahead, with the setting sun shining in all its splendor of color on the marble cliffs beyond. It was such a glorious sight, after being for days in the narrow canyon, that it inspired everyone, and Potter and the negro boys spoke up first, and said: "We'll go back in the morning and bring down the survey," which, of course, we did.

HOW IT AFFECTED THE MEN

Before going farther, I wish to give credit and due praise to the four men who voluntarily remained with me on this particularly arduous piece of work. They were of the stuff that heroes are made of. They had, with the exception of Hislop, no professional pride at stake. For six days in all we toiled on, continuing the survey at the rate of four miles a day, with one small piece of bread, a little coffee and milk for our morning and evening meal, and three lumps of sugar and as much of the River water as we wished at noon. Under such circumstances the true nobleness of men's character are either shown in bright colors, or entirely lost. The men worked on without a murmur, carrying the survey over the rocks and cliffs on the side of the canyon and handling the boat through the rapids of the River. At night, when they laid down upon the sand to sleep, after a meal that was nine-tenths water and hope, and one-tenth bread and coffee, it was without a complaint. The deprivation did not of course affect all alike. Hislop and I cared little. It was not the first time that each of us had gone days with little or nothing to eat, and kept at our work. Potter, I think, deserves most praise. He started out in the morning cheerful and willing, and worked without flinching all day; but he was working upon his determination and nerve, for as soon as we stopped for camp, and the boat was tied up, he fell on the ground a total wreck. Each night I would mix him a cup of milk and water with a few spoons full of brandy (a small bottle of which I had saved from the devastation, by our guests, of our medicine chest) and make him drink it, before he could sit up and eat his supper of three ounces of bread and coffee. After a night's sleep he was as ready and willing to push on as he was the day before. Richards, though perfectly willing, could not stand the loss of food as well as his Negro brother, and Gibson, unselfish fellow that he was, would each time divide his scanty meal and make Richards eat half of it.

It is but justice to say here that Nims, the photographer, was willing to stay with us, but, having only one boat, it was impossible to let him. Gibson took it upon himself to find some wild game to help out our scanty store, and was up by daylight wandering up the side canyons and over the cliffs with his rifle. He had no cooking to do now, but he never as much as had one shot. We put our fishing lines out every night, baited with lizards, but never a fish.

Our work was all earnest labor and much of it sad toil. One afternoon, as we were coming in our boat to camp, our cook spied, sitting on a rock down the River—not three, but only one black crow. The work was stopped, the boat was landed, and the whole railroad interest of the country stood still for the while. The cook crept out upon the sand bar with his Winchester. Our hearts beat quick in joyous expectation. Crack! went the rifle, and behind the rock fell the crow. Into the boat we jumped, and as we floated down the River, our cook grew eloquent on the supper he was going to prepare. Broiled crow, baked crow, and stewed crow with plenty of gravy! We stopped on the little sand bar on which he was, there he lay—our luscious supper—behind the rock. But, just as Gibson went to pick him up, he raised his wings and gracefully flew away. Poor fellow, he had only one leg broken, and we had lost our supper. It is said that blessings brighten as they take their flight. As that one black crow soared far above us into the light of the setting sun, he looked as large as a Rhode Island turkey.

It was on June 20th, in this narrow part of Cataract Canyon, that I discovered the inscription on the wall of "D. Julien" . . .[12] In the afternoon, we came to the half-mile chute of water so graphically described by Major Powell in his Report . . . but the water was undoubtedly much higher than when he was there, and, with only one boat, we were obliged to use great caution. Portaging the boat, etc. over the head of the rapid, and then running our survey line down to where the current beat up against a sixty foot marble wall, we took a bearing to a rock down the River, and set up a driftwood stick, twenty-eight feet high, with cross arms nailed at every foot, for a stadia rod. Hislop and Potter then ran the rapid in beautiful style.

The description of this rapid, referred to above, is so true as given by Major Powell, that I take the liberty of quoting it:

> We made two portages this morning, one of them very long. During the afternoon we run a chute, more than half a mile in length, narrow and rapid. The chute has a floor of marble; the rocks dip

12 "For myself, I claim to have discovered but few things in all of the Canyons through which we traveled in 1889 and '90. One of these few new things, that I did find, was an inscription on the left hand wall near the lower end of Cataract Canyon, recording the adventure of another early explorer of the Canyons this time of the Colorado itself. This was first seen on June 20th, 1889." Stanton, "The River and the Canyon," I, 135.

For additional description and comments on this inscription dated 1836, see Stanton, "Availability of the Canyons of the Colorado River," *Transactions* of the American Society of Civil Engineers, Vol. XXVI (1892), 284–85.

in the direction in which we are going, and the fall of the stream conforms to the inclination of the beds; so we float on water that is gliding down an inclined plane. At the foot of the chute, the river turns sharply to the right, and the water rolls up against a rock which, from above, seems to stand directly athwart its course. As we approach it, we pull with all power to the right, but it seems impossible to avoid being carried headlong against the cliff, and we are carried up high on the waves—not against the rocks, for the rebounding water strikes us, and we are beaten back, and pass on with safety, except that we get a good drenching.[13]

Thus on this 20th. of June, our party of five with our one little frail boat, made exactly the same two portages, "one of them very long," that were made on July 28th, '69 twenty years before . . . ran five other rapids, crossed the River ten times, for angle points to triangulate around cliffs where the water filled the whole gorge, besides rowing up stream three-quarters of a mile, and made four and a half miles of railroad survey, doing all instrument work, and sketching complete contour topography; which I think is a pretty fair answer to the criticism referred to [above] . . . that we "seldom attempted to cross the river . . . never entering the boats at all except where absolutely necessary, [and] Thus they were greatly hampered in their movements."[14]

PROVISIONS REACH US FROM BELOW

Our provisions being so very valuable just now, we did not trust them to the boat, but we carried the grub, and all instruments, over the cliff past the rapid, which filled the canyon from wall to wall. At 6:30 this evening, as we were coming down the hill, we met Howard, Coe, and Hansbrough, who had come up the River from Dandy Crossing, with plenty of supplies, through

[13] Powell, *Exploration of the Colorado River,* 66.
[14] Dellenbaugh, *The Romance of the Colorado River,* 351.

Narrow Canyon to a point some four miles above Millecrag Bend. Our only trouble now was not to eat too much at our first supper. Two of the men forgot the necessity to be careful, and were made very sick, but Hislop and I ate two griddle cakes, drank one cup of coffee, and went to bed well satisfied with our supper and the work of the past week.

Now having two boats, and all the heavy rapids of Cataract Canyon being behind us, we skipped along, making six to eight miles of survey each day, at the cost of some exertion, however, for a plentiful supply of food made us tired, listless, and sleepy. We reached Dandy Crossing at the mouth of Trachyte Creek the evening of June 24th, having rested the day before, over Sunday, at the lower end of Narrow Canyon, at a number of magnificent sulphur springs—hot ones at one side of the river, and cold ones on the other.

In the afternoon of Sunday, President Brown came up from Dandy Crossing and congratulated us on our bringing the survey successfully through.

The distance through Cataract Canyon is forty-four and two-tenths miles, and Narrow Canyon, eight and three-tenths miles. *By our survey,* which, on the broad flats, cut off as much distance as possible, these distances were—Cataract, 39.585 miles and Narrow, 7.575 miles, with the fall of the River in this distance of our survey of 47.16 miles, of 355 feet, having at one point the extreme fall of 55 feet in two miles.[15]

15 "In [Table 1 page 226] . . . will be found the tabulated results of this work of the first railroad division on the Colorado, and also that from Grand Junction, Colorado, to the head of the River, together with the other divisions extending to the Gulf of California."—Stanton.

CHAPTER FIVE

The glories of our blood and state
Are shadows, not substantial things;
There is no armour against fate;
Death lays his icy hand on kings:

—JAMES SHIRLEY[1]

BEFORE leaving Denver, I had made an estimate of six to eight months as the time required to make a rapid preliminary survey, as far as the Needles, California. President Brown, with his sanguine disposition, expected it could be done in much less time. The delays which had already occurred, and the engagements he had made in New York, which he had fully explained to me, led President Brown to change the whole plan of the expedition. It was decided, at this time, to leave Mr. W. H. Bush and his men to continue the survey through Glen Canyon to Lee's Ferry, while President Brown and myself, with a smaller party, would go on through Marble and Grand Canyons and to the Needles, and make a preliminary report, *from observation,* upon the feasibility of the railroad route, supplemented by a complete set of photographs of the interior of the Canyons.

With our experiences in Cataract Canyon, with the boats and outfit we had, such a procedure was unwise in the extreme. Besides the reasons already given—his want of appreciation of the dangers of the journey, with the frail boats we had—President Brown was influenced by his strong desire to meet his engagements in New York, and the belief, which he still had, that he could accomplish the whole journey with the boats then on the River. In my own case, I considered it my duty to remain with my superior officer. Two of the men, Rigney and Terry, withdrew from the party at Dandy Crossing. Bush and four men were left with one boat, to continue the survey along the smooth

1 *The Contention of Ajax and Ulysses,* Act I, scene 3.

waters of Glen Canyon. Of the two guests, Hughes left after going fifteen miles below Dandy Crossing, and Reynolds returned home from Lee's Ferry.

The party that started to go on through the lower Canyons consisted, besides myself, of President Brown, Hislop, Hansbrough, Richards, Nims, the photographer, Gibson, the cook, and Harry McDonald. The last named joined the party at Dandy Crossing. He had been in Glen Canyon for several years, was an experienced boatman on that part of the River, and a combination of trapper, hunter, and miner. We left Dandy Crossing June 26th, with three of the original cedar boats and supplies gotten from the little store at that place. Additional supplies were ordered to meet us at Lee's Ferry. By noon we reached Tickaboo, a placermining camp fifteen miles below Dandy. We remained at Tickaboo mines two and a half days, using their blacksmith and carpenter tools, and McDonald's skill as a carpenter, in repairing and rebuilding the three boats. They were strengthened in every way, with some new and heavy planking, and, when we left, were in good condition, and I may say here, that these boats, in themselves, gave us no more trouble as long as we used them. The journey through Glen Canyon, from the mouth of the Dirty Devil to Lee's Ferry, was one of pleasure and enjoyment, without danger or excitement, and, after our hard work in Cataract Canyon, was a great relief.

GLEN CANYON

The River, from Narrow Canyon to Marble Canyon, has a fall of 256 feet in 185 miles, a little more than 1.38 feet per mile. There are a few heavy rapids with falls of 10 and 12 feet, with a number of others of much less fall, but great stretches of the river, of 10, 20, 30 and in one case 50 miles, are like lakes, from 200 to 500 and 600 feet in width, in places with a swift current, but generally smooth and glassy, when the wind does not blow, requiring constant rowing to make any considerable progress.

The River is very tortuous in its course, forming great bends in the massive rock through which it has cut its channel. The formation in Glen Canyon is through its whole length in sandstone. The extreme upper end in the Permian, and the remainder all in the Triassic. The sandstone is of two forms, massive, hard, homogeneous rock, or softer, thin, horizontal beds. The nature of the walls depends upon the relative position which these two kinds of rock sustain with reference to the River itself.

The general position of the beds is horizontal, though not entirely so. Where the thin bedded strata are next to the River, the walls are sloping with a heavy talus at their foot, and vertical cliffs of massive sandstone above. When the homogeneous sandstone comes down to the water, the walls rise vertically to heights, in places, of over 1,000 feet. Here, in Glen Canyon, are the true vertical walls, but what bearing these have upon the object of our survey—a railroad route—will be seen by inspecting the table of classification given in [Table 1 page 226] . . . .

One of the peculiar features of this Canyon are [sic] the extensive broad level flats of bottom land in the great bends of the River, in places covered with black willow and scrub oak, which, with the red walls of the Canyon, form such pleasing pictures.

These large flats, by actual measurements—in later years—contain over 15,000 acres of gravel and fine sandy loam, much of which, in by-gone ages, was cultivated by that long-forgotten race that built their homes, their grain-houses or corncribs, and their extensive system of fortifications, along and on the Canyon walls. Call them what you may—cliff dwellers, or what not—they were the same people, it seems to me, that, in forgotten ages, built those great systems of irrigation canals in Arizona, and cultivated the soil of the more open valleys. Here in the canyons of the upper Colorado, they had more in view than mere living. They were on the outskirts of their country, and while they cultivated the flats on the River, they also built on the rims of the Canyon, and far back to the northeast, a system of fortifications to pro-

73

tect them from outside enemies, and thus, as it were, stood guard on the northern frontier of their country. . . .

In our journey through Glen Canyon, we stopped to examine and enjoy many of the beautiful glens, and the great chambers and amphitheatres that have been carved out of the massive sandstone, by the action of the River, in which there are often springs and streams of clear water, with moss covered walls, and banks of ferns. The coloring of the Canyon walls is generally red, streaked with black by the weather. The red is not in itself brilliant, but the effect of the morning and evening sun shining upon the cliffs, through the peculiar atmosphere of that dry country, produces a most startling effect, till the whole side of the Canyon seems ablaze with scarlet flame. It is difficult to understand how this effect is produced. In the late evening, as one is looking up the River at some massive wall that seems, in the shadow, to be black rather than red, suddenly the sunlight streams through a side canyon, and in an instant the whole cliff flashes out in living fire, so bright, so startling, as to be unreal, for it is the color of the sun's rays, not the wall; but the wall is needed to bring the color to your eye, and it stands out as if painted in veritable scarlet.

We passed the historical point, "El Vado de los Padres," where Father Escalante crossed the river in 1776, and the point where later the Mormons first crossed, when carrying their settlements south into Arizona.[2] At the mouth of Escalante Creek, or River, where there is another crossing, I, later on, found carved on the wall of the Canyon what I considered was a map of the river. By whom this was done, I do not know, but it was cut deep in the rock by some Indian, cliff dweller or possibly, (?) white man,

[2] "In Glen Canyon there are five places where, at extreme low water, the river can be forded, even with wagons.

    1st   At Dandy Crossing, in Utah.
    2d   The Mormon Crossing, about the middle of the Canyon.
    3d   'El Vado de los Padres' in Arizona.
    4th   At the mouth of Escalante Creek, Arizona,
    5th   At Lee's Ferry, Arizona."—Stanton.

who knew the River from its head to its entrance into Marble Canyon. The cutting was not new, but in appearance as old as any of the picture writings found elsewhere. It was cut into the rock deep and plain, and, at its lower end, ran into a much deeper cutting, just as the river sinks into Marble Canyon, and there the map ended. The sketch here reproduced was made in my note book at the time.

4. "Map of [the Colorado] River cut in rock at mouth of Escalante Creek, Glen Canyon."

WAITING FOR SUPPLIES

Our advance party reached Lee's Ferry, at the mouth of Paria Creek, on the evening of July 2nd. Our supplies not having arrived, President Brown started next morning on horseback for Kanab, ninety miles north, to get provisions for our journey.

The rest of us remained in camp, near the ranch of Warren M. Johnson and his Mormon families, and feasted ourselves upon his fresh vegetables, fruit, milk, eggs, and fresh beef. And now that we did not need them, we could catch a dozen fish every night.

During this time, Bush was continuing his survey through Glen Canyon. It had been arranged to send supplies to Bush's party up River, from Lee's Ferry. Why this was not done is one of the mysteries I never could solve. Bush and his men kept up their survey work until July 20th, when, being entirely out of food, they left next morning, and went down the River to the Ferry, and from there home. They could no nothing else, and deserve credit for the rapid and successful work they did for 130 miles, below Dandy Crossing.

On July 8th, President Brown returned from Kanab with a

wagon load of provisions. Next morning we loaded the three boats, and our little party of eight bade farewell to our kind Mormon friends, and swung our little fleet into the head of Marble Canyon. The first day we made only ten miles, running five smaller rapids, but, in order to take all precaution, we portaged over the heads of two heavy ones at Badger and Soap Creeks, and camped near the center of Soap Creek Rapid.

THE FIRST NIGHT IN MARBLE CANYON

As soon as we made camp I wrote up my notes, and after supper, making my bed down, lit my pipe for an evening smoke, when President Brown called me and asked me to come and sit on his bed and talk with him. On the journey, especially through Glen Canyon, we had become great friends. Brown was a most delightful companion, kind and genial, and as another has said, "no one could live near him, and not love him." We had found that we were both members of the same college fraternity, the Alpha Delta Phi, and the glens and alcoves had frequently rung with our old college songs. Usually, however, our beds were placed some distance apart when we retired for the night. This evening, he asked me to bring my bed and sleep beside him. I pulled up my blankets, and we sat down together. I noticed that President Brown seemed lonely and troubled, but I attributed it to the fact that his two special companions, Hughes and Reynolds, having both gone, this was the first night he had been entirely alone.

We sat there late, smoking and talking of our homes and the journey on the morrow. At this time President Brown's family were all traveling in Germany, and he spoke of them, and how far they were away.

When I awoke in the morning, President Brown was up and at the edge of the River taking a bath. As soon as he came to where I was, he said: "Stanton I dreamed of the rapids last night, the first time since we started."

Our breakfast was eaten in silence, and, as I can recall it, President Brown hardly said a word to me, or any one after that, until he was on the River.

Our boats were soon loaded and ready to start in the heavy waves of the lower half of Soap Creek Rapid. Beyond this was another rapid, short but heavy.

President Brown's boat, with himself and McDonald, was ahead, and my boat, getting off from shore with some difficulty, was a little distance behind. It was my custom, all through the River journey, to take the exact time of starting in and coming out of every rapid, and record it in my note book.

THE FATAL PLUNGE

In two minutes we were at the next rapid. Just as we dashed into the head of it, I saw McDonald running up the bank waving his arms. We had, for a few moments, all we could do to manage our own boat. It was but a moment. We were through the upper part of the rapid, and turning out into the eddy, I heard McDonald shout: "Mr. Brown is in there." As our boat turned around the whirlpool on the left, the note book, which Mr. Brown always carried, shot up on top of the water, and Hansbrough picked it up as we passed;[3] but we never saw the face of our noblehearted leader again.

Let me quote the details of this sad day from notes written in my note book at the time, and signed by each of the men—together with the sketch explaining the situation, also taken from my note book—under date of July 10th, 1889.

"[My boat left river bank at 6:23 A.M. At 6:25 entered head of rapid No. 108.] My boat with Hansbrough & Richards Struck

[3] The notebook is owned by Otis Marston, Berkeley, California.

77

the rapid head on in good shape intending to run all the way thro' I telling Hansbrough who was Steering to pull to the left of the heavy waves at the lower end of Rapid. Just as we got into the swiftest part at head of rapid I looked up and Saw McDonald bareheaded on left bank running towards us with his hands in the air. I called to Hansbrough, 'There they are waving to us we must pull out into the eddy/' Fortunately we were going so fast we went head on thro' the heaviest waves & turned into the eddy, only shipping a few gals of water. McDonald, continually calling to us, we heard Say just as we got into the eddy. 'Mr Brown is in there.' We realized in a moment that their boat had upset. I turned quickly & looked over the water, Saw nothing & then Shouted to men to pull hard for shore, & just as we turned at point marked 'D' in sketch I saw Brown's note book shoot up out of the water and . . . I called out 'there's his note book/' Hansbrough picked it out of water as we turned through eddy [to the shore]. I jumped over Richards to shore with line & immediately looked over the whole eddy & rapid but could see no other trace of him— . . . The whole of this did not take ¼ of a minute, even much less/

"I then called to men to unload boat which was done in a moment/ By this time McDonald had reached us, & he & Richards jumped into our boat & pulled out into eddy close to rapid, & rowed all round [for some time,] but never saw any trace of Mr. Brown or his body. When they came ashore, McDonald related the following

> We Struck rapid head to all right. Just when we were in the Swiftest part of water above breakers Mr. Brown said 'Mac, We want to make this eddy (McDonald was steering & B. rowing) and look at rapid below, this is where Stanton wanted to stop & look at the rapid which he could not see.'[4] I replied 'Alright' & turned the boat to come in. Just as we turned, in what seemed to be smooth waves, a heavy wave came up out of a whirl on upper side of boat

4 "The evening before, I had walked down the River bank about a mile, but could not see clearly the second rapid around the bend."—Stanton.

& instantly upset boat, throwing us both into river away from the boat.

We both went under, when I came up Mr. Brown was already up, I being in stern of boat was thrown into current & Brown being in bow was thrown in whirl[pool] between Current & eddy—I was carried down & turning my head 'hallooed' to Brown 'come on' he answered 'Alright'—in a cheerful voice. I was carried by Current and landed on point of rock in little eddy about 200 yards below— The boat, upside down, went down stream 50 to 75 ft ahead of me.

As soon as I got out of water I climbed up on rocks & turned immediately & saw Brown still in whirl[pool] swimming round & at same moment saw Mr. Stantons boat just coming into head of rapid not over two hundred feet above where Brown was. I ran up shore hallooing to Mr Stanton, 'Mr Brown is in there.' till I got up to Mr. Stanton's boat, which was then unloaded & immediately jumped in with Richards & rowed around whirls & eddys but could see no trace of Mr. Brown or his body & after Some time searching went ashore. *This is correct.*

Harry McDonald
July 10th 9:10 A.M.

Witness
   Rob B Stanton
   P M Hansbrough

Continuing to quote the notes in my note book: "This Sketch [below] Shows position of Rapid &c.

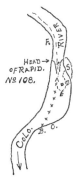

5. Sketch map of the river where President Brown was drowned

Point 'A' where Brown's boat upset/ Dotted line [_ _ _ _] course
of Stantons boat/ Cross line [xxxx] course McDonald drifted.
'B' point where McD. got out & first saw Stantons boat which
was at 'E'/ ['S,' Sand Beach where Stanton's boat landed.] . . .
'C' where Stanton first saw McDonald—'D' Position of Stantons
boat when note book came up. at point '□' which is place where
McDonald last saw Brown & must be pt where Brown sank not
five seconds before Stanton came/

"Boat No. 3 with Hislop, Nims and Gibson started from
Camp about ¼ minute later than we did, but did not get out in
good shape/ caught on rock & were delayed a little. They came
down through rapid [safely,] & into eddy at same point my boat
did . . . passed us as McDonald & Richards were pushing off from
sand beach.

"From McDonald's Statement & what I myself saw—our boat
was at head of rapid, in the draw—when I saw McDonald first
(pt C [in sketch]) & he saw Brown Still above water, & Our boat
was not over 175 ft from Brown/ (I paced this distance [after-
wards on shore.]) We ran this distance in 5 Seconds, no more,[5]
and reached the point where Brown sank not over 2 or 3 seconds
after he sank for the last time. His note book he carried in his
shirt [pocket,] and I suppose when he sank it escaped & shot
up out of water just as I saw it.

"The whole accident happened inside of a minute & a half . . . .

"[When I first saw McDonald,] we were in the heaviest [part]
of the rapid, and all hands & eyes [were] engaged in getting
our boat through safely [so that] none [of those] of our boat
saw Brown at all/ Even if we had [seen him], it would have been
utterly impossible to get to the place where he was any sooner
than we did—but if he could have remained afloat till we got
there we could have easily thrown him a line or reached him with
an oar as our boat circled round the whirl[pool] of the eddy

[5] "This would make a speed of a little less than 24 miles per hour. Not unusual
in running these rapids, as we proved, by actually timing the boats on a measured
course later."—Stanton.

he was in. Mr Browns boat upset [probably] before we rounded point marked F in sketch, tho' we might have been further on—
"This [above] we believe [to be] entirely correct

Rob B Stanton	P M Hansbrough
Harry McDonald	H. C. Richards

and we know as to boat No. 4 which was all we [actually] saw

John Hislop	F. A. Nims
G. W. Gibson	July 10th 1889"[6]

WE STILL HAD OUR WORK TO DO

Thus it was that President Brown sacrificed his life, which could so easily have been saved if he had had a life preserver to keep him afloat one-half minute longer. A noblehearted man and a true friend, he had won the love of everyone associated with him.

We sat that whole day, watching the ever changing waters of that rapid, its whirlpools and eddies, and searched the banks of the River for miles below, hoping, at least, to find his body and give it decent and honored burial; but it has been said, by those who know the River—"It seldom gives up its dead."

It was a day of terrible experience. In the depths of that lonely canyon, we sat for hours utterly paralyzed, beside the roaring waters that leaped and lashed and foamed without ceasing, and we could not realize until the darkness closed in around us, and we turned away to our camp, that our friend had gone forever.

In this world we are left but little time to mourn. We had work to do, and I determined, if possible, to complete the whole of that work. That such a determination *at that time* was unwise, I can freely admit, as I look back upon it today, but neither Hislop nor I ever thought of leaving the River then. That we did not sufficiently appreciate the difficulties, even after such a warning, knowing the outfit we had, is also clear as I see it now,

6 Entry for July 10, 1889, Field Notes, Book B.

81

but who is there that can say our decision was culpably wrong?

Next morning we sorrowfully embarked in our three little boats—having found boat No. 1 about a mile below in an eddy, where it was safe and uninjured. The River was some ten feet above its low water stage, and in the narrow part of the Canyon, where it was much higher, ran between low vertical walls a rushing torrent. We ran three lively rapids without trouble, stopping to take full notes and photographs of our railroad line.

Early on this same morning after the accident, at 8:20, we reached the head of a roaring rapid, No. 115. This section was called Echo Canyon, where the roar of the rapids rebound from wall to wall, resembling mighty thunder. The practically vertical part of the cliffs, next to the River, continued to rise, and, in a short time, we were between walls 300 to 500 feet high, and 200 feet from wall to wall, in general form as shown in the accompanying sketch.

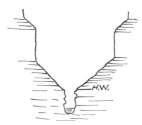

6. Sketch of cross section of Echo Canyon with high water mark indicated

The walls are rugged, broken into points which stick out over the water, forming little coves with quiet water above the rapid. In one of these we stopped, catching on to the points of rock while we examined the rapid ahead. It was too rough to run, in fact, as far as we could see, it was a roaring cataract, with huge rocks in the center, among which no boat such as ours could live.

We could not really see half the rapid, yet we were not 200 feet above the draw, and we were not in a frame of mind, that morning, to run any risks. So we attached our 210 feet of small line to my boat, and McDonald, Hislop and I got in and pushed along the wall, by catching on to the points of rock, while the rest of the men held the line to keep us from being swept into the head of the rapid. About seventy-five feet down, we held on to the cliff, McDonald with his hands and I by sticking an oar into a crack, while Hislop scaled a vertical wall some twenty feet, on little projecting points for toe and finger holds. When on top, we threw him a fish line by which he drew up our second heavy line, thus with the two lines attached, and hard rowing against the current which was rushing out from the cliff, we were dropped around the next point into a little eddy seventy-five feet above the rapid. Hislop, then making our heavy line fast, came across the cliff above us, and we cut loose our small line which was pulled back to let the other two boats down. This was more easily done, as the heavy line was still fastened above. After getting the last boat to where we were, we let the two down into a small cove, about thirty feet above the rapid, to a sand beach below a rock extending into the water. We then cut loose our heavy line, and Hislop, McDonald, and I, in the first boat, were pulled into the same cove by the small line, as we swung out into the stream. It was a nervous piece of work, after our experience of the day before, and we were glad to stop and lunch in the shade of an overhanging cliff. In the afternoon we portaged the supplies, swung the boats down by the lines for some 200 feet, reloaded, lined them down to the end of the rapid, and, rowing about 1,000 feet, came to Rapid No. 116, which was lined down with full loaded boats. Where the rapids were free from rocks, we ran them, only getting well wet by the splashing of the waves. In this narrow part of the canyon, even between the actual falls, the water at a high stage rushes along at great speed, is full of whirlpools, which, with their changing currents, sweep us from wall to wall, and we are sucked through swift and narrow draws, V shaped at their heads, like rapids, but with no breaking waves, only rolling torrents, too smooth to be given the name of rapids.

Thus, Thursday, Friday, and Saturday, we pushed on with our usual work, shooting through, or portaging, or lining down twenty-four bad rapids, in a distance of 18 or 20 miles, some of them very short, others a half-mile in length, thus leaving very little quiet water between. These rapids in this section are caused or formed in three ways. 1st, by the water dropping over a ledge of rock in the bottom of the River, of ten, fifteen, and in one place, I remember, of what seemed twenty feet. The amount of water being so great in these small falls, it does not drop vertically, but has a steep incline and then rolls back in high, but regular waves—These we called "water waves," and though lively and exciting, with the waves from five to ten feet high, are safe to run. 2nd, other rapids are formed by huge boulders, washed in from side canyons, thus forming dams; and, 3rd—by dams formed from portions of the cliffs which have fallen into the River. In both of these latter, boulders are washed down the River, and the whole rapid in some cases is full of rocks and huge boulders for a half mile or more in distance. These rapids are more dangerous to run, for the current is so changed and driven from side to side, that new currents and cross waves are formed suddenly by the boulders, so that they rush first from one side and then the other; are lashed into white foam, breaking in spray, 10, 15, and 20 feet in the air. The sunken boulders, with the powerful rush of water over the dam, cause the up-shoots, or boiling fountains, that so suddenly and unexpectedly rise up in the River when you least expect them, one of which was the cause of upsetting President Brown's boat.

SOME FACTS, WITH NO EXPLANATION

On Sunday, July 14th, we camped for our Sabbath rest in a beautiful spot, between variously colored marble cliffs, at the mouth of a side canyon which had divided and left standing in the center a solid marble pier forty feet high. The occurrences of this day are not related here as evidence for the Society of Psychic Research; but as facts that happened on a railway survey.—I leave to others their explanation.

It will be recalled that the night before President Brown was drowned, he insisted upon my sleeping beside him, as he was lonely and troubled. He talked of his home and his family so far away, dreamed that night of the rapids, and in less than two minutes, after he embarked on the River the next morning, he had gone to "that bourn from which no traveler returns." I can never forget the Sunday of July 14th. I had slept Friday night in the narrowest part of the Canyon, on a shelf of the cliff some twenty feet above the River, so worn out, that, though the marble slab was only covered by two blankets, I hardly moved all night, until Hansbrough woke me out of a sound sleep, at four o'clock in the morning, to tell me he had not slept at all, and was frightened by a pain in his big toe. I was vexed to be thus awakened for so trivial a reason, and told him to get out and let me rest. As he went away, I noticed how distressed he looked, and immediately repented of my sharp words and called him back.

The whole day he was troubled and worried. The next morning, after our Sunday breakfast, he came to me and sat near me, or walked with me around camp, the whole day, talking of his past life, of death, of Heaven and his trust in a future state. I tried to cheer him up. Although no thoughts of coming danger came into my mind, I entered into the spirit of his talk and read to him several chapters from the Bible, which seemed to comfort him.

The two Negro boys had their camp some distance away, so I hardly saw them all day; but learned later from Gibson, that Richards spent the whole time, and the greater part of Sunday night, talking to him in the same way as Hansbrough had to me, of the River, of death, and the future life to come.

I suggest no explanation of this, but simply record the facts as they occurred, in connection with what followed.

Monday, we were on the River again, and soon came to two

very rough and rocky rapids. We portaged the first and swung the loaded boats around the point at the head of the next (No. 133). The lower part of this rapid was very steep, though not rocky, and the powerful current, turning to the left, beating against a low cliff of marble perhaps 20 or 30 feet high, had worn out the bottom so that it overhung the water four or five feet. The boats were to run the lower part of this rapid, while Nims and I went down the shore, which was easily done for the walking was good, to take the photographs and record my notes.

McDonald and Gibson pushed off in the first boat, but, not getting a good start, landed on the right some 200 feet below and tried it again. From the point they went out, it was difficult to keep the best course; but, by hard pulling, they landed safely on the sand bar a half mile below, where we were to meet. Hansbrough and Richards in my boat went next. There had been some discussion between the men as to how they had better go, and Richards said to Hansbrough: "Well, if you say so, we'll go that way. Its a bad place to smash a boat, but of course, there's no danger to us," and with that he sat down and pulled off his shoes. When ready, I helped them push the boat from shore, telling them to keep well out in the current away from the cliffs. Hansbrough answered: "Yes we will." For the first few hundred feet, they went down near the center of the stream, when, suddenly, we saw them swept towards the left cliff and, in a moment, they were against it at a point where there was an overhanging shelf of about three feet in width. The current was swirling along the cliff. They quickly put up the oars, and began shoving the boat out from the cliff, as they were being carried along under the little shelf. I saw Richards get his bow end out clear from the wall into the stream, and Hansbrough had pushed out the stern so his head was from under the shelf. I turned to Hislop and said: "they are all right now," expecting to see them pull out into the stream, when, suddenly, their boat turned completely over and both went into the water. I screamed and waved to McDonald, and he and Gibson, jumping into their boat

86

MARBLE CANYON

"There is marble enough to build forty Babylons, wall and all."

BELOW MARBLE CANYON

"Portions of the cliffs which have fallen into the river form partial dams and rapids."

pushed out from shore towards Richards, who was swimming down the center of the current; but he sank before they reached him. Hansbrough was never seen by any of us after the boat was upset. Both of these men were powerful athletes and good swimmers, but they were powerless against the current and condition of the River. The Saturday before, we had heavy rains, and, Monday, the water was thick with sand and mud. Even with the few clothes the men had on, they were soon weighted down by the sand and held under the water. I then realized fully what it meant to be without life preservers, in such work on such a River. If all had had them, there would have been no reason why these two men, or President Brown, need have been in any danger in the part of the River into which they were thrown.

A CHANGE OF PLAN

Two more faithful and good men gone! Astonished and crushed by their loss, our force too small to portage our boats, and our outfit and boats unfit for such work, I decided to abandon the trip, with then and there a determination, as soon as a new and proper outfit could be secured, to return and complete our journey to the Gulf.

From then on, our only object was to find a side canyon leading out to the north, through which to make our retreat. Tuesday, and until nearly noon on Wednesday, we continued running, lining down, and portaging eleven more rapids, getting deeper and deeper into the marble gorge. At a point about thirty-two miles below the head of Marble Canyon, where the River makes a right-angle turn to the east, is a narrow side canyon; and a short distance below it a large living spring gushes out of a crevice on the side of the cliff, just under which is a broad marble shelf; on this has gathered large patches of rich soil, probably accumulated there from the dust blowing and being caught by the water from the spring trickling over the rocky shelf. In this

87

soil grow beautiful flowering bushes, grass, ferns, and vines, the latter hanging down in festoons over the face of the cliff. This was named by Major Powell—"Vasey's Paradise."[7] From it we gathered ferns and flowers and took them to our camp where we expected to spend our last night in the Canyon. The little flowers, in their innocence and beauty, seemed to speak to us of better things, still the sad thoughts of the past few days crowded in upon us.

A STORM IN DEATH'S CANYON

A great storm was gathering over our heads. The rain was falling in a steady shower. No shelter below; not a dry blanket or coat. About forty feet up on the side of the marble cliff, I saw a small cave with a marble shelf projecting over it. With some difficulty I climbed up to it. It was hardly large enough for my body, and not long enough for me to stretch fully out; but I crawled in, and, worn out by the work and excitement of the day, soon fell asleep.

About midnight, I was awakened by a terrific peal of thunder, and around me and over me raged one of the most awful storms it has been my fate to witness. I have seen the lightning play, and heard the thunder roll, among the summit peaks of the Rocky Mountains, as I have stood on some rocky point far above the clouds, but nowhere has the awful grandeur equalled that night in the lonesome depths of what was, to us, death's canyon.

The lightning's flash lit up the dark recesses of the gorge and cast ghastly shadows upon cliffs and sloping hillsides; and again all was shut in by darkness thicker than that of Egypt. The stillness was only broken by the roar of the River as it rushed along beneath me. Suddenly, as if the mighty cliffs above were rolling down against each other, there was peal after peal of thunder, striking against the marble cliffs below, and, mingling with their echoes, bounded from cliff to cliff. Thunder with echo, echo with

[7] Powell, *Exploration of the Colorado River,* 76.

thunder, crossed and recrossed from wall to wall of the Canyon, and, rising higher and higher, died away among the side gorges and caverns thousands of feet above my head. For hours the tempest raged. Tucked away as a little worm in the cleft in the rock, the grandeur of the storm spoke as to the Psalmist of old; and out of the night came a voice mightier than the tempest, and said: "Be still! and know that I am God."[8]

Our last camp, No. 40, in Marble Canyon, a short distance above Vasey's Paradise, was at the mouth of the side canyon leading out to the north, into House Rock Valley. We had climbed up on the cliffs the day before, and looking ahead were sure we could go out by this canyon. So, preparing then for our return, we cached all our supplies in a large dry marble cave.

About noon, July 17th, I looked up the main canyon and saw something like a large bundle floating down the River. As it came nearer, we all saw that it was President Brown's body. We recognized it by the coat he had on in the early morning, when he was drowned. McDonald and Hislop jumped into an empty boat, and, at the risk of their lives, attempted to get it. This was impossible, as it was so near the head of the powerful, high water rapid just below. I followed the body for some distance along the shore, and saw it go around the big bend, through another rapid, and float on down the River. This was a sad disappointment, for I so hoped, when I first saw the body coming toward us, that we might give the last remains of our loved friend a fitting burial among the flowers and shrubbery of that beautiful evergreen spot, Vasey's Paradise. In the afternoon, we climbed the cliff to explore the side canyon, for, where it entered the River, it was but 10 or 15 feet wide and was filled by a roaring muddy stream, from the heavy rains of the past few days. On a bench, some hundred feet up, we found the remains of a whole village of cliff dwellers, with a narrow street before the houses with a natural marble pavement, except at one point, where the cliff was broken down, and there a retaining wall had been built to make the

8 Psalms 46:10.

street complete. From this, a well worn trail led up the walls of the side canyon, which we followed, till we could see far up the valley, and then returning to camp, we named the magnificent marble promontory at the bend of the River—"Point Retreat."

A RETREAT, WITH A PLEDGE TO RETURN

This retreat was a sad disappointment, especially to Hislop and myself. But as I recorded that day in my note book, "it would not only be unwise [and wrong] to attempt to go further with our present outfit, but would be impossible as we have not enough men to portage our boats."[9] Hislop and I then pledged each other that we would return as soon as possible and complete our work—a pledge which we both redeemed.

Early in the morning of July 18th, we took up our sorrowful retreat, following over the cliff dwellers path into the more open valley of the upper side gorge. This upper part of the side canyon is in the Permian Sandstones, which skirt the tops of the marble walls of the main canyon below Lee's Ferry, and is composed of hard and soft strata, the latter being easily crumbled and washed by the rain. When a few miles up, there came on another of those sudden and furious storms, so common at times in the dry Southwest.

The rain did not fall in showers, or in "bucketfulls," but in what could almost be termed solid sheets of water. We took shelter under an immense leaning rock, in the bottom of the canyon valley, near the creek. As the rain increased, I heard some rock tumbling down behind us, and, looking up, I saw one of the grandest and most exciting scenes of the crumbling and falling of what we so falsely call the everlasting hills. As the water began to pour over from the plateau above, it seemed as if the whole upper edge of the Canyon had begun to move. Little streams, rapidly growing into torrents, came over the

9 Entry for July 17, 1889, Field Notes, Book B.

hard top stratum from every crevice and fell on the softer slopes below. In a moment they changed into streams of mud, and, as they came farther down, again changed into streams of water, mud and rock, undermining huge loose blocks of the harder strata and starting them, they plunged ahead. In a few moments, it seemed as though the slopes on both sides of the whole Canyon, as far as we could see, were moving down upon us, first with a rumbling noise, then an awful roar. As the larger blocks of rock plunged ahead of the streams, they crashed against other blocks, lodged on the slopes, and, bursting with an explosion like dynamite, broke into pieces, while the fragments flew into the air in every direction, hundreds of feet above our heads, and as the whole conglomerate mass of water, mud, and flying rocks, came down the slopes nearer to where we were, it looked as if nothing could prevent us from being buried in an avalanche of rock and mud. It was a scene of the wildest fury of the elements!

The rain ceased as suddenly as it began, and, in a few minutes, the whole Canyon resumed its deathlike stillness, only broken by the rumble of the stream of muddy water, running in the creek bed at our feet. It is a noticeable fact that in all of the weeks we had been in the Canyons, before this day, we had never heard as much as a pebble drop, or anything roll down from the cliffs, not even during the heavy storms in Marble Canyon. This latter is accounted for by the different nature of the walls—the hard limestone and marble.

We finally reached the top, at 4:00 P.M., after a hard climb of the last 200 feet of the slopes, made dangerous by the loosening of the rocks by the recent storm, and, continuing north over the plain, slept that night by the side of a pool of fresh water. It was a cold night, with everything wet. By midnight we froze out, and then huddled around a sage brush fire until morning. Friday, early, we came to an outpost of the "VT" Cattle ranch. After resting, the foreman drove us twenty miles to House Rock. Next day Mr. S. W. Taylor, in charge of the ranch, took us with his team forty miles to Johnson P.O., where we were most kindly received by Mr. W. D. Johnson and his family and furnished a most elegant dinner, and after sleeping, as we preferred to, in the hay mows, and a hearty breakfast Sunday morning, we drove on to Kanab.

The reception given us by Bishop Lawrence C. Marriger and his family at Kanab is one of the brightest memories of several years spent among the Mormons of Utah.

That evening, I telegraphed to my family and to the secretary of the Railroad Company, announcing the death of President Brown and the two boatmen.

All the money of any consequence that was in the party was on Mr. Brown's person and we had not a dollar. Without my asking Bishop Marriger offered me all necessary funds to take us home, and did loan me $600.00 for that purpose. By means of which, and his team to take us to the railroad at Milford, we reached Denver the evening of July 27th.

It is with the greatest pleasure that I record here, what I have stated elsewhere, my profound thanks to Bishop Marriger and his good wife for the kind manner with which they received me and my shipwrecked companions into their home, their hospitable care of us while there, and the generous and trustful manner in which they speeded our sorrowful homeward journey. Kindhearted, true Christian folk, it has been a pleasure and an honor to keep up their acquaintance, and our friendships for many, many years.

CHAPTER SIX

"Glen Canyon"

Ne'er saw I, never felt, a calm so deep!
The river glideth at his own sweet will:
Dear God! the very Canyon seems asleep;
And all that mighty gorge is lying still!

—ADAPTED FROM WILLIAM WORDSWORTH[1]

ON reaching Denver, I immediately began to prepare for our second expedition, or, as it has been called, our "second attempt"; but which, I think, it is only just to designate as the continuance, or completion, of the Survey.

Whichever it may have been, during the first journey I had no authority, beyond the actual survey work, except what may have come to me, as the next in command, after President Brown's death.

From August 1st., 1889, however, I assumed all responsibility, not only for the determination to complete the work, but for the raising of the necessary money, as well as the conduct of the second expedition.

After the disasters in Marble Canyon, it required some little exertion for me to raise the required amount to secure a new outfit to complete the survey to the Gulf of California. I went to New York in August to consult with my friends. The one who gave me the most encouragement was Arthur M. Wellington, C.E., then editor of the *Engineering News*.[2] . . . I did not seek

1 "Composed upon Westminster Bridge." Stanton's adaptation consists of changing two words: from "houses" to "Canyon" in line 3; from "heart" to "gorge" in line 4. The title is Stanton's.

2 "Three Denver gentlemen made it possible to settle up all past accounts and *start* the new, and final expedition, and to those men I express my sincere thanks and everlasting gratitude.

Hon. T. C. Henry donated $10,000.00
Mr. H. B. Chamberlin donated 2,000.00
Mr. S. S. Harper, donated 1,500.00

financial assistance in the East, but . . . Mr. Wellington's strong backing stiffened the backbones and loosened the pursestrings of some of my Denver friends, so that sufficient funds were raised to order the boats and other needed supplies.

Profiting by the experience of the summer before, our new outfit was vastly different from the first. I had built, at Waukegan, Ills., three boats, twenty-two feet long, four and a half feet beam, and twenty-two inches deep. These were made of oak, from plans of my own, with ribs of one and a half by three-quarters of an inch, placed four inches apart, and planked with one-half-inch oak, all riveted together with copper rivets. Each boat had ten separate air-tight compartments, two large ones in the ends and four along each side.[3] Two cross seats were built into the sides, which, with the bulkhead division in the center (without deck), completely braced and stiffened the sides. A fifty-foot line in the bow, and two hundred and fifty feet of three-quarter-inch line at the stern, a life line rigged all around the whole boat, and a plentiful supply of selected eight-foot oars for rowing, and twelve-foot oars for steering, constituted the equipment of the boats.

I detailed Harry McDonald, himself a boatbuilder, to go to Waukegan and stay with and superintend the building of the boats, that nothing might be overlooked to make them perfect.

The best cork life preservers, made expressly for us from my own pattern, were provided for all the men, and during the expedition, everyone was compelled to wear them whenever on the water. They were of such a form as not to be the least inconvenient, so that, in the winter, the men put them on when they first got up in the cool of the morning and never took them off until they went to bed. On the bow of each boat was placed a

Others, both West and East, made fair promises.—Promises that were forgotten when the work was done, and the depression of 1890 came, and it devolved upon me, out of my own pocket, to make up the deficiency amounting to $12,500.00."—Stanton.

3 "Two water-tight lockers were built in the ends, for meats and other things, which, if possible, we did not wish to unpack when making a portage."—Stanton.

circular cork life-buoy, with line attached, to be used in case a man was thrown overboard.

All stores and provisions were packed in water-tight rubber (mackintosh) bags, made expressly for the purpose. Remembering that in Cataract Canyon, the much abused and condemned air-tight zinc boxes saved us from starvation, when they were cut loose and went over the rapid, by patiently waiting for us in the eddies below, I had left in the sides of each boat two spaces, by omitting the air-tight compartment, large enough to take in a five-gallon keg. These kegs were intended to be filled with rice, beans, coffee, sugar, &c, the idea being that if all our boats were smashed and our provisions all lost in one great disaster, these kegs would float and be picked up in the eddies, and furnish us sufficient food to take us safely out of the Canyon. This necessity did not arise; but, when our one boat was lost, my calculations proved entirely correct, for the two kegs that were left in the boat when it was swung out into the rapid were found later, safe and sound, in the eddy below, and the provisions perfectly dry.

THE MEN OF THE SECOND PARTY

The new party and the assignments to the boats were as follows. Each boat was named by its own Commander.

My boat, No. 1, "The Bonnie Jean": Harry McDonald, Langdon Gibson, Elmer Kane, and myself.

Boat No. 2, "The Water Lily": Assist. Engr. John Hislop, Photographer F. A. Nims, Reginald Travers and W. H. Edwards.

Boat No. 3, "The Sweet Marie": A. B. Twining, H. G. Ballard, L. G. Brown and James Hogue the Cook.[4]

[4] "To prevent confusion in names, it should be remembered that, in the first party, there were President Frank M. Brown and G. W. Gibson, the colored cook, and in the second party L. G. Brown and Langdon Gibson. No confusion can come from the name Brown, for where the first is referred to he is always spoken of as President Brown; and from here on where Gibson is referred to it is always Mr.

These men were selected for the double duty of boatmen and an engineer party.

In the discussion of my paper before the American Society of Civil Engineers, it was suggested that I would have done better by employing northern river lumbermen for my boatmen, as being experts on such waters. With no disparagement to the rest of the men, I quote the following from my part of the discussion of that paper answering Mr. Alfred F. Sears:

"I am fully aware of the value of 'skilled labor' in any undertaking, under ordinary circumstances. Yet in selecting my men for the second expedition, although strongly advised to secure the lumbermen Mr. Sears refers to, I rejected all such labor with but one exception, an experienced boatman in such waters, and he deserted the expedition in the Grand Canyon when we most needed him. It has been my experience many times during the past twenty years that for such work, whether on land or water, where prolonged hardships and privations, and especially scanty food, and perhaps starvation, are to be faced day after day, the man who has an object to gain, with of course the qualities of body and mind to quickly acquire 'experience,' is far more efficient, and the better man to tie to in a wilderness, than the laborer, however skilled he may be, who is simply hired for so much a day.

"No one could have rendered more faithful service or have more skillfully saved our lives by his quick-witted work just in the nick of time, than my First Assistant, Mr. John Hislop, C.E., and while all the men who made the entire trip with me did their whole duty, yet the one who in less than a week developed the most perfect skill in navigating that rushing torrent with a heavy boat, was Mr. Reginald Travers, whose only preparation for such work, from the time he was seventeen till he was twenty-eight,

Langdon Gibson who is meant, and who objects very much to being *identified* as the brother of Charles Dana Gibson [the popular artist and magazine illustrator], which, however, he is."—Stanton.

when he joined the expedition, was that of a stockbroker on one of the New York exchanges, and an amateur oarsman on Flushing Bay."[5]

Since then, I have spent some time on northern rivers and among Canadian lumbermen and have questioned the men employed there, and, from all they said, my opinion was more than ever confirmed—that as long as these skilled laborers have their dry beds and their bellies full of grub, they are most expert in such work, but that it would take more than their wages to keep them, when they had nothing to eat and only a pile of sharp rocks to sleep upon.

THE TRIP TO THE RIVER

As explained before, we were not seeking adventure, but a railway route; I, therefore, decided not to subject our new outfit to any unnecessary risk. Our survey was completed 130 miles below Dandy Crossing and it would have been foolish, just for the adventure of running the rapids of Cataract Canyon, to come all the way from the railroad by water. I arranged to haul our boats by wagon from Blake, or Green River Station, Utah, to the nearest point in Glen Canyon, which was the mouth of Crescent Creek, about four miles below the mouth of the Dirty Devil River.

The party left Denver Monday, November 25th, 1889, reaching Blake the next noon. To load the heavy boats securely on the wagons required a whole day. The overland expedition left the railroad in the afternoon of Nov. 27th. Our route was across the San Rafael River, seventeen miles south of Blake, and the Dirty Devil in Graves' Valley, where the town of Hanksville now is, and thence to the head of Crescent Creek Canyon, and down it to the Colorado, a total distance of, probably, 120 miles. Any

---

[5] Stanton, "Availability of the Canyons of the Colorado River," *Transactions of the American Society of Civil Engineers*, Vol. XXVI (1892), 355.

one who, from Western experience, knows what "four spokes in the sand" means can appreciate what it was to transport long unwieldy loads, as these boats were, over such a country. The latter half of the journey was without roads or trails, simply across the Mesa, down into and across the gulches, and finally down Crescent Creek Canyon, a dry wash, only a water course in time of storm, hundreds of feet deep, and, part of the way, at the bottom so narrow that the hubs of the wagons in places scraped along the walls on both sides at the same time. It snowed, or rained, during nearly the whole journey, but we arrived without accident at the Colorado on the evening of Friday Dec. 6th. Looking over my note books, I find little things that I had long forgotten—"[On reaching the River] we raised a pole . . . [and hoisted the Stars and Stripes and my little Alpha Delta Phi pennant intended for my boat.] The boys fired a salute of 13 Shots [my lucky number], gave three cheers for the flags and three cheers & a tiger for myself."[6] The next day, the teams started back, but, in the afternoon, one of the teamsters returned and told us that when they were in the narrowest part of Crescent Creek Canyon, they were met by a flood of water four feet deep, from a storm farther up the Canyon, though it was not raining where they were, and the narrow gorge being dammed up by their wagons and horses, the flood rose till the whole outfit, teams, wagons and men, was tumbled, turned over and mixed up, in one mess and washed six hundred feet down to a wider part of the gorge, and two of the horses drowned.

Our outfit, teams, boats and men, was in the same narrow spot the day before, and I have often wondered what would have been the history of our final railway survey if that storm had happened twenty-four hours earlier.

Our boats, even after their railroad ride from Waukegan and the rough handling of the wagons over the plain and down the rocky canyon, when put into the water, did not leak a drop.

6 Entry for December 6, 1889, Field Notes, Book A.

It took us several days to separate and pack our stores. All provisions, clothing, and supplies, except bedding, canned goods and meat, were packed in the forty-eight heavy rubber bags.

They were 12 inches in diameter and 20 inches long, with mouth pieces 16 inches in length. After the bag was filled, this mouth piece, or flap, was folded and rolled very tight and laced over, through eyelets, with a strong cord. Over each one was fitted a heavy canvas sack, to keep them from being chafed. When filled with provisions, each bag weighed about seventy pounds, and, when laced tight, proved to be very effective in excluding the water, one boatload being under the water several hours without injury. Besides these rubber bags, the six five-gallon kegs, two in each boat, were filled with rice, beans, sugar, coffee, etc., for the special precaution explained above. The "etc." was one keg of the best brandy, and one of fine old whiskey. This was taken for medicine and precaution—not snake bites—and it must be said to the credit of the expedition that no time, with two exceptions, was it ever touched, except as medicine when in the middle of winter we were thrown into the River and needed a quick restorative. At the mouth of Diamond Creek, while I was out at the railroad, the boys had a little celebration. I think, possibly, they deserved it.

All supplies, including this time the cooking utensils, were divided equally between the three boats. A supply of medicines, rifles, shot guns, ammunition, etc. was taken. Expecting to be out all winter, four small tents were provided, but these were soon thrown away, as being cumbersome luxuries. On account of the winter weather, overcoats, more blankets and clothing were necessary. Four months' provisions were taken at the start, and each boat carried, when fully loaded, about 3,200 pounds besides the four men.

A false bottom was placed in the boats, under which all canned goods were packed next to the keel, with the salt meats and hardware in the lockers at each end. Everything was so packed and strapped to the boats that in case of an upset nothing could be detached unless the boat was completely smashed.

The new photographic supplies consisted of two 6½x8½-inch cameras and one 4x5-inch detective instrument, and 2,000 films, in rolls, with extra roll-holders. Each roll of films was in a tin box made water-tight by a strip of adhesive plaster; and these packed in the rubber bags. As each roll was exposed, it was again *soldered* up in its tin box, and the duplicates carried in separate boats. All necessary instruments, transits, levels, rods, barometers and thermometers were, of course, supplied.

THROUGH GLEN CANYON AGAIN

Everything now being in readiness, we started once more on the River, the morning of Dec. 10th. For nearly two hundred and twenty miles, we were to retrace the same journey we had made in the summer, and a hundred and eighty miles of that was over the quiet stretches of Glen Canyon. This gave us time to break in the new men, and me an opportunity to study more in detail the questions of the railway problem.

I had also an opportunity to note the change in the River from medium high water to extreme low water. It is my opinion after traveling parts of the River (the best and some of the worst) in both stages—at high and extremely low water—that the safest time to navigate the Colorado with a boat is at a stage of water, in the open parts of the Canyons, of about ten feet above low water. This would give a much higher rise in the narrow crooked parts, and would cover up the greater number of dangerous rocks in the rapids and make them safe, and, at the same time, not create such a powerful current as to be in itself dangerous.

There are places in the Canyons where the narrowness of the defile, and right-angle turns in the solid rock, and where the River being at its extreme height—100 to 120 feet above low water in the narrowest parts—it would seem to me, no boat could possibly live, for the want of "sea room." The current would curl back in breakers, perhaps thirty feet high, from the vertical cliffs in marble Canyon. No one, as far as I know, has ever been in these Canyons at the time of *extreme* high water. What this means requires some little explanation. Generally the River begins to rise at the head of the Colorado *about* the first of May for its annual high season. High water is caused by the melting of the snow in the mountains. This is seldom the same for two seasons. Some years there is more, some years less snow. If the snow melts slowly, freezing up each night, the rise of the River is not excessive. An extremely warm June in the mountains, heavy warm rains among the foot hills, and general cloud bursts in the summer over the arid region (which sometimes occur) *combined,* would make the most extreme stage of high water. Such a combination seldom happens. So far as is on record, no one has traversed the Canyons during one of these *highest* floods. The highest stage noticed, in boats, was recorded by Dellenbaugh in 1872. It was the intention, as stated by Dellenbaugh, for the Powell expedition of 1872 to go on through the whole of the Grand Canyon, but when they got to the mouth of Kanab Canyon; "Powell . . . announced that he had decided to end the river work at this point on account of the extreme high water, which would render impassable the rapid where the Howlands and Dunn had left,"[7] and Dellenbaugh has told me that during this same trip at the rapid known as the "Sockdologer," above Kanab and in a wider part of the Canyon, and where they thought the water was extremely high for their boats, he noticed the highest high water marks "50 to 100 feet above the then stage." This being the case, it shows that, when Major Powell stopped his second trip on account of high water, the River in the *narrowest parts* still lacked fully 75 to 100 feet of its highest stage as recorded by the driftwood lodged on the cliffs. In my summer and winter experience, we traveled through Cataract, Glen, and part

[7] Dellenbaugh, *The Romance of the Colorado River,* 341.

THE NEW OUTFIT AT THE HEAD OF CRESCENT CANYON

"The new boats were of solid oak, sturdy and in all ways well suited for the work which they were to perform."

THE FIRST MILE IN THE GRAND CANYON

"Where the alignment of the river and slopes of the walls were of such a nature that no question could arise, the instrumental work was left undone."

of Marble Canyons on what would be about one-half of the usual high water stage, and through Glen, Marble, and half of the Grand Canyons on a very low stage. In the unusual winter rise of February 1890, in the *wide* portion of the Grand Canyon above Kanab Canyon, while we were there, the River rose between 10 and 15 feet, caused by the great floods and bursting of the dams on the Little Colorado, as explained later on. This meant, in the narrowest part of the inner gorge below Kanab Canyon through which we traveled during the next few days, a rise of from 30 to 40 feet. So that when anyone speaks of *high water* on the Colorado, one must know not only the season of the year, but the year itself.

Another point; the condition of high or low water bears directly upon the number of real rapids in each Canyon. At places, where a severe rapid exists at low water, it may be entirely obliterated during higher water. I know a number of points where a narrow part of the Canyon, below a severe rapid, backs up the high water and smooths the whole cataract out.

The less important rapids, made by boulders, are at times formed in new places by heavy storms in side canyons, and, at others, by these same sudden storms, are washed out. All this goes to show why the counting of the rapids by two parties in different years varies so materially.

Other changes are taking place. Great rocks from the cliffs are falling in and forming temporary rapids and new channels, in the broad and Shallow River in Glen Canyon.

Our second journey through Glen Canyon, though made in December, was in the weather of early fall. The excessive heat of the summer had gone. The nights were cool, but the wild flowers in the lower stretches of the Canyon were still in bloom. Though the willows were touched by frost their leaves were still on. The exquisite shade of the first yellow; the light green of the young protected sprouts, mingling with the browns of the dry grasses on the great flats; the bright red of the autumn oak leaves; all seen against the walls of variegated shales, of creamy

103

orange above, then bright vermilion, and below purple and chocolate beds, with, at their foot, hillocks of green and yellow sands,
all made a color scheme and a picture most pleasing to look upon,
worthy of an artist's brush, but which, much to my regret, my
camera could not catch.

ICE BOATING ON THE COLORADO

Some years afterwards, I traversed in boats this same Canyon
several times.[8] Once in the winter of 1897–98, the most severe
known in Utah and Arizona for many years; when, in places, the
River was frozen over in the quiet portions in Glen Canyon, and
I went from Dandy Crossing to Lee's Ferry with my friend John
Ginty and his son, of San Francisco, and a couple of men, where,
for miles, we had to cut our way through the ice with axes. The
ice was thick enough for us to walk and skid our boats upon.
At places, the whole mass would be moving down the River
while we were cutting our way through it, and, coming out at
the head of the rapid, we would be carried through, surrounded
by huge cakes of ice that were broken off the advancing sheet
at the head of the rapid. Such an experience, in some of the
heavier, low-water rapids of Glen Canyon, was more nervous
work and more dangerous than running many of the rapids of
the Grand Canyon, for, going through the rapids, even though
their waves were only three or four feet high, surrounded by
cakes of ice, surging, swaying, grinding and crushing against
the boat, we were entirely at the mercy of the current and the
ice, as we could neither row nor steer. Fortunately, by using poles

[8] Stanton was engaged in gold placermining activity in the Glen Canyon. See
Dwight L. Smith, "Hoskaninni: A Gold Mining Venture in Glen Canyon," *Prob-
ing the American West: Papers from the Santa Fe Conference,* ed. by K. Ross Toole
et al. (Santa Fe, 1962), 125–32, 203–04; also, "Hoskaninni: A Gold Mining Venture
in Glen Canyon," *El Palacio,* Vol. LXIX (Summer 1962), 77–84; and C. Gregory
Crampton and Dwight L. Smith (eds.), Robert B. Stanton, *The Hoskaninni Papers:
Mining in Glen Canyon, 1897–1902* (University of Utah *Anthropological Papers*
No. 54, Glen Canyon Series No. 15 [Salt Lake City, 1961]).

with spikes in their ends, pushing against the ice and the cliffs as we went by, we reached Lee's Ferry in safety, and had the pleasure of a nine days' tramp to the railroad, sleeping out in the snow every night, without tents or other shelter than our blankets, while the thermometer ranged from 10 to 30 degrees below zero. . . .

WE MEET JACK SUMNER

Returning to our railroad survey; Friday the 13th of Dec. '89, was to me again a lucky day. In the afternoon we were hailed by a man at one of the placer mines on shore asking us for tobacco; he was entirely out, and those who know what this means in a wilderness can appreciate his position. We landed a little below, gave him a pound plug of good tobacco, and discovered the man was "Jack" Sumner. I had a half hour's talk with Sumner, which was the beginning of a friendship that lasted to the time of his death. He gave us great good cheer, and the simple advice to "Go slow and be careful, and you will be all right." I asked him many questions about the River below, particularly about the cataract where the three men left the party of '69, and going out, were killed by the Indians, telling him that was the one rapid and the one place on the whole River, from Major Powell's account, which I feared.[9] He assured me there were no unsurmountable difficulties at that point, and encouraged us in every way. . . .

I took Sumner's photograph and bade him goodbye. . . .

The next day we came upon one of the troubles of low water in Glen Canyon, where the River is very wide and shallow. For about one half-mile the level bed rock is broken into steps of a few feet over which the water pours and is churned into a mass of white foam. On these steps the water was not deep enough to float our loaded boats, the River being spread out over so wide

9 J. C. Sumner was a member of the 1869 Powell expedition. Powell, *Exploration of the Colorado River*, 9.

a channel. We were obliged to make a portage of all our supplies for some eight hundred feet, and the light boats were run below. The next day the same operation had to be repeated for a distance of another half-mile. It was the longest portage we had ever made, requiring four round trips, making four miles' walk for each man, not such a great distance in itself, but the loads we had to carry were heavy. This shallow, shelving bed rock continued for several miles farther, and was very trying at low water, requiring very hard work, with our heavily loaded boats. Years after, I became well acquainted with this section and learned how to navigate it through cracks in the bed rock, which, even at the lowest stage, carried water enough to float our boats in narrow crooked channels. In the summer of 1889, this stretch, with six to ten feet higher water, was only a broad, smooth, but very swift, current.

At the mouth of the San Juan River there was no rapid at all. The rocks from this side canyon crumble into sand and go on down to the Gulf. We walked up the San Juan for several miles. At its mouth the Canyon walls are low, but grew higher and higher the farther we went, until, in a few miles, the Canyon became as large as that of the Colorado.

ANCIENT ENGINEERS OF THE COLORADO

Below the San Juan, Hogue discovered a large number of cliff dwellings. We stopped to examine them and noticed some curious structures at the mouth of the side canyon, which I could not at first understand. In the side canyon, for a long distance up, were the remains of a great many cliff dwellings, large and small. Back a mile or so from its mouth, which was very narrow, the Canyon widened, and there were extensive bottoms that once, centuries ago, were cultivated in corn—the stone corncribs still remain with corn cobs in them. In the main Canyon, below this side canyon, there were also great flats that had once been cultivated. After studying the whole situation for some time, I came to the conclusion that we had discovered the works of some of my professional brethren, the prehistoric Civil Engineers of that long forgotten race of centuries upon centuries ago. The case was this. The mouth of the side canyon was narrow and deep, with walls Vertical perhaps, 100 feet up. At high water, all communication was cut off between the town, in the side canyon, and the farms on the main River. On the lower vertical wall was a shelf, four feet or so wide, twenty or more feet up, but this also was covered at high water. Communication must be kept up, and these engineers, my oldest professional brethren, were, perhaps, the first engineers to bridge the Canyon of the Colorado lengthwise.[10] On the shelf of the rock wall, they erected a set of dry rubble masonry piers, about six feet apart, in size four feet by four feet and six feet high. Over these they laid their foot bridges, so that they could go to their fields at any time. The timbers are not there now, but most of the piers still remain. The bridge spans were not long, it is true, but tall timber is not easy to find in that part of the country—only scrubby pinon. This, to my mind, was true engineering, and possibly one of the oldest remains of bridge construction on the continent, showing also that even the first engineers of our country had no dreaded awe of building a road, if not a railroad, in the Canyons of the Colorado.

On the 19th, we met Edward Mesken, an old trapper and prospector, and his dog Sport. They had been on the River nearly all of five years, though we passed, the last summer, without seeing them. Our night at their camp was at least one bright spot in their lonely lives.

December 21st., we reached the point where Bush dropped his work. We picked up the line and continued the survey down the River over some difficult points, arriving at Lee's Ferry, December 23rd., '89. The last afternoon, the wind blew a terrific

10 See Howard V. Hinckley, "Bridging Canyons Lengthwise," *Transactions* of the American Society of Civil Engineers, Vol. XXVI (1892), 521.—Stanton.

gale up stream, forming waves four and five feet high, breaking into white caps over our boats, making fearfully hard rowing for the last seven miles.

We spent Christmas with our Mormon friends the Johnsons, and Al. Huntington, a California '49er, and Mr. and Mrs. (No. 1) Johnson took dinner with us. Our table, decorated with wild flowers picked that day, was set in the open air in front of an old stone fort built by John D. Lee, who took refuge in this part of the wilderness years before, in 1871 or '72, and finally, in 1877, was executed for his connection with the Mountain Meadow massacre of 1857.

Expecting to be on the River somewhere at Christmas time, remembering the scanty meals we had had, and thinking of those we might have in the future, I had packed in the bottom of the boats, unknown to the boys, some little extras for that day, which with fresh fruits, beef, and milk from the Johnson ranch, made up our Christmas dinner.

MENU
Colorado River Survey Christmas Dinner, 1889

SOUPS
Oxtail, Tomato, Chicken.

FISH
Colorado River Salmon.

ROAST
Turkey. Beef. Ox Heart.

ENTREES
Braised Chicken. Game Pie.

VEGETABLES
Mashed Potatoes. Stewed Onions. Tomatoes. Rice.

Potato Salad.

Wheat, Corn and Graham Bread.

Tea, Coffee, Chocolate, Milk.

THE SECOND ATTEMPT

DESSERT

Plum Pudding, Hard Sauce. Mince and Apple Pie.
Apple and Cherry Sauce.
Bents Crackers and Utah Cheese.
Arizona Apples, fresh Peaches and Pears, Raisins
and Nuts (all grown at Lee's Ferry).

Havana Cigars. Turkish Cigarettes.

CHAPTER SEVEN

All your better deeds
Shall be in water writ, but this in marble.

—BEAUMONT AND FLETCHER[1]

(All our disasters came in Marble Canyon.)

SATURDAY, December 28th., we started to traverse, once more, that portion of Marble Canyon made tragic by the death of three of our companions the summer before.

How different this time were our preparations for the work—three magnificent boats, heavy and strong, easy to manage, answering their helms quickly, and in every way seeming perfectly fitted for the work. We added to our provisions from Johnson's store, and on top of the load of each boat was lashed a fine hind quarter of fresh beef. We did not intend to go hungry for a few days at least.

The rapid at the mouth of Paria Creek was described by Powell, in his Report, as "a long, rocky, mad rapid,"[2] and it was even worse when we ran it. Storms in the Paria must have built up the dam since '69, and made it what it was in '89. It was nearly a mile long before quiet water was reached, full of rocks, with one clear channel next to the partially vertical wall on the left, and with a fall of fully twenty feet. Our good friend Johnson and all his families, thirty-two members in all, came out to see us start, and gave us a cheer as we ran the long rapid. It was the first real rapid our new boats and new men had run. I was proud of them both.

The strata, at the head of the Canyon, dip up stream, rising higher and higher as the winding River cuts its way between the marble walls. Between these walls, we started on smooth water,

1 *Philaster*, Act V, scene 3.
2 Powell, *Exploration of the Colorado River*, 73.

but soon came to and ran three lesser rapids. In the afternoon we reached Badger Creek rapid, with very low water and full of huge boulders, portaged our supplies, lined down our boats, and went into camp for our Sunday's rest.

At Lee's Ferry, we had had little real rest. The last night before leaving, we worked until four next morning, and were up at five-thirty for breakfast. On account of shortage of funds provided for the expedition, it was impossible to carry a complete survey along all the River below Lee's Ferry. It was decided to make instrumental surveys at all difficult points and take complete notes and a continuous photographic panorama of the whole route, for the preliminary report.[3] Sunday afternoon, Hislop and I walked several miles down the River, to where our first tragedy of the last summer occurred, and President Brown lost his life. What a change in the appearance of the place at this low water time! As we sorrowfully stand on the bank and look over the scene, there is the same current; the same great eddy; between them the same whirlpool with its ever changing circles, and, every now and then, comes up a swirl, or fountain, as before; but all so different with ten feet less water, that, at some distance away, shows a swift current; but the great power of the rapid is gone, for this rapid—No. 108—was one without boulders in its channel.

Monday morning, we found Soap Creek Rapid with many more boulders exposed than in the summer, which required a portage of nearly the whole distance, and we went into camp at the same spot where we had camped July 9th. It brought up sad memories of the last night President Brown was with us, how I had made up his bed for him, as he seemed unable to do it, and divided my blankets with him, for he was cold and unhappy. Next morning, when we strapped on our cork jackets, I was forcibly reminded of all three of our former party, who in all

---

[3] "A continuous transit line was run for the first 355 miles. Over 600 miles of transit line was run altogether, the additional amount in shorter stretches over difficult portions."—Stanton.

human probability would have been alive still—if they had been as well provided.

We followed with our boats the same course through rapid No. 108 and landed on the same little sand beach, and there resumed our survey, hoping that the railroad at least might eventually be a monument to the memory of its first President. In pulling out from shore, my boat was caught in the same whirlpool, and, although the water was so much lower, before the two powerful oarsmen could get control and pull her out, she was whirled round a number of times; swirls and fountains coming up and around the boat with a dull angry snarl. As I stood in the bow, they lashed and broke over our sides as if eager for another victim to their never satisfied greed.

THE UPPER PART OF MARBLE CANYON

In the narrowest section of the Canyon, including the next six rapids, we had a good illustration of how some rapids can be more severe, and with much higher waves, in low water than in high. The rapids in this section are really falls over ledges of rock formed as shown in the sketch.

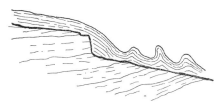

7. Profile sketch of a rapid in the upper part of Marble Canyon

There were few boulders in any of these six rapids, so we ran them all at the rate of fifteen, twenty or more miles per hour; but the low stage of water made the waves much more powerful than they had been the summer before. Over the ledge the current dropped more suddenly, in almost real falls of from five to ten, fifteen, and, in one place, twenty feet (as it seemed to me) and, after the first drop, curled back in wave after wave, breaking in white foam high above our heads. The channels were crooked, in some instances, and it required quick work on the part of the steersman to guide the heavy loaded boats through them. The excitement of such runs became wild at times, as I stood up in the bow of the leading boat. After the first drop, the boat would suddenly rise over the first smooth wave, and, plunging down into the first huge breaker, I would duck my head to go through it as it broke over me and fell on the bow oarsman, so that for a time, to the steersman, we were entirely out of sight in the foaming water. On we went, plunging through wave after wave, our heavy boats, with load of over three thousand pounds, coming up as light as corks, though partially filled with water; and every man completely drenched. And so we went dancing over the lighter waves at the foot, and through the smooth, swift water between the rapids until we reached rapid No. 115. Here we used the same method of rounding the point with lines as we did in July fearing the many more exposed rocks, at low water, since we could not see ahead. Through this narrow part of the Canyon, our survey line was on the broad slope above the first bench, one hundred or so feet above the water . . . Marble Canyon seemed destined to give us trouble.

AN UNFORTUNATE ACCIDENT

January 1st., 1890, was a beautifully clear, bright New Year's day. After rowing down River about a quarter of a mile, we stopped to take photographs. We tied up our boats some distance above the next rapid, and Nims the photographer, with Hogue to help him, went ahead, behind a large rock and out of sight, to take the pictures. I had always told Nims that the object of our photographs was to show the nature of the canyons for the purpose of illustrating the railroad route, and not to risk anything in his work, simply to get a pleasing picture.

The rest of us lounged in the boats or in the bright sunshine on the sand bar, talking of home and the New Years reunions we should miss. All was quiet around us, except the dull roar of the rapids we had run some distance up the River. Suddenly we were startled by a cry from Hogue. In an instant we were at the foot of the cliff, gathered, horror stricken, around the photographer stretched upon the sand, insensible and bleeding at the nose and ear. It seemed that Nims had climbed up the cliff, a short distance, to set up his camera, but, wishing to put some life in the picture, he insisted against Hogue's protest, on going higher so as to take in the boats and life of the men on the beach; thus his artistic sense caused his undoing. He slipped, and, his foot striking on a ledge as he went down, he was turned over and fell a distance of twenty-two feet, landing on his head and shoulders upon the hard sand below.

On careful examination we found, besides the terrible jar, he had broken one of the bones in his leg just above the ankle. Well provided with medicines, bandages, and twenty years experience in the far west, we set to work to prepare our hospital and care for our first patient. McDonald and I soon had his broken leg and smashed foot in splints and bandages. He rested easier, poor fellow, but we feared internal injuries, for he was still bleeding at the mouth.

It was now noon, and we had time to realize our situation. We were now well in the Marble Canyon, at the bottom of a chasm, whose walls of limestone stood seventeen hundred feet high. There was no path from the bottom to the top. We had just enough provisions to carry us to Diamond Creek, but, of course, for the sake of the wounded man, we must stay where we were for the day.

But I must confess, what worried me most was the fact that no one remained in the party who had ever so much as focused a camera. It was a matter of most vital importance. The Canyons of the Colorado had been pronounced impracticable, and even impossible, as a railway route. Even if a survey were made in the usual way, would doubters accept this testimony as against their own opinions? The case became one of Mohammed and the Mountain reversed. We could not take these doubters and the prophets of Wall Street to the Canyons, hence we must bring the Canyons to the prophets. How was it to be done? By Photography! We had made plans for taking photographs in such numbers all along the survey, so as to show, as near as possible, a complete panorama of the River banks and the walls of the Canyons, from the head of the Colorado to the Gulf of California, a distance of about 1,050 miles, and now, by this most unfortunate accident, I saw before me the possible failure of this—the most vital necessity of our railway survey—for there was not another professional photographer to be had within, perhaps, a thousand miles. Besides this, we had to get a man with a broken leg out of the Canyon to a place of safety. The nearest place of safety we knew of was seventeen hundred feet up in the air, and thirty-five miles across a desert mesa.

My life on the frontier had taught me to believe in Sam Patch's[4] motto: "Somethings can be done, as well as others," and a decision was made at once. We must get the wounded man out; we must go on with the survey; a new photographer must be invented. It would not be safe to move that day, so we had a few hours in which to take our first picture. I had never adjusted a camera, had never seen the inside of a roll-holder. How did the thing work anyway? The photographer's book of record was at hand. It was full of columns, headed with all sorts of abbreviated notes and signs. They were so much Choctaw to me. All that was known, and all that could be found out from anyone in the party, was that the film should not be exposed so long in a bright sun

4 Sam Patch was an early nineteenth-century bridge jumper whose heroics became subject matter for several plays.

as in a dark night. With that stock of knowledge and information the work began. The camera—a 6½x8½ Scovil & Adams instrument, one of the old style, no shutter, only a cap to be taken off the lens by hand, with roll holder—was focused, adjusted, turned and twisted. Every moment I became more excited and worried. At last the roll-holder was put in place; the instrument carefully covered up with the focusing cloth, and the slide drawn; but, as I attempted to take off the cap, I hesitated, dashed my hat upon the ground, and tore my hair in desperation at the complicated state of affairs. While thus engaged the cook picked up our little camera, took a snapshot at me, and preserved for my future contemplation the absurd picture I was making of myself.

This was the first of January, and it was not until March that we knew how our first picture turned out. In the meantime, I had made over twelve hundred exposures. As soon as we reached Peach Springs, a telegram went to W. H. Jackson, of Denver, to whom two batches of rolls had been sent for development. It was a happy moment, when the answer came: "Negatives all right." It may be stated here that out of some sixteen hundred negatives taken from the time of the accident to the end of our journey, full ninety per cent were clear, well-timed pictures. This was not skill—it was accident, but that kind of accident that is invention, which owes its birth to that troublesome matron, so often found wandering in the wilds of the west—commonly called necessity.

The next morning, our patient was much better. I determined to push on some miles down the River, where, from my notes of the last summer, I knew there was a side canyon leading to the north through which to take the photographer out. We loaded one boat so as to make him a level bed, and, preparing a stretcher of two oars and a piece of canvas, put him aboard and strapped him safely on. He was soon sound asleep, or he again became insensible, and we ran down some ten miles over one quite lively rapid with him in that position, but he knew nothing of it. At 2:00 P.M. we made camp at the mouth of the side canyon to prepare for our trip to the top on the morrow. Nims, being made as comfortable as possible in a dry shelter beside a fine driftwood fire, under an overhanging shelf of marble, slept more quietly.

SEEING A RAPID RUN

Our Camp (No. 57) was at the same point where we had camped, (No. 35) July 11th, at the head of Rapid No. 118, which required a portage, at least of the stores. The greater part of the afternoon was spent at this work. The rapid being carefully examined, we concluded to run it with the empty boats. It was too shallow, rough and rocky to attempt it with the full loads, and it was a wild looking place even for light boats, with the waves so much more powerful, among the exposed rocks, than they had been at a higher stage of water. There was a clear channel, though a crooked one, which we thought was safe. The party was to go no farther than the foot of the rapid, and I concluded to forego the pleasure of a complete ducking so late in the evening, and decided to watch the boats and try to get some photographs of the operation from shore, and so took my position beside the heaviest of the waves, to see for the first time, without being in it, the running of a great rapid.

Boat No. 1, with McDonald, Gibson, and Kane, went over the first fall and the smooth upper waves in beautiful form. As she rose over the next high wave she shot out into the air, and I could see clear under one-half of the keel, before she turned down and plunged into the bottom of the next breaker, where the two oarsmen and two-thirds of the boat went completely out of sight under the water. Out she came, and swept by at the rate of twenty or more miles per hour, climbing and dashing through the waves like a thing of life.

Boat No. 2, with Hislop, Travers, and Edwards, came next. Hislop missed the course a little, and in the worst place went over a huge boulder that lay under water. The bow of the boat shot out in the air, and, as she was going so fast, she did not *turn* down, but dropped bodily, and the stern struck on the rock, which keeled her over on her side at an angle of forty-five degrees, and in this shape she fell into the vortex of the suck behind the rock. She lay but a moment, righted herself like a feather, and shot on down the rapid as if nothing had happened.

In Twining's boat, No. 3, Ballard and Kane took the oars. They were the most powerful oarsmen of the whole party, and they gave this boat more headway, on entering the rapid from the smooth water above. They entered at a fearful rate, and by the time they struck the great, rolling waves, were going at fully thirty miles per hour. Over the first smooth roll the boat went. As she rushed down into the trough she forgot to turn up, and the whole boat and the whole crew went completely and entirely out of my sight under the next wave. From this, she rose as light as a cork without damage, except being well filled with water, and shot on to the end of the rapid like a flying fish, skimming through the lighter waves.

After securing the three boats on a safe sandbar below, we all returned to camp to nurse our wounded photographer and prepare for our journey up the side canyon on the morrow.

SPEED OF THE BOATS

Our estimate of the rate the boats traveled through the rapids was not a matter of guesswork. The summer before, we had found an Indian canoe—a dugout—and, measuring the distance alongside a rapid, had turned it loose and timed it as it simply floated down with the current, thus getting approximately the rate of flow of the water. Added to this was the force of two powerful oarsmen, when the boat was started a thousand feet or so above the head of the rapid, and rowing with all their might to enter it. We also, occasionally, timed the boats themselves, on carefully estimated courses, and it is from these data that the speed of fifteen to twenty and thirty miles per hour, while running the rapids, is given. I attempted to get some pictures of such work on a dozen instantaneous glass plates which I had brought for that purpose; but, either on account of my want of knowledge of how to do it, or the want of a proper shutter to my camera, every attempt was a failure. The only pictures I succeeded in getting were on slow timed films. . . .

A TRAMP TO THE UPPER WORLD

Next morning, January 3rd., Hislop, McDonald, and I started early up the side canyon to find a way out.

After some pretty hard climbing in places, where the men assisted me up the cliffs with a rope from above, we reached the top a little before noon. After a lunch, the two men started back to the River, and I to go thirty-five miles to Lee's Ferry to get a team for our wounded photographer. I had come out on the west rim of this side canyon, and, after traveling up it several miles, concluded to cross it where it was about one hundred feet deep. The descent where I started was simple, but to get out on the other side was another matter. There was no way out except up through a crack in the limestone, by putting my back against one side, with my knees and hands against the other, and squeezing, and edging my way by inches up the crack. From there it was but six or seven miles to the wagon road which led to Lee's Ferry; but the last twenty miles of a sixteen hours' climb, of seventeen hundred feet out of the Canyon, and thirty-five mile tramp over the Mesa, began to wear upon one's muscles, and, before I reached that Mormon settlement, I several times wished all photographs and photographers at the bottom of the deep sea, or the Colorado River, for, as I sat down by the roadside, at 11:55 P. M., still one mile away from rest, and pulled off my shoe, there shone out in the moonlight a blister on my heel about the size of the No. 4 Dallmeyer lens in Nims's camera.

But all troubles come to an end sometime. It was not long after midnight when my Mormon friend spread a good bed upon the floor and gave me possession of the outside kitchen. By that time I was well filled with photographic contemplations—and little else. Before I lay down to rest, I took a panoramic view of my surroundings. By a slight adjustment of a cupboard door, my eye was focussed on a two-quart pan of sweet milk, and another half full of cold rice pudding. It did not take me many minutes to develop a negative, or at least a minus quantity, in those two pans. With a full stomach and a clear conscience within, and a half-dozen Navajo blankets without, I slept the sleep of a latter-day saint, except for the throbbing of the Dallmeyer on my left heel.

I had a welcome compensation for my tramp in finding several letters at the Ferry from home, which, otherwise, I would not have gotten for two months.

TO THE RESCUE

Next morning, our good friend W. M. Johnson, with his team and son, started back with me to get our wounded man. How different were my surroundings the next night! The picture is photographed upon my memory, if nowhere else. We had traveled many miles with the wagon around the heads of the side canyons, into and out of which I had climbed the day before, on the plain west of Lee's Ferry, but could not reach the sick man that day as we had hoped. It was late, and we camped for the night on the open prairie—the old Mormon, his little son, and I. A snow storm was driving from over the mountains. Our supper was cooked by a sage-brush fire—the bacon, the coffee, and the bread—but, before it was eaten, my friend knelt upon the ground, and turning his face to heaven, while the snowflakes fell upon his white beard, offered up a fervent prayer for blessing upon ourselves, upon those at home, for care for the wounded man, and strength for ourselves and the horses, till we could reach him and take him to a place of safety.

I wish that all of my Christian friends had the spirit of kindness and charity that it has been my good fortune to find among the Mormons in northern Arizona and *southern* Utah. This man was generous to a fault, sincerely honest, and honestly sincere. What more can a man be?

Sunday morning, being so worn out we overslept ourselves, and as the team had to head another side canyon, I started across on foot and found the men, with their wounded companion, by nine o'clock. They had reached the top of the Mesa early Saturday afternoon, and, expecting to meet the wagon and return to camp the same day, had made no preparation for staying over night, and so were obliged to sleep out in a snow storm without supper, blankets, or breakfast.

We had brought a mattress in the wagon, and made the wounded man as comfortable as possible, putting in his sack some things that the Johnson's did not have at the ranch, such as medicines, cocoa, corn starch, tobacco, etc., and, late Sunday afternoon, we left our photographer, Nims, to the kind care of Mr. W. M. Johnson, who carried him back to Lee's Ferry, where under Mrs. Johnson's good nursing, though after much suffering, he was able to return to his home in Denver.

The bringing of the wounded man on a stretcher, out of the Canyon 1,700 feet to the mesa above, was no small undertaking. I, of course, did not see the work, and have asked my friend and fellow boatman, Langdon Gibson, one of the "Ambulance Corps," to relate the story.

THE JOURNEY OF THE AMBULANCE CORPS

"Things shape themselves in most unexpected ways. In the summer of 1889, while a broker's clerk in Wall Street, with visions of some day becoming a successful banker, I received a letter from my father, who was at that time traveling in the West. This letter marked a turning point in my career, and, as it resulted in my becoming a member of the Denver, Colorado Canyon & Pacific Railroad Survey, I quote it as a means of introduction. The original of this letter is still preserved among my most treasured possessions, for, while I was in the canyon, my father was taken ill and died of pneumonia. The letter follows:

MY DEAR SON:—

For three days I have been in the heart of the Rocky Mountains, and yesterday made the ascent of Pike's Peak. Of the party of road masters who reached Manitou, only Mr. Stimpson and myself went up the mountain.

The difficulties grew more formidable as we approached the top, and the others gave up the trip. With us, however, went a member of the Stanton party who are organizing to explore the Colorado River.

They mean, I understand, to push the explorations through to the Gulf of California. The man I met was the photographer of the party. His name is Nims. He tells me that the party is made up excepting two men. Mr. Robert B. Stanton, who is to head the party, is at present in Stapleton, S.I. How would you like to go on such an expedition?

Of course the men who go are picked men. The journey is all made in boats, and the boats are specially constructed for the trip. Naturally, the men who make up such a party have to combine brains with muscle and health. Intelligent, observing, capable of making useful notes concerning land, stone, water, birds and beasts, and expert boatmen.

The object of the trip is, I am told, to open up that wonderful region to the improvements of civilization.

The trials and experiences, of such an expedition as this, develop the true inwardness of human character, which you would have a chance to read. The trip might prove a liberal education. You would be in the University of the Almighty, a place for big hearts and big souls and great faith.

The very idea may strike you as absurd, but when I was your age, had it been possible for me, I should have been only too glad of such a chance.

Your affectionate father,
CHARLES DeWOLF GIBSON

"This letter awakened in me a spark, which, fanned by my natural born love of nature and the wilderness, rapidly developed into a flame, to be partially quenched, only, by the muddy, restless and turbulent waters of the Colorado River.

"It is not my intention to lead up by degrees to the incident of our trip which Mr. Stanton, our commander, has requested me to describe, but with this brief introduction I will run a few imaginary rapids, leaving the description of the real ones to an abler pen than mine, and come at once to New Year's morning, 1890, when at the head of Rapid No. 116 in Marble Canyon, our photographer, F. A. Nims, met with his terrible accident, falling from the cliff, breaking several bones, and as we feared, received almost fatal injuries. Nims's accident cast a gloom over our party, and what to do with him and how to get him back to civilization, were subjects of long and earnest discussion around the camp fire. I remember the first night after the accident I sat beside Nims's bed, taking my turn in giving him at intervals sips of hot chocolate, while the rest of the party slept. It was a gloomy and depressing ushering in of the New Year. Nims's moans harmonized in chilling rhythm with the wind that blew from all directions; one instant, a choking puff of fat black smoke, from the burning pinon logs, the next instant, a cold gust laden with dry sand, would assault from the opposite direction. Ice formed that night in the shallow places near shore, and some of it went crackling and drifting by. It was a lonely New Year's night.

"The following morning, Nims was placed on a stretcher, made of two oars and a piece of canvas with spreaders of drift wood, and strapped on the load of boat No. 1. We dropped down the River about 10 miles, through swift water and one quite lively rapid. Here we found a side canyon, on the north side of the River, and Mr. Stanton determined to camp here for the purpose of finding out whether this canyon, which looked promising from our camp, offered a possible means by which to get our companion on top, and ultimately from there back to Lee's Ferry, a distance of some 20 miles but nearly 40 miles the way he would have to be carried.

"The following morning (Friday, January 3rd.) Mr. Stanton, Hislop, and McDonald started out to locate a trail. Shortly after lunch McDonald and Hislop returned, reporting that they had reached the top, and that Mr. Stanton had proceeded to Lee's Ferry to get Warren M. Johnson, the Mormon, with a team. 'If the trail isn't a bad one it's a pity,' said Mac. He reported snow and ice on top, and his description of the places over which we would have to carry our unconscious companion, was, to say the least, not encouraging.

"That night, poor Nims was very uncomfortable. He begged us to take the rubber boot off his foot (the crude splint in which we had set his broken ankle). The night finally wore itself away, and early Saturday morning, after giving Nims as much chocolate as we could get him to swallow, (it being absolutely impossible for him to eat solids) we started off with eight men: Hislop, Mc-Donald, Travers, Ballard, Brown, Edwards, Twining and myself, and Nims on the same stretcher of canvas and oars, leaving camp about 8:30 o'clock. We took turns about, four men carrying the stretcher at a time, while the other men went ahead with our lunch and some extra blankets, at the same time picking out the best trail for us to follow.

"The lower part of the side canyon through which we went was very narrow, with almost perpendicular walls, but with small rock benches near the bottom. For some distance we were able to carry our burden by walking in the bottom of the gorge, as there was no water in the little creek, but soon this became impossible on account of the huge boulders. Then it was necessary to walk along the little benches, and in places they were so sloping that one could not stand upon them alone. Twice it was necessary to set the stretcher down, by piling up some rocks on the lower side to rest it on, while four of us climbed from nitch to nitch to the ledge above, and came back to a point over where the wounded man was, where ropes were passed up to us and attached to the oars, and while we, lying down on the sloping rock holding on with our toes, held the weight, the men below slid the stretcher along the rock wall, they, in places, going on their hands and knees, for the bench was so steep they could not stand upon it. In one instance the upper ledge was so sloping, that only two men could hold the ropes, while the other two lay, in more secure places above, and, holding on to their legs, kept the first men from being dragged over the cliff.

"Further on, the creek dropped over perpendicular ledges of eight and ten feet; over these we drew Nims up with the ropes, from one bench to the other. This hard work brought us about one and a half miles, and then, for about a mile and a half, we had fairly good going, on the flat rocks in the bottom of the Canyon, but, in places, so covered with broken rocks that our footing was none too secure. All this time we were making a gradual ascent, and in the three miles climbed some 700 feet. Then came the final climb of over 900 feet, up over a slope of loose rocks and earth lying at an angle of nearly forty-five degrees, where progress was very slow, and, above this, was a perpendicular wall of limestone over 100 feet high. The only way up this to the mesa above was through a huge crack, filled with immense, sharp boulders broken from the cliff. At one place, two great boulders filled the crack, with a small space left under them. This opening, or tunnel under the boulders, was cleaned out, and the wounded man on the stretcher was pulled and pushed through the hole. The last rise at the top was a wall of about 15 feet. The ropes were attached to the oars and (Nims being strapped to the stretcher during the whole climb) we all went above and hoisted him to the mesa, at an elevation of 1,700 to 1,800 feet above the river, which we reached at 3:30 P.M., having stopped a half hour for lunch. We were glad our task was over, and our wounded companion safely on top, and, with heaving chests, we laid Nims a few yards from the edge of the cliff and sat about him, resting our weary and bruised limbs. It had been trying work, forced as we were to climb and struggle upwards in places where not only our muscles but our heads were tested for their steadiness. We discovered new muscles, and learned new expressions; the latter from McDonald, who at critical moments had most original and unconventional ways of expressing his thoughts.

"As we had mounted higher and higher on the canyon walls, we looked back less frequently, but when we did, a terrifying and grand scene lay spread out before us.

"Occasionally large rocks would become dislodged and go crashing down the walls, leaving behind a trailing odor of brimstone.

"I do not think Nims realized his position, where a false step or a slip would have sent him hurling down the canyon side, perhaps even to the very bottom; though at one time, in a very difficult place, he raised his head and looked over the side of the stretcher to the depths below. It was a mercy that the injured man was for the most part unconscious. Had he been fully conscious, the realization of what we were forced to do with him, would have made his suffering much more intense.

"As we sat on the mesa at the edge of the canyon, a cutting wind was blowing from the desert, and it soon became necessary to build a fire. There was no shelter of any kind, and, in the absence of wood, we started out in squads to gather sage brush and tumble weeds to take its place. We built the fire as near to Nims as we could, in order to give him the full benefit of the heat.

"The sage brush and tumble weeds would blaze up merrily, but it was a mere flash in the pan. It was a rocky mesa and the bushes were very small, each one furnishing little more heat than could be produced from a burning sheet of newspaper. As the stock became exhausted in our vicinity, we had to make longer trips to collect it, and it was thus that the party, who remained on top that night, kept themselves warm by their exertions during an almost continuous snow storm, and Nims, wrapped in all the blankets we had, was kept from freezing by the burning of the weeds that were brought in continuously during the night.

"We had expected to return to the river the same day, and had brought no bedding for the men, and breakfast was needed for the following morning. Travers, Brown, and I returned to the River Camp, arriving there some time after night. We were, however, fortunate in being able to make the descent of the difficult places before dark.

"Bright and early next morning, Travers, and I climbed once more to the top with food and water, reaching the party by 9:30, where we found Mr. Stanton, who had come ahead of the wagon, but it was not until two o clock in the afternoon that the team was sighted, and, a short time later, the old, weather-beaten, covered wagon, innocent of springs, rolled up to our bivouac, with Johnson and his little son. After this, there was little time lost. Nims was loaded into the wagon, carefully wrapped in blankets, good-byes were spoken, and we disappeared over the brink like a lot of frightened mountain sheep; down the steep sides we ran, crawled, climbed and tumbled, sometimes starting little avalanches of rock, which rolled down the slopes ahead of us.

"The boat camp was finally reached, without further incident, and we were ready once more to tackle the River which reached out down stream, describing great interrogation marks in its circuitous route.

LANGDON GIBSON."[5]

5 "Langdon Gibson, with a letter of commendation from the President of our Railroad Company, secured the position of Ornithologist, on 'The First Peary Expedition of 1891 and 1892' and spent those years with Commander Peary, in the Arctic Regions."—Stanton.

Out of this accident there grew one of the most cruel hoaxes connected with the whole expedition. Nims, on reaching the railroad, some weeks later, telegraphed to Denver for funds and told of his accident. This was perfectly proper, but, out of this simple message, a Denver newspaper, *The Times,* manufactured a story that a whole boat's crew of the expedition had been lost, Nims being the only one left.[6] Although denied in the next morning's paper by my wife, who knew all the circumstances which I had written her from Lee's Ferry,[7] *The Times* persisted in the story, with telegrams from Winslow, Arizona,[8] *all manufactured in their Denver office,* as they later acknowledged to me. Anything for a "scoop"—but the telegrams received by my wife, from the parents and friends of the members of the party throughout the country, showed what was the price, in anxiety, the "scoop" cost them.

ON TO POINT RETREAT

Monday morning, we started again with one man less in the party and his work falling to me. In two days we ran some eight rapids and dropped our boats with lines over four more, all of these being small falls over ledges of marble, with heavy waves, and, as the weather was cold, with snow blowing in gusts, to be drenched by the waves breaking over our heads was far from cheering. In lining through Rapid No. 131, boat No. 3, the "Marie" received her first injury, having one rib broken by being jammed against a rock. We camped at the Marble Pier for repairs, at the point where we spent Sunday July 14, '89. It

[6] Under headline, "The Fate of Stanton's Party," *Times* (Denver), January 28, 1890.

[7] Under headline, "Stanton's Men Safe," *Rocky Mountain News* (Denver), January 29, 1890; also letter, Mrs. Robert B. Stanton to *Republican* (Denver), January 29, 1890.

[8] Under headline, "Stanton's Accident a Reality," *Times* (Denver), January 29, 1890.

required two days for our Survey work and to make all repairs in proper manner. A heavy snow storm was driving up the Canyon, the clouds hung almost to the River, and, with the blinding snow, made it difficult even to see.

While the boats were being repaired, we also, between the gusts of snow, continued our instrumental survey for the railroad line. Jan. 10th, while lining the boats around the head of a very rocky rapid, just above where the two boatmen were drowned the summer before, the "Lily" was washed in broadside and lodged against a boulder. By rigging a gin pole with block and tackle she was lifted out, with little real damage except a severe strain on her keel. The heavy oak construction of the boats stood well the rush of the strong current into the open compartment. Everything being strapped in securely, nothing of value was lost, except a few cooking utensils and cans of milk, as we were taking them out. Repairs were made next day. Sunday, the bright sunshine cleared away the snow that had fallen on the lower benches. Monday, Jan. 13th, we made twelve miles, portaging two and running eight heavy rapids, being wet every time by the waves breaking over our heads, and in the evening reached Point Retreat, where we left the River on our homeward march six months before. Here we found everything we had cached in the marble cave in good condition, except some little damage to the flour by the mice. Thousands of these little pests are found in all the Canyons, but we saw and felt the worst of them in Marble Canyon. They would gnaw into our provisions, run over us at night, and affectionately nibble at our noses and ears while we were asleep.

BELOW POINT RETREAT

We noted one remarkable change in the River, at the big bend just below Point Retreat, which is opposite Vasey's Paradise. What had been, the summer before, a very heavy rapid of "water waves" (as we called them) caused by the swift heavy current dashing high against the solid marble wall where the River makes a right-angle turn at Vasey's Paradise, and being thrown back up stream in formidable billows, now, with a stage of water about fifteen feet lower, had entirely disappeared and there was no rapid to speak of. With the water fifty feet higher, this bend would be impassable for any boat, for these refluent waves would throw it back from one side against the solid rock wall on the other side.

From the head of the Colorado to Point Retreat, we had encountered one hundred and forty-four rapids, not counting small "draws," in a distance of about two hundred and seventy miles. From Lee's Ferry to Point Retreat, in a distance of some thirty-two miles, there are forty-four rapids. With our new boats we ran nearly all of these, and portaged but few. To stand in the bow of one of these boats, as she dashes through a great rapid, with first the bow and then the stern jumping into the air, and the spray of the breakers splashing over one's head, is an excitement whose fascination can be realized only through experience.

We stopped two days to complete our railway survey around a very difficult point, and, on Wednesday, January 15th, having added to our supplies the blankets, flour, coffee, sugar, etc., from our cache, and replaced our recent loss of cooking utensils, we repacked our boats and were ready to start into, for us, a new world of Canyon wonders.

This part of Marble Canyon, from Point Retreat for nearly thirty-two miles down to near the mouth of the Little Colorado, was by far the most beautiful and interesting canyon we had yet passed through. At Point Retreat, the marble walls stand vertically three hundred feet from the water's edge, while the marble and standstone above bench back in slopes and cliffs to 2,500 feet high. Just below this, the Canyon is narrowest, being but a little over three hundred feet at the bottom, from wall to wall. As we go on, the marble rapidly rises till it stands in real vertical cliffs seven hundred to eight hundred feet high, colored with all the tints of the rainbow, but mostly red.[9] In many places, toward the top, the cliffs are honeycombed with caves, arches, and grottoes with here and there a natural bridge, left from one crag to another, over some small sidewash, making a grotesque and wonderful picture, as our little boats glide along this quiet portion of the River so many hundred feet below.

Near the foot of these cliffs, in many places, and sometimes higher up, are fountains of pure sparkling water gushing from the rock, like the one at Vasey's Paradise, and dropping among shrubbery, ferns, and flowers, some of which, even at this time of the year, were in bloom.

Ten miles below Point Retreat, as we went into camp one evening, we discovered the skeleton of Peter M. Hansbrough, one of the boatmen drowned on our trip the summer before. His remains were easily recognized by a peculiarly made pair of shoes, which we knew and that were still on his feet.

It was a sad and ghastly sight, to see the bleached bones of my faithful foreman, who had served with me for years, stretched out on the rocky shore of the River, caught, as they had been, in an eddy at high water on a rock, and left high and dry when the water went down. The next morning, we buried them under an overhanging cliff. The burial services were brief and simple. We stood around the grave while one short prayer was offered, and we left him with a shaft of pure marble for his headstone, seven hundred feet high with his name cut upon the base, and in honor of his memory we named a magnificent point opposite—*Point Hansbrough.*

Our progress from Point Retreat to the Little Colorado, a distance of about thirty-two miles, was slow, as there were many places where it was necessary to stop and make careful surveys. The narrow portion, for ten miles or so above Vasey's Paradise, had forced our railroad line out of the inner gorge onto the first

[9] "We triangulated these cliffs and got their extreme heights by instrumental measurements."—Stanton.

bench, and crossing the River at Point Retreat to the right bench, the heaviest portion of the whole route was found to be for ten miles down to the more open Canyon and talus slopes that begin below Point Hansbrough. From there on for twenty miles the whole line is on a hillside of mountain talus. We stopped at many points to make surveys and sketches, and take photographs, more particularly at the mouths of the side canyons to illustrate their crossings, as shown in the following sketch of the mouth of the Nan-co-weap, made January 18th.

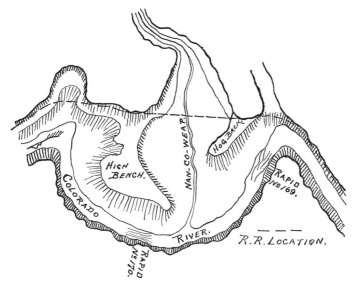

8. Sketch map of the mouth of the Nan-co-weap

As we climbed up the hillsides, we found wild flowers in full bloom, with new spring grass, three inches high, and birds of many kinds singing on almost every bush. And, although in the early morning the spray from the waves had frozen in a sheet of ice over our coats, the musical part of the corps sang of "the flowers that bloom in the spring, tra-la," and recounted pleasant memories of Barnabee[10] and "The Mikado."

10 Henry Clay Barnabee, an American actor and singer.

From Point Hansbrough to the Little Colorado, the Canyon widens, the marble benches retreat, new strata of limestone, quartzite, and shale come up from the River, the debris forming a talus equal to a mountain slope. Here the bottoms widen into little farms, covered with green grass and groves of mesquite, making a most charming picture, in strong contrast with the dismal, narrow canyons above. And as we pass the valleys of the Nan-co-weap and the Kwagunt, the contrast is more strongly brought out. Here, among green grass and flowers, yonder, far up the valley on the lofty mountains covered with their winter mantle of pure, white snow for a background, stand out sharp points of scarlet sandstone, and the darker green of the cedar and pine is heightened in color by the rose-tinted light which the morning sun flashes over the eastern walls of the Canyon.

In this last section of Marble Canyon we encountered some forty-three new rapids, but had little difficulty with any of them. Nos. 171, 172, and 173 were the most powerful; they were close together, with high waves, but clear channels, though one was in the shape of a complete letter S, and the three, covering a distance of one and a half miles, were run in less than six minutes. Beyond these, there was a two mile stretch of smooth water, but the wind was blowing in great gusts and whirling the dry sand from shore into our eyes, almost blinding the steersman, so that our progress was very slow. We had hoped to reach the mouth of the Little Colorado that night, but it was impossible on account of the strong head wind coming up the River, and we camped about four miles above, though in sight of, the head of the Grand Canyon, and remained there for our Sunday's rest. The wind storm ceased, but at night it began to rain, and we slept till near morning in a steady pour, with only our bed canvas drawn up over our heads.

Monday, January 20th., after making some slight repairs to

our boats, we again set sail, on nearly a mile of smooth water, to Rapid No. 182. This was a long, shallow, crooked rapid, in the form of the letter S, with a huge rock at its head, towards which it was necessary to steer and shave it as close as possible, in order not to be driven upon a worse point below. It took strong, quick work, going at fifteen miles per hour, but was successfully done. The lower part of the rapid seemed clear of rocks as we looked at it from above, but we were mistaken, and we bumped upon three submerged boulders, though without damage.

Below this rapid begins the broken up portion of the Canyon, which extends for about sixteen or eighteen miles down the River, and sandstone, conglomerate, and mineralized matter, with dikes and seams of iron, began to rise from the lower levels, in colors of yellow, gray, brown and black, and the marble was benched back and largely disappeared above.

At about ten o'clock we came to two of the most difficult rapids to navigate we had so far found. The fall was not so great, nor the waves so high, as many we had passed, but four great boulders of hard conglomerate had rolled down into the stream and formed a channel with sharper turns than any we had made with our loaded boats. The two rapids were almost one, and the combined distance so great that it would have been a full day's portage to pass them that way. We decided to run them.

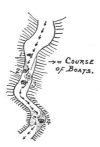

9. Sketch map of Rapids 184 and 185

The sketch will illustrate our experience here. In starting in

Rapid No. 184, it was necessary to shave as close to rock No. 1 as possible, and then steer direct for No. 2, and just before reaching it to turn suddenly from it, but to keep close to it, so as not to be driven across the channel on to the left bank. Rock No. 3 stood in the center of the channel, and the whole force of the current beat directly against it. To keep out of the whirlpool below Rock No. 2, it was necessary to steer directly toward No. 3, down the center of the current and through the heaviest waves, and, just before reaching it, turn sharp to the left. Here the space between the rock and the big eddy, in the cove next the shore, was so narrow, and the current being so powerful, it was impossible to follow the current, which fact required us to drive into the eddy itself. Going, as we were, at the rate of fully twenty miles per hour, the sudden dash across the edge of the two currents gave our boat a fearful twist. As the bow struck the eddy flowing upstream, the main current caught the stern, and with a sudden jerk, we were turned completely round and round and our speed quickly checked, so that we only continued our downstream course, though the upstream flow of the eddy, by hard rowing. Pulling out of it below the rock (No. 3) we made a new start for Rapid No. 185. The difficulty here was that the whole current beat against the shore *behind Rock No. 4*, against which it lay, and then curled in front of it in angry breakers. To avoid the rock and the breakers, we were to cut across the current to the right, and we hoped to pass along the edge of the main current close to the large eddy opposite rock No. 4. There was plenty of room at the head of the rapid, but we got a little too much speed, and, just as in the rapid before, our bow struck the upstream current of the eddy opposite the rock, and again, like a shot, we were whirled round and round, and with a jerk suddenly stopped, and were again obliged to pull hard downstream against an upstream flow.[11] Thus we waltzed down through the

11 "It, probably, will appear to some to be a contradiction of the laws of physics to say that a heavy boat, going at the rate of twenty miles per hour down

two rapids—making two reverses and complete circles—and reached the lower end of the second rapid in exactly two minutes by the watch.

The next two rapids were light and easy, and at eleven o'clock we landed at the mouth of the Little Colorado, and . . . we found it coming in perfectly naturally, *from the left,* through a canyon nearly 5,000 feet deep.

We walked about two miles up the Little Colorado Canyon, and, after a substantial lunch, continued our survey on the opposite bank of the main River into the head of the Grand Canyon.

one current, and meeting another current flowing in the opposite direction could be stopped suddenly, spun round like a top, and at once start upstream, without smashing boat and men to pieces.

"If a railroad train, on land, were treated so, there certainly would be a wreck. But there is a difference, and an explanation.

"The speed of twenty miles an hour was not guessed at. It was measured, as already explained. Still, while the stopping and turning seems to one in the boat to be all done 'in a moment,' and 'like a shot,' and is so sudden as to sometimes jerk a man out of the boat, yet the time required—in seconds—is much longer than it seems, and the boat does not strike a solid object, or even still water, or at once, the upstream current.

"The downstream current and the upstream eddy is not divided simply by a line. There is—a not very wide, but—a clear zone of neutral water between the two currents, badly mixed up—to be sure. The bow of the boat, coming down stream, & first entering this neutral zone, is not immediately stopped and whirled round, but at that moment the speed only *begins* to be checked. At the same time the bow is being slightly checked, the current catches the stern and the turning also *begins,* but during this time, and after, the whole boat continues going down stream, while gradually losing its speed. Sometimes the stern is thrown round and enters the neutral zone, and the boat goes on into the upstream flowing eddy stern first. Again the power may be so great as to throw the bow back into the main current and a second or third turning be effected, the whole boat all this time progressing downstream. Even when, as in some cases, the boat at once goes across the neutral zone into the eddy, there is quite a time—in seconds—before the boat is really stopped—as it must be—before it starts upstream in the up flowing eddy.

"How far a boat continues downstream, from the first checking to the final stopping and starting upstream, is hard to tell. It may be one or more hundred feet. To those in the boat, it seems but an instant, and the jerk is so sudden, so powerful, and so confusing, one loses all idea of time and distance."—Stanton.

The distance by the railroad survey from Lee's Ferry to the Little Colorado is 62.50 miles, the small distance saved by tunneling was made up by our crooked crossing of the River. In [Table 1] . . . will be found the classification of the railroad work. In general, the walls of Marble Canyon are composed of various strata of limestone, in places, turned into true marble. The strata are of different degrees of hardness, lying upon each other, first a hard and then a soft. The softer strata are generally composed of layers of horizontally stratified rock, worn away in slopes of from 30 to 50 degrees from horizontal, with vertical cliffs between them. These slopes of rock, in place, are covered with loose, broken rock or debris. This is the nature of the near fifty-nine miles of "heavy talus slope" and "cliff bench work" given in [Table 1]. . . . The cliff bench work only differs from the talus slopes in that the railroad line was located on the slope above a vertical cliff of solid limestone one hundred feet or more above the River.

Where the River at its present level has cut through the harder strata, it has formed a narrow inner gorge, with vertical walls next to the water. This inner gorge is very narrow, but of necessity the railroad line was located on the first sloping bench above and well away from high water, which here has an extreme rise of 108 feet, as measured on the walls.

The most difficult portion of the whole line is for about ten miles, in the neighborhood of Point Retreat, in the very heart of Marble Canyon. But even here, where the canyon makes two almost complete right-angle turns, a good line can be located by crossing the River—the only time in the whole survey—with a single span bridge, from marble cliff to marble cliff, at an elevation of some 200 or more feet above low water, and with a tunnel at either end. Beyond this section of tunnels and bridge, the same cliff bench work continues for about twelve miles, with a tunnel through Point Hansbrough effecting a saving in distance. The last 17½ miles above the Little Colorado the Canyon widens, and the changed rock strata form successive slopes and benches. These slopes, covered with debris in places, rise from the River at an angle of about 40 degrees to a height of a thousand feet. . . .

CHAPTER EIGHT

A thought of God on earth expressed!—

The silence of His perfect rest;—
The patience of eternal power;—
The ceaseless change from hour to hour;—
Forms in alternate gloom and flame,
That bide yet evermore the same,
And do but wear a fitful guise
Reflected in our human eyes,
Which only compass in their range
The things that change, or seem to change;—

The blended hues of heavenly birth
Beyond the tenderest tints of earth,
That fill and flood these spaces wide
With surges of celestial tide;—
The mystery of this awful brink
Where meaner thoughts in rapture sink,
And souls see clear, tho' eyes grow dim,
While time and space are lost in Him!

Methinks I could not fail or flee
In any conflict yet to be,
Whatever pathway must be trod,
Might I but keep this thought of God!

—ROSSITER W. RAYMOND[1]

W E were now about to enter, and attempt to pass through, the most stupendous chasm on the globe. Approaching it after months of hardships, dangers, starvation and death, the feelings that came to us during the first few days in the depths of the black granite gorge would be most difficult to describe. Twenty years before, the first little band to brave its dangers entered the then absolutely "Great Unknown," and even now (in 1890) it was in a great many ways still the "Great Unknown," except to the few members of Major Powell's parties of '69 and '72.

I shall not attempt a description of the Grand Canyon as a whole. As I have already said, its sublimity and grandeur, and even its beauty, are far beyond the human mind to grasp, for they are infinite. Individual scenes and impressions may be understood, and imperfectly put into language; thus far I shall attempt to go and no farther.

We spent nearly a whole winter in Marble and Grand Canyons, and I take the liberty of here quoting, as an introduction, that wonderful description of the real poetic nature of the Grand Canyon, written by its first and greatest explorer, published in 1895, five years after I had written the partial story of my journey . . .

In winter some of the characteristics of the Grand Canyon are

---

1 "Used by permission."—Stanton. Raymond was a mining engineer and an occasional poet.

emphasized. The black gneiss below, the variegated quartzite, and the green or alcove sandstone form the foundation for the mighty red wall. The banded sandstone entablature is crowned by the tower limestone. In winter this is covered with snow. Seen from below, these changing elements seem to graduate into the heavens, and no plane of demarcation between wall and blue firmament can be seen. The heavens constitute a portion of the facade and mount into a vast dome from wall to wall, spanning the Grand Canyon with empyrean blue. So the earth and the heavens are blended in one vast structure.

When the clouds play in the canyon, as they often do in the rainy season, another set of effects is produced. Clouds creep out of canyons and wind into other canyons. The heavens seem to be alive, not moving as move the heavens over a plain, in one direction with the wind, but following the multiplied courses of these gorges. In this manner the little clouds seem to be individualized, to have wills and souls of their own, and to be going on diverse errands—a vast assemblage of self-willed clouds, faring here and there, intent upon purposes hidden in their own breasts. In the imagination the clouds belong to the sky, and when they are in the canyon the skies come down into the gorges and cling to the cliffs and lift them up to immeasurable heights, for the sky must still be far away. Thus they lend infinity to the walls.

The wonders of the Grand Canyon cannot be adequately represented in symbols of speech, nor by speech itself. The resources of the graphic art are taxed beyond their powers in attempting to portray its features. Language and illustration combined must fail. The elements that unite to make the Grand Canyon the most sublime spectacle in nature are multifarious and exceedingly diverse. The Cyclopean forms which result from the sculpture of tempests through ages too long for man to compute, are wrought into endless details, to describe which would be a task equal in magnitude to that of describing the stars of the heavens or the multitudinous beauties of the forest with its traceries of foliage presented by oak and pine and poplar, by beech and linden and hawthorn, by tulip and lily and rose, by fern and moss and lichen. Besides the elements of form, there are elements of color, for here the colors of the heavens are rivaled by the colors of the rocks. The rainbow is not more replete with hues. But form and color do not exhaust all the divine qualities of the Grand Canyon. It is the land of music. The river thunders in perpetual roar, swelling in floods of music when the storm gods play upon the rocks and fading away in soft and low murmurs when the infinite blue of heaven is unveiled. With the melody of the great tide rising and falling, swelling and vanishing forever, other melodies are heard in the gorges of the lateral canyons, while the waters plunge in the rapids among the rocks or leap in great cataracts. Thus the Grand Canyon is a land of song. Mountains of music swell in the rivers, hills of music billow in the creeks, and meadows of music murmur in the rills that ripple over the rocks. Altogether it is a symphony of multitudinous melodies. All this is the music of waters. The adamant foundations of the earth have been wrought into a sublime harp, upon which the clouds of the heavens play with mighty tempests or with gentle showers.

The glories and the beauties of form, color, and sound unite in the Grand Canyon—forms unrivaled even by the mountains, colors that vie with sunsets, and sounds that span the diapason from tempest to tinkling raindrop, from cataract to bubbling fountain. But more: it is a vast district of country. Were it a valley plain it would make a state. It can be seen only in parts from hour to hour and from day to day and from week to week and from month to month. A year scarcely suffices to see it all. It has infinite variety, and no part is ever duplicated. Its colors, though many and complex at any instant, change with the ascending and declining sun; lights and shadows appear and vanish with the passing clouds, and the changing seasons mark their passage in changing colors. You cannot see the Grand Canyon in one view, as if it were a changeless spectacle from which a curtain might be lifted, but to see it you have to toil from month to month through its labyrinths.[2]

2 Powell, *Canyons of the Colorado*, 393–97. Stanton might have finished the quotation: "It is a region more difficult to traverse than the Alps or the Himalayas, but if strength and courage are sufficient for the task, by a year's toil a concept of sublimity can be obtained never again to be equaled on the hither side of Paradise."

THE FIRST DIVISION OF THE GRAND CANYON

On January 20th. we passed the mouth of the Little Colorado and slept that night in the Grand Canyon.

The first section of the Grand Canyon from the Little Colorado to the beginning of the Narrow Gorge, some fourteen miles in distance, is one of great interest. The whole section seems to have been upturned, tumbled over and mixed up in every imaginable shape and form, showing most gorgeous colorings of mineralized matter, from dark purple and green to bright red and yellow. The River runs through quite a wide valley, with bottom lands and groves of mesquite. The top walls of the Canyon are miles and miles apart, and hills and knobs rise between the River and the walls beyond, these being separated by deep washes and gulches, running in every direction.

These washes have brought into the River many boulders, mostly smooth and round, which form rapids at their mouths. The first two were very light, but No. 189 had a sudden drop of four or five feet, and boulders scattered through its whole length of crooked channel, which was divided into almost two distinct rapids. With some pretty hard rowing and quick turns, all went through without serious mishap, except Twining's boat No. 3, which struck a rock near the lower end and smashed a great hole in her side, so that we had to go into camp early for repairs, which occupied our time until the next noon. That day we only made three miles, passing three light rapids, and stopped early for photographs of the iron dike, which cuts across the River and through which the River, ages ago, cut its way.

Here we found another evidence of the changes that had been going on in the Canyon during the eighteen or twenty years preceding—changes which have already been explained as caused by the washing in and washing out of boulders from the side canyons. Major Powell, in his Report, describes a volcanic dike, about six miles below the head of the Canyon, "through which ... the river has cut a gate-way ... several hundred feet high, and as many wide. As it crosses the wall, there is a fall below, and a bad rapid, filled with boulders of trap; so we stop to make a portage."[3] In the winter of 1890, the dike, of course, was there, and the gateway, but no fall and no bad rapid. At the low water stage of winter, we found in the first fourteen miles of the Grand Canyon, twenty-four rapids. Many of these would be obliterated in the time of high water, though the fall in this section is nearly nine feet to the mile.

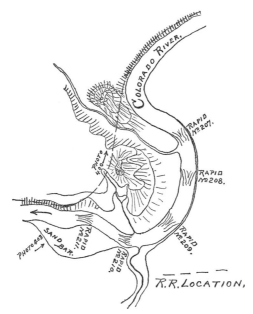

10. Sketch map "in first 14 Miles of Grand Canyon."

Here is a sample of the open valley, and also a sample of the simple railroad alignment along this crooked part of the River above the "narrow gorge," as I called it, which begins where the River, as it were, enters the mountains some few miles above the granite.

[3] Powell, *Exploration of the Colorado River*, 81.

A LONE PROSPECTOR AND HIS DOG

January 22nd., coming into camp, we were much surprised to hear the barking of a dog, who, as soon as he came near us, ran away across the flat, keeping up a continual yelping. In a short time he returned, bringing with him his master, Felix Lantier, a prospector of Flagstaff, Arizona, whom the dog had plainly told of our presence. Lantier spent the evening and next day with us, as we laid over a day to fix up our notes and photographs and write letters home, which he took to the post office at Flagstaff. These were the first photographs I had been able to send out since Nims's accident, and I had assumed the work of photographer. I was most anxious to have them developed and know if my work had been in any measure a success. It was not until March that I received, at Peach Springs, that joyous telegram from Denver—"Negatives all right."

We bade Lantier good-bye (not forgetting his dog) and pushed on down the River. In the afternoon we entered between the close walls of the "narrow gorge" and camped (No. 70) early at the head of Rapid No. 213, which required a portage, and as we had already made two long, hard portages that day, this one was put off for the morrow. Although we had had ice and snow in the wide valley above, here in the deeper Canyon the tender green willows had not been touched by frost.

The next morning, early, we began our portage of something less than a half mile by the shallow, rocky rapid, lining the boats down, but were not reloaded and ready to start again until 2:00 P.M. Then we ran a small rapid, after which came a beautiful stretch of smooth, quiet water for a half mile, which, being backed up by the dam below, of course brought us to the head of an immense, long, rocky, rapid, full of boulders, both above and below the surface, impossible to run with such large, heavy boats as we had at the then stage of water, as it was very broad and shallow, and there was no distinct channel anywhere. We at once portaged the supplies, and with two men in the boat to keep it off the rocks, lined down the "Lily." As a storm was coming up, we secured the boats, one below and two above the rapid, and we made our camp, well tired out and ready for our Sunday's rest. It blew a perfect hurricane all night. Sunday morning, the wind went down, and it was cloudy and oppressively warm, with flies, millers, and moths in the air. I climbed up on a bench of the Canyon wall and walked down the river about a mile to get my first view of the granite gorge.[4] I thought it was the most wonderful sight I had ever looked upon—perhaps heightened in its grandeur, and the awe it inspired, by the surroundings and circumstances under which I viewed it.

Monday, January 27th., we completed the portage of Rapid No. 215 by noon, and about a half mile below came to the next rapid, over the head of which we lowered the loaded boats with lines, portaged the center part, and loading up, ran the lower half, which lay between the first real granite walls. The next two rapids we ran without stopping even to examine them, as the Canyon was narrowing and the water was confined in one deep, clear channel. We stopped for the night at the head of No. 219. Our camp was on a narrow bit of beach, and all hands climbed up the crevices of the granite to gather small pieces of driftwood to cook with. Fortunately, the weather was mild, and we needed little fire for warmth.

INTO THE GRANITE GORGE

The first Granite Gorge of the Grand Canyon has a peculiar form of its own. Unlike the towering masses of granite of some of the canyons of the Rocky Mountains, its walls start from the water's edge with generally a few feet—ten to fifty—of vertical cliff, and then slope back in a ragged, irregular slope, eight hun-

---

4 "The Metamorphic Crystalline Schists, with dikes & beds of granite and the black gneiss formations of this Archaean portion of the canyon are commonly called granite."—Stanton. This note is borrowed from *ibid.*, 81n.

147

dred to one thousand two hundred feet, at an angle varying from a few degrees to forty-five degrees from vertical, with some small patches jutting out boldly into the River and towering hundreds of feet high, forming *almost* vertical cliffs; or rather, more accurately speaking, they form buttresses and towers to the generally sloping walls.

On the top of this granite, some little way back from the crest of the slope, is a dark brown and black stratum of hard sandstone —part of the Tonto formation—standing generally vertical, fifty to one hundred feet high. This stratum, cut up into small points and rounded knobs, these stained black, has the appearance of a black beaded fringe, running the whole length of the granite, and in keeping, both in form and color, with the gloomy depths of the narrow gorge below.

Above this formation, the various strata of limestone, quartzite, marble, and bright red and white and yellowish sandstone, and limestone, pile up on each other in receding steps, cut into every imaginable shape by sidewashes and canyons, till the whole main Canyon is from six to thirteen miles wide at the top.

Into this narrow granite gorge, on January 27th., we rowed our boats with caution. The fall of the River for the first ten miles averages sixteen and a half feet per mile (the greatest average fall, except that in Lodore and a portion of Cataract Canyon), and this is contracted into individual falls and rapids, of greater depth and more powerful in the concentrated strength of their raging waters than any upon the whole River, with the exception of a few at the extreme lower end of the Canyon.

With this same care, we worked on slowly and cautiously, making but short distances each day, running such rapids as had sufficient water over the boulders, letting our loaded boats down by lines from rock to rock over some, and portaging our whole stock of supplies, and lifting our boats over the rocks at the head of others. We stopped frequently between the rapids to take photographs, make short surveys around difficult points, and, occa-

148

sionally, it was necessary to tie up to shore while I wrote up my notes, which it was impossible to do from memory at our night camps. The work we were doing required a detailed description of the Canyon walls, the nature of the material, the side drainage, and all data possible, for my railroad report. To cram such details into one's memory, for even a half day's run, was an impossibility; hence I took plenty of time to write my 1,600 pages of field notes and make sketches.

We were now on the steepest portion of the River grade, in the Grand Canyon. Here in the first few miles we had our second real falls, and began to realize the power of the current, confined between the solid granite walls, driven by the crags jutting out into the water, so close together, first from one side, then from the other, while the foam of the waves, ten and fifteen feet high, lashed and broke from every direction. On account of the low water, the rapids full of rocks, of course, we were obliged to portage or let our boats down by lines, but the falls over ledges of rocks made exciting runs. To feel the boat under you go over and down a slope of ten, or twenty feet, on the incline of the rushing waters, and then dash into and split the huge waves at its foot, with their angry power slapping you first on one side, then on the other, is an excitement grand in the extreme, and this, in the narrow channel hemmed in so close on either side, was wild and full of awe.

No comparison can be made between the several parties, who have passed in boats through the first eighty-five miles of the Grand Canyon—that is, no comparison of the manner in which they navigated the River. All the others passed through this portion earlier in the season and on a higher stage of water, Major Powell, in '72, on the highest stage of any. Our expedition, as far as Kanab Canyon, traveled on *extreme low water,* so that many portages had to be made on account of the exposed rocks in the rapids. With ten to twenty feet higher water, the channels would have been clear, and *no portages* required, even with our heavy boats.

149

Our progress on January 28th. was only one mile, and nearly the whole time, till 3:30 P.M., was occupied in passing the one rapid, our No. 219. By that time, all hands were completely tired out, and we went into camp and used the remainder of the day for rest, notes, and photographs.

This rapid was formed by the wash coming in at the foot of the *original* Hance's Trail, from what is now known on the maps as Hance Creek, and is not the "Hance Rapid," of the newer maps, which is two miles above at the mouth of "Red Canyon," and is our No. 215. We found on the granite ledge some curious remnants of a woman's garments of a tourist party, that had been down the old Hance trail. The River between the granite walls had washed the boulders, from the creek on the left, down the Canyon for a considerable distance, many of which stood above the extreme low water. With even three or four feet more water we could have run this rapid. Our portage was a most difficult one. There was no bench or talus—only the boulders in the River offered a footing—and to portage the supplies to the boats after they had been lined down, the men climbed from granite crag to crag around the open bays to the boulders below. The rapid had three falls, and at the time I felt sure it was the one that the first party, in 1869, noted as "a fall of thirty or forty feet,"[5] and made this entry in my note book: "We find the creek [on left], the 1st & 3d dam & the 30 or 40 ft. fall perhaps, but the middle dam has changed."[6]

[5] *Ibid.*, 82; ". . . though there is no such estimate in his original journal."— Stanton.

The entry for August 14, 1869, in Powell's original journal reads: "Made a portage from camp then ran 2 miles to bad falls in narrow chute, no talus, no foothold of any kind, must run it or abandon the enterprise! Good luck! Little boat fills with water twice. Chute ½ mile long. Fall 30 ft. probably, huge waves. Then run of 2 or 3 rapids, then a long portage. Dinner in a cave. Camp at night on rocks in middle of long portage on right bank. No. 31." William Culp Darrah (ed.), "Major Powell's Journal, July 2–August 28, 1869," *Utah Historical Quarterly,* Vol. XV (1947), 129.

[6] Entry for January 28, 1890, Field Notes, Book C.

THE GRAND CANYON TWO MILES BELOW THE LITTLE COLORADO

"Remembering that the notes I was taking and the impressions I was recording were to be put in a Report and upon Maps."

IN THE GRAND CANYON BELOW CATARACT CREEK

"The Chief Engineer waits for the Survey to catch up."

Since then this rapid has been measured and the sum of the three falls found to be thirty-five feet.

With two men in each boat to ward them off the rocks, the three boats were safely lowered over the first fall, and passed the dangerous boulders about one half way down the rapid, then, reloading, we ran the lower half like a whirlwind, for the drop was sudden, and the waves, driven in every direction by the sunken boulders, lashed us from every side and broke high over our heads.

Our night's rest, though refreshing, did not take the soreness out of our limbs, from the hard climb over the granite crags of our portage the day before; and, although we had breakfast at six o'clock, it was not till 8:20 that the boats were loaded and we were on the River again. The next four rapids, though heavy and steep, had clear channels and we ran them all—clear, that is, of the exposed boulders, but the boulders were there under the water, and tore the current into twisting, lashing waves that broke high in the air. In just one minute after starting we dashed into No. 220. It had a sheer drop at its head of perhaps ten feet over a ledge of granite—that is, as sheer a fall as the volume of water rushing down the narrow channel could make—and then the usual great waves at its foot. It was my custom, in running these rapids, to stand in the bow of the first boat with my knees braced against the gunwales and hold on to the short bow line. In the next rapid, which also had a fall at its head of about eight feet, the waves at the foot of the fall tossed our boat from side to side like a cockle shell, and one particularly severe one slapped me with full force on the right cheek and sent me sprawling down on my seat and against the bow oarsman, but fortunately not overboard. I did not rise and follow the Scriptural injunction and turn my other cheek to be smitten; but, possibly on account of my non-Christian spirit, in the next rapid, three immense waves served me in the same manner in quick succession, one striking me in the throat, a favorite spot for their duckings, and a bucket or two of water went in and under my flannel shirt and ran out

151

at my boots—a cheering and refreshing douche so soon after breakfast on a winter's morning.

The last of the four we ran without examining it, and, at 9:30, stopped for photographic work, and to write up my railroad and other notes.

We were now on a quiet, smooth lake of water, and the backed-up, placid stream in its very stillness spoke warningly, if not loudly, of a great dam and trouble ahead.

The smooth water tempted us to loiter, and we drifted slowly along among scenes of grandeur and beauty beyond compare. At ten o'clock, we stopped again for photographs and a climb up a little side gorge on the south to the broad bench above the granite, while the cook prepared a hot lunch. Hislop, McDonald, and I clambered a thousand feet or more up over the granite ledges and had our first view of that wonderful, broad, open "Upper Canyon" on top of the Tonto platform, flanked on either side, miles back from the River, with the green sandstones, the mighty red wall limestone, and the banded sandstones in many colors, all capped by the towering white limestone that reached to the plateau 4,000 feet above us, and at their foot the broad, nearly level floor of the upper gorge.

As I wandered among the grassy coves, dotted with little wild flowers in bloom, and saw from where we stood what looked like level plains stretching for miles down the River, and here and there a spring of clear water trickling from the upper cliffs, I dreamed one of my day dreams and saw each cove with its picturesque Swiss chalet, and its happy mountain people with their herds of sheep and mountain goats, developing local business for our future railroad. It was, perhaps, a wild dream, but as I stood years after, (in 1907) at the Hotel El Tovar on the rim of the Canyon, and looked down on the trail the same 4,000 feet, this time below me, and saw that little cottage (not Swiss, to be sure) with its shade trees and its little garden full of fresh vegetables, grown by the water from one of those same springs, I recalled my day dream of eighteen years before and wondered if it ever would be fully realized.

A RAPID OF GREAT RENOWN

After a hearty lunch, we resumed our drifting on the quiet lake, but soon that well-known, sullen, ominous roar came up the Canyon which told us that the lake had an end and beyond was more trouble. We soon came to what was claimed by Major Powell as being the greatest single declivity on the River, at the head of this most noted rapid; it is not a fall, but, after the first drop over the dam, is a regular incline, the actual descent from head to foot of the rapid being some 35 feet.[7] This is the one great rapid which, as early as 1872, received a distinct name and has kept it ever since. It was called the "Sockdologer." It is formed at its head by a dam of boulders washed out of the little side gulch, with immense blocks of rock broken down from the adjoining cliff lying just above the beginning of the fall, and, below that, the water tumbles over quite a number of *ledges* in the granite, making one continuous, raging torrent for a distance of 1,800 to 2,000 feet. In low water, that portion at the head is for some distance very dangerous, on account of the exposed and sunken rocks; while below, it is but a matter of the power of the waves breaking in every direction as the current rushes down a rock hewn trough.

On account of the many exposed rocks in the dam, we decided to lower the loaded boats over the head of the rapid and run the balance. At the low stage of water, there was a good shore

7 "While we were at this rapid in 1890 I made a measurement of its fall—but this with some other *level notes,* of the Railroad Survey, were lost in Denver, where all notes of the Survey were left until I took possession of them later on.

"When I began to write this work my memory was that the fall of the 'Sockdologer' was about thirty five feet, but, it being so many years after, I could not be sure."—Stanton.

line, of boulders and broken granite, on which we could walk. At a higher stage, a portage or lining down of the boats even over the head of the rapid would be impossible, as there would be no footing on the smooth, granite wall. Still, in that case, the whole rapid could easily be run (as it has been several times) for then it is only a mad, rushing incline of water, much more simple than many others on the River, the only danger being the great power of the "water waves."

We at once started to work and soon had all three boats safely over the first portion of the fall. The next short distance was easier, and Hogue and I walked ahead to a little gravel beach. As No. 1 was swung round a rock, held by the men with the long line above, the full current caught her, she dipped her nose un- der, filled with water, and came near getting away; but as she came by, Hogue and I both jumped into the River, caught on her gunwale and pulled her in on the gravel beach, tied her up, bailed her out, and waited for the other two boats, which were soon lined down to the same position without difficulty. Just beyond this gravel beach was an ugly pile of boulders with the water boiling over them, and it was necessary to get past these before running the rest of the rapid below. The "Marie" was started first, was caught by a crosscurrent, turned sideways, and swung against one of the rocks, turned one quarter over, filled with water, sank, and was jammed in between two boulders. We fought desperately to save the stores. With a line tied around his waist, and two men holding it, Travers jumped over the water into the boat, unstrapped and lifted out the bedding and sacks of provisions, and, with lines and grappling hooks, they were pulled to shore. Travers soon froze out, for the water was very cold, and Ballard took his place. Standing nearly waist deep in the rushing current, he saved nearly all the rest of the stores. Only two sacks of provisions were lost. Our next effort was to save the boat. We worked at it till dark, but made no progress, and gave it up as lost and began to prepare for the night. All the blankets in two boats were soaked, there was no wood in sight to make

coffee, and only a huge pile of broken granite to sleep upon. However, everyone was good-natured and full of hope, even if empty
in other respects. We gathered some little driftwood sticks and a
few bushes off the cliff, had bacon, coffee and flapjacks for supper, smoked several pipes of tobacco, divided the dry blankets
among all the men, and lay down upon the sharp granite to sleep
—if it were possible on such a bed. It was a beautiful clear night,
and, by various turnings and twistings so as to make our bones
fit in the depressions in the rocks, or by changing the pressure
of a sharp point from the middle of the back to the middle of the
stomach, we managed to get some sleep and quite an amount of
rest. Before we were asleep, we heard the boat move, and, getting up, we found the River was rising, and the boat had been
moved over the rocks into the hole below. We spent an hour
trying to pull her out, but without results, and again gave her
up as lost, not expecting to find a remnant of the boat the next
day. The morning came, the River had risen two feet during the
night, and the boat was in the same hole below the rock. After
two hours' work, we succeeded in getting her ashore. But such a
boat! One side half gone and the other smashed in, yet her keel
was not broken. We hauled her up on the rocks, and Travers, Mc-
Donald, and Edwards at once began repairs. They cut four feet
out of her center, drew the two ends together, and with five days'
hard work we had a new boat. In those five days we were not a moment without the awful roar of that mighty torrent in our ears,
with hardly enough wood to cook our meals, (the last two days'
cooking was done with the shavings from the broken boat), and
the ever-returning question—which boat would go next?

Here we had a fine illustration of that saying of Joseph Cook,
that a Western man is only an Eastern man spread out. Mc-
Donald, Travers, and Edwards were the boatbuilders. McDonald
and Edwards had had years of experience; but Travers, until
three months before a stockbroker in New York City, now suddenly became even a more complete Western man than anyone
in the party. The mechanical ability and power of adaptation

were in him, the opportunity and necessity were offered, and he was able to grasp them with a will. All three men deserve praise for their skill, and their cheerful and quick use of it. They did the real work, while the rest of us helped as best we could.

During those five days, the men not engaged on the boat spent most of the time doing Survey work and gathering wood for the cook. The latter was no small task in that locality—but we had to eat. The cook's camp was moved down below the boat yard, where there was most wood, and we had to climb over a high cliff three times a day to our meals. During this time, we lowered the other two boats past the point where we had wrecked the "Marie," loaded them up, and ran the lower 1,600 feet of the rapid, over the great, rolling waves; but, as the channel was clear, it had fewer crosswaves and lashing side-currents than some of the rapids above. The boats were secured in a cove below, and the men came back over the high granite wall, for we kept our camp still at the boat yard!

February 4th., our work was done; we had a new "Marie," eighteen feet long, and, as it proved, as good as new, and as serviceable as ever, lighter and, perhaps, easier to steer. She was soon loaded, and, at nine A.M., started on her first trip down the lower part of the "Sockdologer" rapid, riding the waves as easily as a duck. To gather up all the odds and ends and repack all three boats took a couple of hours, when at last, after our long delay, we started once more to conquer or be conquered in some other great rapid yet to come.

ON TO THE BRIGHT ANGEL

Glad to be released from our workshop, we stopped only for our photographs and notes, and dashed through the next six rapids. The second, though clear of visible rocks, seemed to have the most powerful waves we had yet run with full-loaded boats. Through the heaviest waves we went head on in good shape, but the side waves struck us, first on one side and then on the other. One huge wave, from the bow, struck me with such force in the stomach that the breath was almost knocked out of me, and as I doubled up in the bottom of the bow, it broke over the whole boat, very nearly swamping it, and, at the end, caught by the whirls and eddies, we were in one place dashed sideways against the cliff with a crash, but not with serious damage.

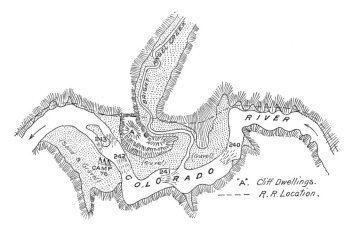

11. Sketch map of the mouth of Bright Angel Creek

After making one short, but heavy, portage we went into camp early, where we had plenty of wood and a quiet stretch of water, to try to rest our nerves after the six nights attempt at sleeping so close to the incessant roar of the rapid, where we had met our disaster. After a refreshing night, the next morning, still in the dark granite gorge, we ran three rapids, portaging over the dam of boulders at the head of the fourth, and then ran the halfmile of tumbling waves that beat at one point against one side of the cliff, the rebounding water only keeping us from being smashed against the granite wall. While our boats plow through the heaviest, wave after wave breaks over our heads, and, in a minute and a half, we stop at the foot, completely drenched through, and make a big driftwood fire to warm by and cook a hot lunch, for it is winter and we are chilled through.

This was the last of the heavy rapids in the steepest fall of this Canyon—one hundred and sixty-five feet in ten miles. For a while the rapids became less powerful, with from one to two miles of smooth quiet water between, till late in the afternoon, we met three lively and very crooked rapids, and here it took quick-witted steering to guide the boats through their winding courses, which finally brought us to Bright Angel Creek.

The sketch above, of the mouth of the Bright Angel Creek, gives some little idea of the rugged form of the Canyon walls.

A PICTURE OF THE GRANITE GORGE

The first great Granite Gorge is about forty miles in length. That portion from its head to the Bright Angel Creek, some twelve miles, is narrow, dark and gloomy. It stands at the upper gateway of the Great Canyon, as if by its very frown to keep back the intruder, and guard from vulgar eyes and sordid greed the grandeur, the beauty, and hidden treasure of the lower canyon. At the Bright Angel Creek everything changes; the granite slopes are flatter; they are of a softer black granite (gneiss), cut into sharp pinnacles and crags, and seem more as if formed of very coarsely stratified slate.

Below the Bright Angel, the Canyon grows more and more picturesque and beautiful the farther we proceed. The granite has lost its awful and threatening look, and slopes back in beautiful hillsides of variegated black, gray, and green.

At the side canyons, and from the bends of the River, the upper portions of the whole gorge are brought into view, showing the great marble and sandstone cliffs, benched back far away from the River, while mountains jut in close between the side canyons and washes, nearly a mile in height. As we sail along the smooth stretches between the rapids, each turn brings some wonderful picture more beautiful than the last. As we look down the River, or up a side canyon, with the placid water between its polished walls of black, and gray, and green for a foreground, there rise above the dark Tonto platform, tier upon tier, bench upon bench, terrace upon terrace, stepping back farther and farther, and higher and higher, and, in immensity of height and proportion, seeming to tower almost over our heads.

First above the dark sandstone come the flattened slopes of the lime and mineralized matter, in horizontal layers of yellow, brown, white, red and green. Then rise sheer walls of stained marble, one thousand feet or more, the lower portions yellow, brown and red, the coloring of red growing brighter as it nears the top.

Above this [are] smaller benches of marble, at the top of each, a little mesa, covered with green bunch grass and bushes, and above these a dozen or more terraces of scarlet and flame colored sandstone, stained on their outer points with black and the little benches between them relieved by the bright green of the greasewood, the whole crowned with perhaps a couple of thousand feet of the lighter gray, yellow, and white sandstone and limestone ledges, capped by pinnacles and spires, turrets and domes, in every imaginable shape, size, and proportion, with all their slopes covered and their tops fringed with pine, cedar, and piñon trees, whose dark green stands out in bold relief against the banks of pure white snow that cover the top, and have run down into the many gulches along the sides.

The sketch below, made February 6th., 1890, shows a portion of the granite gorge, a short distance below the Bright Angel, where the River makes two right-angle turns, and also gives the location of the railroad line. The two short tunnels, about 400 and 200 feet long, [are] at points "B" and "E," ... the road, when located above high water, would be simple and permanent, with possibly the necessity of blowing off a portion of point "A" to make more room and prevent the current of the River striking against and piling up on the wall in the bay opposite.

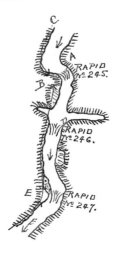

12. Sketch map of section of the river just below Bright Angel Creek

WE FIND IT AT LAST

February 6th., we ran in the morning six more rapids, all clear of rocks except one, (No. 246) where the boats were lined around a low vertical cliff from the first bench, 40 feet above, with two men in each boat to ward it off the rock wall. At eleven o'clock, we came to No. 249, the most powerful rapid, at the then stage of water, we had seen on the River, not excepting the "Sockdologer." It had a fall of some sixteen feet at the head over huge square and angular pieces of rock, fallen from the cliffs, forming a complete dam across the River. The fall itself was not over two hundred and fifty feet long; but, as the current dropped over the rocks, it made holes behind them eight to ten feet below the level of the water on the downstream side, and the rebounding waves dashed high above the level of the dam.

We at once unloaded everything and portaged the supplies. After lunch we crossed to the right side as being the better side on which to line down the empty boats. The two hundred and fifty foot line of the "Bonnie Jean" was strung out ahead, and the boat swung into the stream. She rode the huge waves with ease and went below the first part of the rapid without injury. The men and the line worked well and payed [*sic*] out smoothly; but when the boat reached the foot of the fall, she acted like a young colt eager for a play. She turned her nose out toward the current, and, as it struck her, she started like a shot for the other side of the river. The men held to her doggedly. After crossing, she turned and came back into the eddy, and for a few moments stood still, just as a colt ready for another prance. The men rushed down along the rocks to get the line ahead, but before they could go far enough, she turned her head again to the stream. The men put their wills into their arms and held her once more. She did not cross the current, but, on reaching the center, dipped her nose under as if trying her strength, came up at once, rose on a wave, and then, as if for a final effort to gain her liberty, dived her head under, filled with water, and went completely out of sight. In a few moments she rose to the surface, slowly and leisurely floated sidewise across the eddy toward shore, and quietly stopped alongside a shelving rock, seemingly well satisfied with her frolic and ready for a rest. Kane ran ahead and caught her. She was bailed out and found to be none the worse for her prance.

To prevent another such experience we adopted Major Powell's plan in such cases, of shooting the boat through and catching it below, and not attempting to hold it against the current with the line.[8]

All being now ready, and the boat below being manned, the "Marie" was swung into the stream. She rode gracefully the high waves at the head of the dam, but, when one quarter of the way through, a side wave struck her stem and turned her under the worst part of the fall in the whole rapid. She dove under, came

8 " 'But where the plunge is too great, or the chute too swift, we must let her leap, and catch her below, or the undertow will drag her under the falling water, and she sinks.' " Powell, *Exploration of the Colorado River,* 85.—Stanton.

up in good shape, was forced upstream by the rebounding wave, but, in leaving it, a fountain or shoot coming up under her side rolled her half over. When she righted, half full of water, she was shot to one side, struck against a rock where the whole force of the current was beating, sank in the heaviest part of the rapid, and came up in pieces about the size of tooth picks—our five days' labor and our boat all gone together!

We then built a skidway of driftwood and skidded our third boat, the "Lilly," over the rocks, this being the first time we had made a real portage of a boat.

During all the troubles of the day, there had not been one cross word spoken; every man, as far as he could, worked faithfully, cheerfully, and with all his might; but the loss of the boat cast a gloom over the party and perhaps instilled a little fear in some.

Next morning at breakfast, I stated that to carry the whole party in two boats each man would have to throw away everything he could spare, so as to save all our food supplies. One man objected strenuously and proposed to abandon the trip and go out from there. On second thought, he was the first to open his sack and lighten it by throwing away half his possessions.

Feb. 7th, all provisions, necessary stores, and the eleven men were loaded on the two boats, and we started on once more, running five very lively rapids and making only one portage all day. The next morning, we had to stop to repair a small leak in the "Bonnie Jean," and then, with two short portages, and running five or six miles without heavy rapids, we reached our Saturday night camp for our usual Sunday rest.

Sunday morning, McDonald and I had a long, pleasant and friendly talk over the situation. McDonald wished to leave and go out to Kanab, but said he would not do so because he had agreed to stay for the whole trip. As McDonald said, extra work was placed upon him by his skill and the want of skill of some of the other men. For this he had been receiving one-half more pay than the rest of the men from the very start. McDonald all his life had been a free lance hunter, trapper, and prospector. Considering this, and the effect his dissatisfaction would have on the other men, I finally said "Well, Mack, if you feel you want to go, I shall not hold you to your contract, and if you leave from here I will give you a check for all I owe you tomorrow." He decided to go, and next morning bade us all good-bye, going up the side canyon and, as we learned later, after a number of days of severe tramping through the heavy snow on the plateau above, reached Kanab in safety. In after years McDonald was in my employ for a number of seasons, and was a capable and faithful man.

CHAPTER NINE

Sometime we see a cloud that's dragonish;
A vapour sometime like a bear or lion,
A tower'd citadel, a pendant rock,
A forked mountain, or blue promontory.

—ANTONY AND CLEOPATRA[1]

AFTER a Sunday of rest, I deemed it advisable to take a little recreation and vary the method of our procedure from traveling down hill by water to climbing up hill by land, and at the same time secure some pictures of the mighty chasm from above.

We had been months at the bottom of the great gorge, with the towering, flaming walls above and, although among flowers and green grass in the valley, we had looked for weeks upon the huge banks of drifted snow that fell over the edge of the rim rock and down on the slopes from the plateaus on either side of the Canyon. We wished to reach, if possible, the level of the snow and, looking upon the chasm from above, photograph some of its changing scenes. The spot where we ascended was some miles below the place chosen by Moran for the subject of his great painting of the Grand Canyon, which hangs in the Capitol at Washington.

I have often stood before that painting in the Senate gallery and studied it, to see if it were possible to place upon canvas the grandeur, the beauty, the fantastic forms, and the startling *changes* of form and color which make this chasm the sublimest thing on earth. To me, Moran's painting—grand as it is in outline, wonderfully beautiful as it is in detail and color—is a disappointment. It is a perfect representation of the scene and the grandeur of the storm, caught as if by an instantaneous plate,

1 Act IV, scene 14.

and colored by the brush of a master. Yet herein lies the disappointment. Even with the artistic life like painting of the storm, it does not move. It is quiet. It is still. The Grand Canyon is never still, it is never quiet. It is a living, moving being, ever changing in form and color. Out of unseen depths its pinnacles and towers suddenly spring into view. From wide-spreading shadows of brown and black, scarlet flames flash out, and then fade away into stretches of orange and purple. How can such a shifting, animated glory be caught and held on a canvas? Much less, how can such life and color be represented in the simple black and white of a silver print?

But I am anticipating. We must climb the great north wall and look upon this wonder for ourselves. My first assistant engineer, John Hislop, and Elmer Kane volunteer to go with me. Kane straps the camera and its tripod upon his back. We are supplied with biscuits, coffee, and bacon, but carry no water, since we hope to reach the snow before night.

After climbing the rugged granite wall for a thousand feet, it is a simple matter to ascend the slopes of the inner gorge above the granite and to reach the top of the overlying strata of Tonto sandstone, and from there to walk up the gentle declivities that reach to the base of the towering marble cliffs which form the innermost detached rim of the upper chasm.

To scale these marble cliffs, which stand from one to two thousand feet in vertical walls, with scarce a bench or ledge wide enough for a mountain sheep, is a task of a different nature. We carefully pick our way around the lower points of the marble, rising higher and higher until we reach the top of a narrow divide over which we go and then up through a crack some two hundred feet in height and out upon a little shelf, perhaps three feet wide, until our progress seems cut off by a sharp buttress which projects out beyond the ledge. The buttress is V shaped, and its sharp point extends out over the bench. On the other side of it runs the same little shelf, to reach which calls for strength of muscle and something like the nimbleness of a cat, for, with toe of boot

"The lower part of this narrow river gorge is more benched in form than that just below Kanab."

THE END OF THE EXPEDITION

"April 26th, 1890. We reached tide water at the head of the Gulf of California."

and ends of fingers precariously held on little points of marble on one side, it is necessary to find and reach just such points on the other.

I hesitate for a moment, look down over the precipice, and carefully calculate how long it would take to reach the bottom, where the wild flowers are blooming all over the slopes at the foot of the cliff.

We cannot help each other, and each must stand back while the other reaches the shelf beyond, or the dark valley below.

Not a word is spoken. Each one adjusts his trappings, so that nothing may be out of place. Hislop first swings around and reaches the farther shelf in safety. I place my foot carefully on the edge of the wall close to the buttress and secure a good hold with my right hand. My left foot is thrown around, and my left hand creeps along till it catches a little jutting finger of marble which seems left just there for the purpose.

Just as I start to make the leap, I am caught by my coat on a point of the marble and held fast in mid-air. Again I look down and wonder how long it would take to reach the bottom. With one strong effort I bend my back, loosen the coat, and safely work my way to the narrow shelf on the farther side.

Kane has longer arms and legs than I, and in a moment all three of us, having swung our bodies clean out in the air—with a thousand feet of sheer wall below us and as much more above —are safely around the buttress. It has required a cool head and steady nerves, for, looking back, it seemed impossible to return.

We follow along the little ledge again, but it soon comes to an end—stops suddenly at the bottom of a narrow crack in the wall which appears to stretch up to the very top of the cliff. So up we go through this crack—or "chimney," with our backs well braced on one side and bracing our knees or catching toe- and finger-holds on the other.

About half-way up this "chimney" we come against a boulder jammed in the crack, and it looks as if our journey [is] at an end. We sit down upon a projecting shelf to rest; and, as I look out over the abyss below, my thoughts for a moment turn homeward. However there is no time to be lost. The wiry, athletic Hislop is soon helped up over the boulder, Kane crouches down upon the little shelf while I climb upon his shoulders and, as he rises up, I reach one hand to the man above, and I am lifted bodily out into the air to the top of the boulder. Kane is soon up over the boulder and we are ready to push on up the crack. Hislop starts first and as he takes hold of a *loose piece* of the cliff, I caution him that it is not safe. He coolly replies, "You need not worry now; it held both you and me as I lifted you over the boulder." I said no more and climbed upon it, although it seemed ready to drop.

After a couple of hours of hard climbing, we reach the top of a bench, not on the main cliff but beside a point, far from the main wall—an island in an ocean of thin mountain air.[2] On the other side from that by which we approached it, a narrow ridge, or "arête," of marble, from one foot to eighteen inches wide on top—a mere knife-blade—connects it with what we suppose to be the main cliff. It is perhaps three hundred feet down on either side to our first little bench below, and from that on down two hundred feet to the wild flowers on the slopes at the foot of the cliff.

The wind is blowing almost a gale; but like squirrels crossing on a swaying limb in a storm, we reach the other side of the cliff, at the other end of the narrow ridge, and briskly ascend the slopes that fall from the bright red sandstone wall some four thousand feet above the River.

To our left is another towering wall, and to reach its top we push on up through a third crack, which, again, near its upper end, is blocked by a huge boulder, which this time we cannot climb over; but behind the boulder is a little hole, through which we squeeze our bodies and finally reach the summit. Once more we are disappointed. Distances are deceiving. We are not

2 "The Tower of Ra."—Stanton.

168

on the edge of the Kaibab Plateau, but on another island, the eastern edge of Osiris Temple, fully four miles to the southwest of the main wall. The Temple itself, at our back, is only a little over one hundred feet below the elevation of the southern edge of the Plateau but yet one thousand feet below the summit of Shiva Temple.

It is growing late, and we prepare for our supper—a huge pile of dry cedar, a crackling fire, some dry biscuits and toasted bacon, but not a drop of water have we tasted since we left the River early in the morning.

Here we sleep. There is no trouble in arranging blankets for the night. They consist of nothing but the light mountain air, which comes only a short distance from the banks of snow that cover the peaks and plateaus around us.

THE BIRTH OF A CANYON DAY

Long before the morning comes, our sleep is ended. I sit by the edge of the precipice with my back to the fire and look out upon the darkness of the night. The whole great chasm is hushed in slumber. The mighty River, shut in by the blackness of the deep, seems resting from its everlasting toil.

Flashes from our fire light up in ghastly red the temple walls above us, while the many caverns, hundreds and thousands of feet below, lie like huge monsters resting at the base of the cliffs, the weird blackness of their fantastic forms just faintly shown in the dim light of the morning stars.

Soon, far out in the east, over among the towers and cloister-like buttes of the three great Temples, break the first faint rays of the coming day. Slowly, the whole eastern sky is lit up with a strange and curious light. Not the gray of an Atlantic dawn, but at first a pale blue which seems to mellow the rays of the rising sun which, in their turn, soon flash through the gray and yellow openings between the upper towers, turrets, and cathedral spires of Deva, Brahma, and Zoroaster, and wake to startling brilliancy Shiva's towering Temple, which stands to the north of us.

Yonder, lower down, through that side gorge, the sun has crept, so noiselessly and yet so suddenly that one is startled at the wondrous change. The farther side of the Canyon is all aglow. The scarlet sandstones and the dark-red marbles flash back the rosy light, which, mingling with the hazy blue of the air, casts over the whole landscape a glamour that is known nowhere else.

We hasten to the top of the butte behind us[3] better to see the drama of the opening day.

Far to the north, the great Kaibab plateau, covered with pure white snow and fringed on its edge with the bright green of the stately pines, is sparkling in the morning sun, as if crowned with a diadem of myriads of clearest diamonds and decked with thousands of emerald plumes. To the south and west the vision is bounded by the same high plateaux which lie south and north of the River.

The whole landscape is a network of caverns, gorges, and ravines, and between them are towers, temples, and buttes of every form, dimension, and design.

As the sun rises over the surrounding platform, what a silent, curious change creeps over the whole scene! The clear light of the sun streams through every opening. The eastern walls of the templed buttes burn with almost living flame, while, to the west, are cast long shadows so dark, so bold that they seem as if portions of the night itself had been left behind.

The whole Canyon is still in solemn repose, but, as the sun's light forces its way down, the dark shadows steal away to hide. The inner gorge now wakes from its night of slumber. As shadow chases shadow, and the bright sunlight leaps first here and then there, now around a buttressed point, then into some deep

---

[3] "Osiris Temple, 6637 ft. above sea level and 4330 ft. above the River."—Stanton.

alcove, the whole scene is a moving panorama, of light and shade and mingled tints of celestial beauty.

It is bewildering. One stands enchanted. As the sun rises higher and higher, the purplish blue of the atmosphere, though not of such a sleepy haze as in the summer time, gradually turns into a steely gray, and the sharp lines of the cliffs, which stood out so boldly at first, are blended into one indescribable mass of mingled symmetry.

From beneath the snow-capped summits the gray and yellow of the highest ledges gradually sink, as the eye descends, into a pale, purplish hue, which suddenly flashes out into the fiery scarlet of the middle sandstones. Across the gray talus at their base, the brighter scarlet blends into the rich, deep red of the marble cliffs, and this, gradually melting away, mingling with the purples and darker browns of the lower sandstones, rests for a base upon the black granite of the inner gorge.

Across the chasm to the southwest, into which the sun now pours in all his glory, the noble amphitheaters are opening up their many-colored galleries to view. "Hundreds of these mighty structures, miles in length, and thousands of feet in height, rear their majestic heads out of the abyss, displaying their richly-molded plinths and friezes, thrusting out their gables, wing-walls, buttresses, and pilasters, and recessed with alcoves and panels."[4] The vast ensemble, so grand, so bold, so wild, and yet grouped together with such symmetry, over all whose outer and inner walls are hung with so much grace those parti-colored draperies in a thousand varied tints, is blended in such harmony that none other than He who first painted the lily and the rose could have been its architect or its painter.

A morning on such a sculptured butte, in the presence of such awful grandeur, while slowly and noiselessly the darkness of night is changed into the beauty and sublimity of a perfect day, is like standing on some new Mount of Transfiguration, where language fails and description becomes impossible.

4 Dutton, *Tertiary History of the Grand Canyon District,* 150.

However much their beauty and their grandeur may appeal to us, we cannot linger long among such enchanting scenes. On the River below, our work still remains to do. We have miles of distance and more than four thousand feet of descent to make. We cannot return the way we came, so we go round the Temple and down the first walls to the head of a small cove where the marble cliff is partly broken down. Over this we climb, holding on to little points and dropping from one little bench to another. The last forty feet, at the bottom of the red wall limestone, is vertical, with a small crack or two and a few small points of marble on its face. Hislop, with his long, wiry limbs and some help from Kane in starting, reaches[5] a point where he can jump to the bench below. On the bench is a fallen, dry, slim tree. With a good deal of exertion, he raises it up against the cliff. It reaches half way up. Kane then takes the heavy straps, with which he has been carrying the camera, makes a loop around my body under my arms and, with the strap, raises me up over the edge of the cliff and lowers me into the top of the dead tree, by which I climb to the bench and join Hislop. Kane then descends, by the help of the strap, over a point of the cliff, and by the tree, and we, all being now on the gentler slopes, find little more real difficulty in our five mile tramp to Camp.

A short distance below the marble cliffs, we come to a pool of water, the first we had had in thirty hours. We stop, make many cups of coffee, and lunch in comfort, reaching the River late the same evening.

ONCE MORE ON THE RIVER

February 12th., after returning from our climb on the north side of the Canyon, the boats crews were rearranged. In my boat,

5 "These pages—to 676 [the first several pages of the Stanton draft of this chapter] were missing & [were] copied from orig. by A. S. B. [Anne Stanton Burchard]." Stanton, "The River and the Canyon," II, 668.

the "Bonnie Jean," I took Hislop as steersman, with the same oarsmen. Gibson stroke, and Kane in the bow. Travers, who in my opinion had developed the most skill in handling his work, was assigned to the "Lilly" as steersman, with Edwards as stroke, and Ballard as bow oarsman. Of the two extra men, Brown sat on the center load of the "Bonnie Jean," with Twining in the "Lilly."

We all regretted McDonald's leaving, except on one account. Still, most of the men took on a new determination to conquer the difficulties ahead, whatever they might be. With this spirit we start again on the River, portage two, and line our loaded boats down another rapid. A half mile ahead, we hear the roar of a powerful rapid, and Hislop, Travers, and I climb over a high point of the cliff and examine Rapids No. 261 and 262, which are close together with little or no smooth water between. The following sketch will explain the situation.

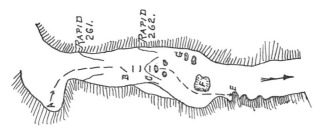

13. Sketch map of Rapids 261 and 262

The first rapid is formed by a dam, over which the water falls some twelve or fifteen feet. The waves are immense, but it is free from rocks. The second is formed by the narrowing of the channel, with three large rocks under water at "C," which divide the rapid into two channels around the high rock "F," in the center of the River. This rock, some fifty feet by fifty feet, stands twenty feet above the water on the downstream side, sloping down and under the water upstream. There are also several rocks above water at "G." The powerful current, striking against rock "F," piles up on its sloping surface. When occasional very

173

high waves or rushes of water come, they break over the entire rock. Studying the whole situation, we concluded it would be best to try the right hand channel around the big rock, but I feared we could not make the offing, through the heavy waves, in time to miss the rocks at "C."

We start at 4:00 P. M., from the Cove at "A" where our boats were tied a quarter of a mile above. The oarsmen pull with all their might to get steerage way, and we enter the rapid at a rate of over twenty-five miles per hour. The waves prove higher and more powerful than we had encountered with our loaded boats. Standing in the bow of the first boat, with knees braced against the gunwale and holding on to the bow line, the excitement is wild. On to the first wave we go, and impelled by the speed of the oarsmen added to a twenty mile an hour current, as our boat rises over it she has not time to follow it down, but shoots *fairly out into the air* and drops on top of the next smooth wave, which is lower and fifteen feet distant, with a terrible crash and loud report and the straining of every timber in her frame.[6]

The third wave is breaking high in the air. Our boat, dropping into the trough, dips her bow and we go clean through the solid part of the breaker, but are going so fast we come up on the other side only partially filled with water. The cross waves in the lower part of the first rapid lash us on every side, and the rebounding waves from the rocks check our speed. We try, at the point "B," to make the right channel, but are too late; the current catches our stern, we are turned and go broadside over the worst wave of the second rapid, and on to the first rock at "C," and our keel catches on the rock, and for a moment we hang. My heart goes into my boots, for, looking down into the vortex of the whirlpool, behind the rock and ten feet below, I cannot

[6] "The whole action here described only took moments in its several stages. But, at this particular moment, I was so interested in seeing our boat go out into the air that I leaned over the side, and looked down and saw the keel of the boat in the air several feet above the water, in the trough between the waves. *The bow* of the boat did not strike the next wave at all. She struck midships, so that for a second at least the *whole boat* was out of water."—Stanton.

see how our boat can go on without turning completely over, and burying us under it. It is but a second. An extra high roll of water lifts us clear, and the boat settles gracefully away from the rock, right side up, with almost perfect head on to the right channel. Every man jumps to his work, and we go by the rock "F" so close that only the rebounding water keeps us from striking.

Safe ourselves, we at once begin to look for the second boat. Even Hislop turned round, and before we knew it the bow of our boat struck against the cliff at "E." The other boat was nowhere in sight. We pull quickly to the shore, as we jump out we see Hogue, standing on the great rock in the center of the River at "F," frantically waving his hat. We jump back into the boat, and pull out into the stream, ready to pick up the other four men as they float down, but, in a moment, they all appear on top of the rock. We pull into the eddy behind the rock to help them and learn that their boat had been turned broadside on, as ours was at the point "C," and caught by the main current in an extra heavy swell, was landed high on the sloping side of the rock "F," filled with water, and, at the same time the wave receding, was left stranded ten feet above the water, and the men stepped out without injury. For some little time no second great wave poured over the rock, but one might do so at any moment, and quick work was required. The heaviest part of the load was taken out and piled on the highest part of the rock, the boat bailed out, lifted off the rock into the eddy behind, and reloaded. We then all rode down a half mile and went into camp, with every man and every thing in our boats—not in the rubber sacks—including our blankets, thoroughly wet. This time our whole photographic apparatus went under the water and I feared the rolls that were in the roll-holders were ruined, but on examination soon found they were uninjured.

It is one of the most curious facts connected with this whole expedition, that while three men were drowned, our provisions lost, boats smashed, and everything and almost everybody swamped and under the river numerous times, not one photographic negative, out of the twenty-two hundred that were taken, was lost, damaged, *or even wet*.[7]

MORE RAPIDS AND BAD WATER

The next morning, February 13th, being so tired out from the work and excitement of the day before, we did not have breakfast until eight o'clock, and it was nearly eleven before we set sail. We immediately ran rapid No. 263, and I took two heavy waves in my lap as a morning douche—when, at the lower end of the rapid, our boat was caught in the swirl and twisted round and round and dashed from side to side, being entirely unmanageable until we reached the quiet water below and landed at the head of the next rapid at 11:10 A.M. This rapid No. 264 could be easily run, except at the then low stage of water, the whole force of the current dashing against the foot of the cliff, which is fifty feet high, and which overhangs eight or ten feet in separate ledges, made it very dangerous. So we portaged our stuff, lined our empty boats down, and then took a long noon rest, as a great storm was brewing and the wind blowing a gale up the Canyon.

The next rapid gave us the hardest portage we had had, over high rough broken pieces of red granite, and, in swinging down the boats, the "Lilly" struck a rock and sprung a leak; but we

[7] "Referring to the very disastrous results of the Kolb Bros Photographic expedition of 1911 and '12 . . . it may be again explained here, how I succeeded in saving all my pictures. Besides the *perfect* rubber bags, in which all the supplies were packed, each roll of photograph films was put in a round tin box, and before exposure were sealed in the usual way with a piece of adhesive plaster.

"*After exposure* the films were put back into the tin boxes, and this time the caps of the boxes were *soldered on* absolutely air and water tight. All pictures were taken in duplicate, soldered up, packed in different rubber bags, and carried in separate boats. A precaution well worth the trouble and extra expense."—Stanton.

The unfortunate experiences which the Kolb Brothers had with their photographic equipment are described in Ellsworth L. Kolb, *Through the Grand Canyon from Wyoming to Mexico* (New York, 1914).

were obliged at once to reload and push on, as there was no landing place along the granite walls where it was safe to leave the boats, nor room enough to pull them out for repairs. In ten minutes we landed on a small bench at the head of rapid No. 266 and went into camp, after the most trying and wearying day to me, perhaps because I slept the night before in wet blankets.

After spending half a day repairing the boats, we started to conquer rapid No. 266. The experiences here are best told by copying the day's record from my note book.

"Friday, February 14, 1890. . . . At 1:45 P. M. we begin & drop boats 500′ to head of rapid, #266. This rapid is very rough & rockey one, and at this stage of water can not be run. [There is] A drop of 10′ to 12′ in 300 ft. [among huge boulders]. Walls from 50 to 100 ft high [vertical at the water]. At the head of it, on Rt for 200 ft there is no footing for portage, & for 600 ft on left—so must let the boats down loaded. We take the Rt side, Hislop climbs over cliff 500 to 600 ft up with small line attached to heavy line, and drops it over the cliff. He gets down to the river and draws heavy line over attaching it to boulder. We draw it taught [sic] & fasten to boulder above. Our boat is then manned and with short line around . . . [the stretched hand] line to slide along so as to Keep her stern from being caught by [the] Current & Swept out, and [with a] long line [attached to the bow and] held by [the] men up stream . . . the 1st boat [the "Bonnie Jean"] is let over [the fall] to rocks below— . . . This is repeated with 2d boat [the "Lily"] . . . Kane [being left] above to hold . . . [the boat's main line]. He then loosens hand line, and it is pulled in, and he being with Hislop the best climber goes up over the [six-hundred foot] cliff & gets [soon] down [to the boats] safely—[We continued our portage to a small eddy below, and there once more embarked. Copying again from my field book:] . . . This rapid (#266) is the worst one [so far that] we have had to get over & around. The rocks all over it are large & the force of the waves [among them] irresistible. After getting over . . . [the upper part of the rapid] as abv. described, We got into our boats in the most—to me—dismal & uncertain place we have ever set sail. The canyon is narrow, the walls come nearer being . . . [Vertical] than at any point we have passed/ it is getting dusk, and the sharp curve in the river to the Rt prevents seeing but a short distance ahead. The walls at the water's edge for 20′ to 50′ are vertical & cut & polished in vertical seams. No wood, no landing place in sight. The [awful] roar of the rapid in our ears, and the huge waves of its lower half dashing in every direction forming whirls, eddys & back currents/ Out into these we pull in any thing but a pleasant frame of mind —We get out of the rough water, after being twisted & turned & dashed about . . . [but, fortunately, not against the cliffs, and finally] row, thro′ [a smooth lake] abt one mile . . . when we [again] hear the roar & see the dashing Waves of a rapid below. Hislop Travers & I . . . [climb] up on the broken granite, just beyond the massive red [granite], and as we get up high enough, we can see around a left turn in the river, & what a view opens to our sight—A wide open Canyon for five miles almost Straight with green grassey slopes at an angle of abt 45° coming down to the very waters edge, the river almost like a placid lake with only a slight ripple at intervals of a mile or two, [as they seem from that distance,] indicating easy rapids. The whole picture charming in the extreme, but to Cap it all, at our feet a short easy rapid [free from rocks] and just below it a dry sand beach covered with drift wood/ what joy, what joy, & what a change of feelings since leaving our last hard portage. We fairly run to our boats, jump in, and dash thro′ the rapid and into the eddy on the left & in a few moments are landed on the beach. The whole party as if overcome by the happiness of the prospect of a comfortable night, fairly scamper out of the boats & make one rush in a friendly scramble for [choice] places on the dry sand to sleep, Like so many school boys let out at recess. . . . we soon have a hot supper, and are sitting [with our pipes] around the most cheerful camp fire we have had for a fortnight—"[8]

8 Entry for February 14, 1890, Field Notes, Book C.

178

After a splendid night's rest and a hearty breakfast the next morning, Kane and I climbed up the granite slopes to take photographs, and by the time we returned the boats were loaded and ready to start. Two and a half miles of almost smooth, quiet water gave us an opportunity to study one of the grandest, and most awe-inspiring sights it has ever been my good fortune to look upon. It was the middle of February, and one of the severest winters known in that section for many years. The mountains and cliffs along the rim rock were covered with from ten to thirty feet of snow, yet in this section of the Canyon, on account of its narrowness and great depth—near 6,000 feet—the winter snows seldom, if ever, reach the River; there spring and summer reign supreme. This particular day was mild and spring-like, at the bottom of the Canyon, though dark and cloudy and damp as we left our camp early in the morning. Green grass was springing up all over the little flats by the water's edge. The early wild flowers were in full bloom, and birds singing on every side. The several stretches of smooth water we had were peculiarly calm and blue. Everything was quiet and peaceful. After our frightful struggle in the rapids the day before, such a morning on so placid a River was restful and reassuring. We sailed along for some time, enjoying to the full the rest it gave our nerves. Before noon we rounded a great granite point, and there was opened to us a vision of winter above—as seen from the flower bedecked fields of spring below—a vision of nature, and the elements in peace and quiet below, in war and tumult above; in the beauty of peace; and in the grandeur of wild and awful struggle that would require the tongue and pen of a combined poet and artist to describe adequately. Above us seemed to hang, almost over our heads, great mountains, five and six thousand feet high, snow-covered from their summits half way down. They were ranged in two battalions, as it were, on either side of the great gorge, those grand old chiefs, standing out in advance near the brink of the

Canyon, while their legions were ranged in well ordered ranks in their rear, with skirmish lines and pickets far in advance, even to the rim of the inner gorge.

From under the dazzling white of the snowy mantles that encircled and hung down from their monstrous shoulders could be seen the bright colors of the cliffs that formed their war girdles and sashes—in scarlet, in orange and in purple.

Among the emerald plumes of hemlocks and cedars upon the crests of their helmets, floated great black clouds, like demons in the air. All was quiet in the peaceful valley below, but the powers of the great winter tempest, the frost kings and their legions, were gathering for the onslaught. From the right came the wild north wind. The winter lightning flashed along the cliffs, and it seemed as if artillery from every castle, from every fort, from every redoubt, hidden among the recesses of the gorge, shot out tongues of fire. And the winter's thunder echoed and re-echoed the roar from the mighty guns, while great puffs of white smoke came from all along the battlements, in the form of enormous drifts of snow shot out into the upper canyon and hurled towards the opposite side. Then from the left came the almost wilder south wind, from the San Francisco mountains, and its gusts of drifting snow were dashed out against their foes from the north. There—over our heads—they whirled, they circled, they rose, they fell and rose again, mingling with the black demons of the clouds, that hung low in the canyon, as if spirits, principalities, and powers were battling in the air, for the glory of possessing the mighty gorge.

At times huge banks of snow—as it were, the very tops of the mountains themselves—seemed to topple over, and come dashing down as if to bury us in an avalanche, but, before they descended halfway through the chasm, they were but floating snowflakes, and as they mingled with the warmer air near the bottom, the thin, frosty crystals melted away and fell around us as a gentle mist and a soothing vapor.

Again the north wind rushed and the south wind raged, the

lightning flashed, and the thunder roared, and the black demons and the white spirits struggled in deadly combat far above our heads. But a mightier power, far above them all, spoke as in a still, small voice. The winds ceased, the lightning and the thunder were no more, the demons in the clouds and the spirits in the air were rolled back to either side, and the hoary warriors, the Frost Kings of the Mountains, though not conquered, folded their arms across their frosty breasts in silence. And from the west the brilliant rays of the afternoon sun flashed in between the contending forces and lit up the whole mighty chasm with a gorgeous beauty from Heaven itself, which seemed to say: "Peace! Be still! Vengeance is mine, saith the Lord."

THE SECTION ABOVE KANAB

From this point for about thirty-five miles to the mouth of Kanab Canyon, the River has much less fall, its average being about six feet per mile. Though in places the rapids are close together, there are longer stretches of smooth water than in the heavy granite above. The rapids are entirely formed by the boulders washed in from the side canyons and hence are at low water full of exposed rocks. In this distance of thirty-five miles there are sixty-three rapids, of which we ran forty-five and portaged over the heads of eighteen. The rapids with the lesser falls were generally the ones that required the portages, but *in all these cases* the portages were only because of the low water, and over the head of the rapids for one hundred to two hundred feet, while the lower ends, sometimes over one-half mile long, *were always run* with full-loaded boats. The fact that the River was so low, in these rocky rapids, made the waves among the rocks higher and more powerful, so that though they were all run without accident—with one exception—in all but a few, the waves broke over our heads with terrific force, their spray dashing ten and fifteen feet high.

181

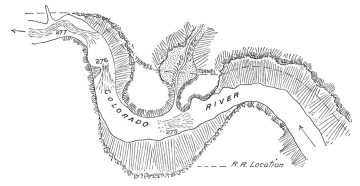

14. Sketch map of the mouth of Shinumo Creek

A QUICK WITTED ACTION

On the afternoon of February 17th., we came to a long, shallow rapid, No. 277, a mile and a half below the mouth of Shinumo Creek. We start into it and find, about half way down, it is divided by a shallow place and low waves, with an eddy on the right and a pile of driftwood on shore, so we pull out and go into camp. Early next morning we start in the high waves and roaring current below. When half way through, rounding a sharp turn to the right, my boat, the "Bonnie Jean," kept a little too far in, to avoid a slide of boulders, and was caught by the whirl and carried towards the right bank, at the same time going downstream at a fifteen or twenty mile rate. Our steersman, Hislop, seeing two large rocks ahead, under water, with large waves breaking over and below them, shouted to pull hard to the shore, but it was too late—we were drifting sidewise and our bow was caught on the first rock, and the boat keeled over, but did not upset. I had time to grab a line and put my foot on the gunwale ready to jump clear if she capsized, but the current swung the stern round like a shot and the boat fell over in the hole behind the rock and, at the same time, snapped Hislop off his stern seat, and he lit in the rapid ten feet ahead of us, but

182

was held up as he went down through the waves by his cork jacket. Our boat drifted down and soon overtook him and he climbed in; but he had lost his steering oar. The second boat, the "Lilly," came through without accident, and the men, rowing hard, passed us as Hislop regained his seat, and here Twining performed his first, last, and only brilliant feat on the whole expedition. Sitting on the bow of the second boat he saw the accident, and that Hislop had lost his steering oar, and, in the few moments it took for the whole occurrence while his boat was going towards ours at something like a twenty mile an hour gait, Twining realized the whole situation, unstrapped an extra oar from the side of the boat, and, just as he passed us, he quickly and skillfully tossed it ten feet across the waves to Hislop, who caught it and soon gained control of his boat. It was a quick-witted, brilliant, and praiseworthy act by Twining, and we cheered him for it.

If only the same spirit and willing action had been exhibited in all his work on the expedition, he would have been one of the most valuable men we had.

TWO VIEWS OF THE GREAT CANYON

The difference in viewing the Grand Canyon from the upper rim and seeing it day after day and month after month from the depths of its inner gorge can hardly be understood except by those who have viewed it both ways. From the top the view is so extensive, so incomprehensible that, as Dutton has so well said, it is one "which at first bewilders and at length overpowers."[9] Spending as we did nearly the whole winter in the Grand Canyon, making slow progress by reason of our railroad work, we could see day by day a thousand scenes, each more grand and more beautiful than those before, and while, although we had more time to enjoy each in detail, even seeing them thus, they

[9] Dutton, *Tertiary History of the Grand Canyon District*, 144.

crowded in upon us so fast that it was not long till one's brain was in a confused whirl with the grandeur and beauty. Yet even after a hard day's work and going into camp, I could not help recording in my note book something of the beauties spread out before me in that wonderful section from Point Sublime to the eastern base of Powell's Plateau.

For instance, let me quote from my note book at Camp No. 83. "Sunday, February 16, 1890. [What] Most beautiful views [are seen] from this Camp both up & down [the River] for several miles each way. The long easy slopes of the inner gorge, covered with grass & greese wood bushes in their bright green spring coloring mingled with the [points of] Shiney polished black granite running down to the waters edge, with two or three rapids in sight, [with their white breakers dashing high in the air,] and glassey lakes of [seemingly] Still water between. The whole [lower] picture hemmed in at either end [and above] with mountains of flaming red, capped with towering pinnacles of grey & yellow & [above] the green fringe of the mountain pine & cedar . . . glimpses of [bands of pure white] snow. . . . And to the West of our camp, a most gorgeous & wonderful amph[ith]eater—Wonderful in the Greatness of its dimensions, and grandeur of its architectural proportions. Beautiful in the curious detail of [its carvings, and] its finish, and the blended colors of its frescoed alcoves and galleries."[10]

From the southern portion of Powell's plateau to the mouth of the Kanab Canyon, the Canyon assumes an entirely new form. The granite, except in a few patches, has sunk under the River, and the softer strata of sandstone and limestone, which formed the great slopes above the granite, have come down next to the River, and rise from the water's edge in great talus slopes from 300 to 600 feet high at a general angle of forty degrees from vertical. The high cliffs of marble and red sandstone bench back from the tops of these slopes. Although these outer peaks and cliffs have drawn in close upon the River, the Canyon itself—

10 Entry for February 16, 1890, Field Notes, Book C.

that is, the inner gorge—is much wider than above, the width being measured between the tops of the great talus slopes. The River is broader, and it sweeps in gentle curves at the foot of the talus, which is covered with bushes, bunch grass, and large mesquite groves.

On many of the long stretches, where the River can be seen for several miles, the picture is one of charming beauty—with the walls of bright colors towering 2,000 and 3,000 feet over head, and those beyond reaching to heights of over 5,000 feet, and its long swinging green slopes, with the quiet waters sparkling in the sun at their foot; for the rapids are much less frequent, and the stretches of still water are growing longer and longer.

In this section, for a few days, we had almost all the rainy weather we experienced during the whole winter. As the clouds gathered thick, they hung down low in the gorge, shutting out from view all the upper cliffs. The rain poured down in torrents, but it seemed lost in the immensity of the chasm. As the clouds rose, we were treated to scenes rare and beautiful in the extreme. Over the brink of the upper walls came—first one and then another—hundreds of little streams, shooting far out into the air, and dropping hundreds and hundreds of feet over the cliffs, breaking up into sparkling spray before they struck the bench below. These formed thousands of smaller rivulets as they dropped farther and farther down, till the whole of the bright scarlet walls seemed hung with a tapestry of silver threads, the border fringed with white fleecy clouds which clung to the tops of the walls, and through which the points of the upper cliffs shone as tassels. As the sun broke through some side gorge, the Canyon was spanned from side to side, as the clouds shifted their position, with rainbow after rainbow as if vying to outdo in brilliancy of color the walls of the Canyon themselves.

For five days the rains kept up almost continuously, but we pushed right on, for the water that fell on us from above did not seem to be so wet as that which soaked us from the waves of the River. During these five days, we ran fifty-three rapids; over

the heads of some of them it was necessary to portage the boats
or let them down with lines, but the lower stretches of the rapids
were always run. The River was rising, and we had one or two
feet more of water, which on the shallow rapids made them vastly
easier. Of the fifty-three we only portaged or let down *over the
heads* of seven, running the remaining forty-six, many without
stopping to make any examination beforehand.

TRAVERS WINS HIS SPURS

In all of these rapids there was danger and wild excitement;
but such experiences had become so common that little note was
taken of the danger, and we dashed through them, only stopping
for our railroad and photographic notes. One rapid—No. 326—
requires special mention. The following sketch will explain its
peculiar nature:

15. Sketch map of Rapid 326

Just at the end of the V shaped entrance of this rapid stood an
immense boulder in the center of the River at "A," against which
the whole current beat, the greater part of the stream being
thrown to the right against the second boulder, "B," lying against
the bank. This action caused a curling wave, or breaker, just
above "B," which extended all across the channel nearly to "A,"
and was higher and more powerful than any *single wave* I saw
upon the whole River. To attempt to run between the two rocks
"A" and "B," and *through that wave* would seem to invite ab-
solute destruction. The water was so shallow, and the rocks so

plentiful on the left of the boulder "A," that it was impossible to run that side channel. Hislop, Travers, and I studied the situation for some time, but the solution was worked out by Travers, that is, how to run the rapid and not spend a whole day in a most difficult portage of the boats and supplies. He showed us that while the boulder "A" was eight or ten feet above the level of the river, it sloped to the right towards "B," and the powerful current rose up over it, covering the greater part of it with two to three feet of water, *which curved around the whole rock,* while the highest part to the left side was bare, and that this water curled over the rock without encountering the terrible wave to the right. Travers proposed to steer his boat directly for the rock "A," and, at the right moment, give the bow the proper turn, and then trust to the powerful current to raise the boat *over the rock* and drop it by and beyond the great wave on the right. We both agreed that it was possible to be done, but that all depended upon the skill of the steersman in turning the bow correctly at the exact moment. Travers's spunk was up, and he asked to be allowed to make the first run. He started back some distance, and his two oarsmen gave the boat a fine send-off and pulled hard to give steerage way. Travers steered direct for the rock "A," as if he intended to smash the boat to pieces, but, just as the bow came within a couple or three feet of the rock, with a skillful turn of his steering oar, he swung the bow into the center of the current, and the next moment, with a powerful reverse stroke of his oar, he kept the stern of the boat from being carried to the left against the rock, and she rose out of the River eight or ten feet, *on the current over the rock,* and although, on account of the slope to the right, she careened nearly forty-five degrees, she followed *over and around the curve of the rock* with the current and dropped beyond, without touching the great wave on the right, scraping her keel, or shipping a gallon of water. It was the most beautiful sight of skillful boating one could imagine, and Travers certainly had won his spurs!

Hislop, as skillfully and successfully, carried our boat over the boulder in the same manner, and we made the next four miles—with three rapids and a swift-twisting current between them—in fine style, for the River was rising, and we did not mind the swirls, eddies and crosscurrents, for the boulders in the shallow rapids were covered. That evening, February 24th, we went into our Camp No. 90, at the mouth of the Kanab Canyon.

CHAPTER TEN

The sounding cataract
Haunted me like a passion: the tall rock,
The mountain, and the deep and gloomy gorge,
Their colours and their forms, were then to me
An appetite; a feeling and a love,
That had no need of a remoter charm,
By thought supplied, nor any interest
Unborrowed from the eye.

—WILLIAM WORDSWORTH[1]

FROM the mouth of Kanab Canyon for about twenty miles down is perhaps the narrowest and deepest part of the great inner gorge. The lower sandstones and limestones have sunk under the River, and the marble and upper sandstones have come close into the water. At the bottom, the gorge is 150 to 200 feet wide, and the River runs between vertical walls—vertical, however, for only about eighty or a hundred feet up—and fills the whole space from wall to wall.

The walls of this portion of the inner Canyon (and it comes nearer being a true canyon than any other part of the River) rise above the water 3,000 feet and they are *almost* vertical. The benches are narrower, and the vertical cliffs between the benches higher, than in any other section. And yet, strange to relate, from one end of this section to the other there is a bench about twenty or thirty feet above high water, running almost parallel with the grade of the River, of solid marble, and wide enough to build a four track railroad upon.

The night before we reached Kanab Canyon the River rose four feet; it continued to rise for two days and two nights. How much the total rise was is not certain, but somewhere from ten to twelve or fifteen feet, that is in the wide part of the Canyon above Kanab—this would make a rise in the narrowest parts of from thirty to forty feet. Just below Kanab Canyon there is a rapid a mile and a half long. On Tuesday morning, Feb. 25th,

1 "Lines Composed a Few Miles above Tintern Abbey." In the third line Stanton has changed the word "wood" to "gorge."

we started down this rapid. We made the mile and a half in just four and a half minutes. We then had for some time few rapids, but a rushing, singing current, forming eddies, whirlpools, and back currents fearful to contemplate, much more so to ride upon.

WATER FLOWING FOUR WAYS

Here we had a very clear, if only partial, demonstration of what the power of the current in such a narrow part of the Canyon might be at the stage of *highest* water, as recorded by driftwood on the walls. The River has never been navigated under such extreme conditions. At lower stages, usually before reaching the head of a rapid, the water is smooth and quiet for some distance back. At this time, with, say, a thirty foot rise as we approach Rapid No. 332, about three miles below Kanab Canyon, we notice, instead of the usual placid water, an enormous whirling fountain some one hundred feet in diameter; we start to pull across it, as it fills the whole Canyon from wall to wall, but find we cannot reach the top, for we are pulling up *a hill of water* fully six feet, possibly higher, above the level of that above or below it. The immense current, driven down the chute, unable to go fast enough over the dam and through the narrower part ahead, is turned back, and meeting the main current on one side, is forced up in a mound of water and flows off from the center upstream as well as down. With all the power of our oarsmen we cannot reach the top, but are driven upstream by the water *rushing off the hill.* We try it a second time, but fail again, and by this time the second boat has overtaken and passed us, and, on the edge of this revolving and rushing hill of water, is caught in the power of a smaller whirlpool, drawn into its deep vortex, is sucked down and half turned over. As we pass, we see the water pouring over the gunwale of the boat and expect the whole crew to be swallowed up, but we can give no assistance, as we are caught in the narrow main current on the side and swept downstream along the right wall, around the foot of our *water hill,* and this time get by. But before we are passed, we see the other boat lifted out of the vortex of the whirlpool and *swept upstream.* A few hundred feet below, we gain the center of the River, and looking back, standing up in my boat, I can only see the tops of the men's heads, as the conical hill of water stands continually whirling and boiling that high between us.

Travers, seeing the course we had taken, pulled out to the side, followed along the right wall, and came through safely. Both boats at once started for the rapid below without stopping to examine it, for we felt safer as the water was all going one way, while that above was going four ways,—downstream, upstream, rising in the air, and being sucked in great holes to the bottom, and, with all, whirling around in every conceivable direction, so that we hoped that to go in one direction at a time, even if the waves were ten feet high, would be a relief. We are, however, again caught in a lesser whirl before entering it and start in quartering. A cross current strikes us and we go down broadside over the worst waves, the boat entirely unmanageable. She goes down stern foremost, then sideways again, and, at the foot of the rapid, the whirls spin her around like a top, and we are dashed from one side to the other clear across the channel. Reaching the end of the rapid, we stop as soon as possible and wait for the other boat, and again stop to take photographs after which we run the next two rapids without trouble.

During the whole morning's run the excitement was wild. Standing in the bow of the "Bonnie Jean," holding on to the bow line, and leaning half over the side to see as far as possible around the bends, we rush along at twenty miles an hour, but we must stop, as often as we can, to examine the rapids where there are rocks and take our photographs and railroad notes. It required more work and more skill to stop than to go on. No sand bars, no beach, only small ledges of smooth rock and a few small slides for our landings.

About half way round a sharp turn to the left we suddenly

came in sight of the head of a Rapid, No. 335, with immense breakers dashing high into the air. We were approaching it at a fearful speed, and it seemed necessary to stop and make an examination before running it, as we could not see around the bend. It required quick work. We crossed the current and struck a small eddy, which suddenly shot our bow upstream, and we pulled hard along the wall till we came to a small shelf of rock. Kane put up his oars, caught the bow line, leaped to the shelf, and with Gibson backing water, checked our speed, though we came near pulling Kane into the River, but he finally hauled us alongside the wall. The second boat followed, and had the help of our men in making a landing. We were only a hundred feet above the first of the breakers, but fortunately on the outside of the curve, and could see down nearly to the foot of the rapid, for we could not at that point climb the vertical cliff behind us. The prospect below looked wild, but apparently safe. After resting awhile, we pulled out into the current, and in a moment went tumbling over the first fall. The channel proved clear of rocks and with fewer cross currents, so we were able to keep head on through the whole rapid, but we had just two minutes of as lively a ride as one wants to take, up in the air, down in the trough, rocking forward and back with a motion like a hobby horse, with a continual shower bath of spray and every now and then a douche from a solid wave thrown in for good measure, until we stopped in the eddy below to take our breath. Beyond was a rushing, singing current, over which we went with caution, pulling against the current, rather than with it, for fifteen minutes, when we stopped for photographs, and concluded to rest awhile and have our noon lunch.

After a rest of an hour and a quarter, the next two rapids were easily and quickly run, and we landed in the eddy below. Starting once more, we were soon in a narrow gorge with vertical and overhanging walls fifty feet up from the water, and saw ahead a slide from the shoulder of a side canyon, which, from the bend of the Canyon where we were, seemed to stretch all the way across the River. In this narrow gorge the current was rushing on with terrific force. The River had been rising all day, and the stream in the narrow trough was gaining force every hour. It was a struggle which tried the muscles of the oarsmen, to check our boat in order to make a landing, by turning upstream and sideling up to the wall, but at last we succeeded in stopping on a few rocks that had fallen from the cliff and were still above water.

Hislop and Kane, being the most athletic, climbed the cliff up a crack to the first bench and went ahead to reconnoiter. They returned and reported that a huge rock from the slide lay in the center of the River, with many sunken rocks to the left, but a narrow, clear channel on the right through which the greater part of the River flowed. Through that narrow channel we ran, at a rate that would have been sure destruction if we had struck the corner of the boulder, but the rebounding waters kept us off, though we went so close I could have touched it with my hand. We stopped below, and I walked back over the slide and took photographs and a snapshot of the rock.

Rapid No. 338—at the mouth of the side canyon—was quickly passed and the canyon again became narrow, with fifty to one hundred feet vertical walls.

HIGH WATER WAVES AND RAPIDS

Thus we went until 2:30 P.M., when we heard a deep, loud roar and saw breakers ahead, breaking into white foam high in the air. We landed and went ahead to examine the rapid. Much to our surprise, there was no rapid, no waves, only a swift, singing current. We chaffed each other on seeing double after the wild run of the morning. Starting again, we ran for a few minutes, when Hislop, Travers, and I all saw, this time surely, a great rapid beyond, with higher waves than before. With great difficulty we stopped upon a pile of broken rock that had rolled in on the side of the River. We climbed up on the first bench and walked down stream, but again the terrible rapid had disappeared, and again, in its stead a wild, rushing, though smooth, current. While we stood wondering, there arose right at our feet those same great waves, twelve to fifteen feet in height and from one hundred to one hundred and fifty feet long across the River, rolling downstream like great sea waves.[2] We watch and wonder and study their action. Out of a smooth current they rise and quickly reach their maximum height, breaking upstream with a fearful roar, at the same time moving downstream, and then gradually subside. The same movement is repeated a little distance farther down, and then farther and farther. Now they begin again above us and in front of us, and the whole operation is repeated again and again at regular intervals. We finally conclude this is the forefront of a great body of water rolling down this narrow trough from some great cloudburst above.[3]

It is difficult to comprehend the force and grandeur of this phenomenon. The greatness of the stream; the height and length and width of the waves; the tremendous force and roaring thunder with which they break, just as a storm surf on a sandy beach; the canyon so narrow; the towering walls; our perfect helplessness on the water; our boats like little chips tossed from side to

[2] "In sea waves the water remains in place, and the *form* of the wave moves on; in the smooth waves of a rapid, the form remains in place and the *water moves on*, but here we had a combination of the two. The current was rushing on at a fearful rate, and the form of the waves was also moving on at a less rate, and breaking back like combers on a beach."—Stanton.

[3] "The cloud burst had occurred on the head waters of the Little Colorado, as we learned some weeks later, and had broken the dams of large reservoirs, and let all the water down at once.

"For explanation of such phenomena, see Henry Darcy and Henri Bazin, *Recherches Hydrauliques* . . . (2 parts in 1 vol., Paris, 1865), Part 2, '*Recherches Expérimentales Relatives aux Remous et à la Propagation des Ondes.*' Also: Clemens Herschel, 'On Waves of Translation That Emanate from a Submerged Orifice, with an Examination of the Feasibility of the Proposed Baie Verte Canal,' *Transactions* of the American Society of Civil Engineers, Vol. IV (1875), 185–200."—Stanton.

side; lifted high in the air and dropped into the "trough of the sea"; turned round and round, and utterly unmanageable. It was something to inspire awe, and cause us to exercise caution. Believing that discretion was the better part of valor, we camped right there on that pile of rocks, fearing that, although our boats would ride the waves in safety, we might be caught in one of these rolls, just at the head of a rapid, and, unable to stop, be carried over the rapid with the additional force of the rushing breakers.

A NIGHT WATCH, AND A SMOKE

There was no place to haul our boats out, only the little pile of rock above water, and then the cliff, up a crack of which we could climb some twenty feet and find room for our beds. We made our camp and had an early supper. It was not safe to leave the boats, as we were afraid the River might rise higher and a sudden rush of water carry them off, and they, being tied to a pile of rough rocks, were liable to chafe holes in their sides against the rocks, so I determined to stay up all night, if it were necessary, and watch them. Hogue volunteered to sit up with me. Hogue was the youngest member of the party and was one of the kindest hearted and most sympathetic boys I had ever known. He could boil rice better than a Chinaman, fry bacon, and make mush to perfection, but of his coffee and biscuits— well, we devoured them, there was nothing else to do. Hogue certainly touched my heart that lonely night, with his cheerful companionship, as we sat around our small campfire, going by turns every few minutes down to the River to watch the boats. We sat opposite each other in silence, looking into the fire, wearing out the night and the flood. We had nothing new to talk about, and not a pinch of tobacco to smoke—all our smoking tobacco had been gone for a week—there was plenty of chewing tobacco, but neither of us used it. About seven o'clock, all the rest being sound asleep, and after the excitement of the day, we both nodded, when, shaking myself to keep from going to sleep, a corner of my memory seemed to open up, and I said to Hogue that I thought I remembered putting an eight ounce package of smoking tobacco in the bottom of my war sack. He fairly jumped into the air and started headlong for the River, and as he went over the cliff, I expected to hear him drop into the water, he was so anxious to reach the boats. I heard no splash, and in a minute he appeared above the wall with my war sack upon his back. It was soon opened, and at the very bottom was found the sack of dry clean tobacco. It was *only Durham,* but it was worth its weight in gold. We gave three cheers—but we gave them in a whisper; we did not want to wake the rest of the men, there was not enough to go around, and that night we were both completely selfish. I got out my pipe, and Hogue his cigarette papers; when they were lit they never went out, nor did the Sweet incense cease to rise over the walls of the Great Canyon for seven continuous hours. It was a joy that I never before, nor have I since, experienced from the soothing and cheering effects of my Lady Nicotine.

By one o'clock in the morning the River had fallen a foot. We watched an hour longer and then pulled the bows of our boats up on a little exposed sand bar where they were safe, went to bed, and as soon as we had pulled the blankets around our shoulders were sound asleep.

A JOURNEY FULL OF THRILLS

The next morning, February 26th, after an early breakfast, we started on what proved afterward to be the wildest, most daring, and exciting ride we had on the River. The Canyon so narrow, the turns quick and sharp, the current rushing first on one side and then on the other, forming whirlpools, eddies, and chutes, our boats caught first in one and then in the other, now spun round like leaves in the wind, then shot far to the right or left almost against the walls, now caught by a mighty roll and first carried to the top of the great waves, and then dropped into the "trough of the sea" with a force almost sufficient to take away one's breath, gave us new sensations. Many times we narrowly escaped being carried over the rapids before we could examine them, making exciting and sudden landings by pulling close to shore, and, with bow upstream, rowing hard to partially check our speed, while one man jumped with a line to a ledge of rocks, and held on for his life and ours too. At last we round a sharp turn and see a roaring, foaming rapid below, and as we come in full view of it, we are caught in a mighty roll of flood waves, we try to pull out to an eddy—it is all in vain, we cannot cross such a current, we must go down over the rapid. In trying to pull out, our boats are turned quartering with the current, and in this position we go, over the rollers and through the breakers of the flood, up to the head of the real rapid.

When we find we must go over the rapid, with great effort we straighten the boats round and enter in good shape, bow on. It lasts but a moment. The crosscurrent strikes us, and we go broadside over the worst part of the rapid. Crouched down in the bottom, it is as much as we can do to keep from being tossed out as the boats roll from wave to wave, but we have learned to know there is no danger of upsetting. The boats are entirely unmanageable, and, as we strike the whirlpools below, we are spun round like tops; but finally, at the end of the rapid, our sturdy boats float into an eddy as quietly and gracefully as swans.

During the day we ran twenty-five of these rushing rapids without a single portage, for the water was high enough to cover up all the rocks.

The lower part of this narrow inner gorge is more benched in form than that just below the Kanab. The two cross sections here given show the form of the Canyon as it appears, looking up and down from a point a short distance above Rapid No. 350.

LOOKING UP.   LOOKING DOWN.

16. Profile sketches of the canyon looking upstream and downstream a short distance above Rapid 350

About eleven o'clock we reached more open country. For ten
miles down to the Great Volcano, the Canyon, with the wide
River, and broad, high talus slopes and receding bench walls,
is more like that above the Kanab, though the inner gorge is not
so wide.

. . . two miles above Cataract Creek . . . . The coloring of the
walls is not so bright, not so scarlet, as the marbles and sandstones in the upper section of the Canyon, but here the artistic
blending of the subdued reds and browns resembled the coloring of oriental rugs and tapestries, which added a soothing effect
to the grandeur of the benched cliffs as they towered thousands
of feet above our heads. We learned, a little later, the cause of
this change in color.

At the mouth of Cataract Creek, we stopped for photographs
and regretted we could not go up the side canyon and visit the
Havasupai Indians who have lived so long in that canyon, well
back from the main River, where Padre Garces visited a hundred
and fourteen years before, to instruct them in religion, and where
John D. Lee, after the Mountain Meadow massacre, took refuge
and taught them new methods of irrigation.

THE COUNTRY OF THE VOLCANOES

Late in the afternoon we entered that most weird and ghastly section, where centuries upon centuries ago—who knows how many?—the volcanoes changed the face of the whole country, and some of them, on the brink of the Canyon, poured their streams of boiling lava over the walls, filling the great Canyon hundreds of feet in depth with solid basalt, through which the River cut its channel a second time. That the Canyon was as deep then—so many centuries ago—as now, is shown by the fact that the basaltic walls, left standing, are resting on beds of gravel, the beaches of the River in those ancient times, and on the same level as the present River bed.

The appearance of the whole country changes a short distance above the first great volcano. From there, for a distance of some thirty-five miles, everything has been torn and rended. The solid cliffs of marble which once stood up so grandly are now in shreds. The former pinnacles and spires have tumbled and gone. Great faults are seen, where mountains have dropped into the bowels of the earth and toppled over as they fell. The whole country looks but the sad and awful reminder of its former greatness. We found standing in the River, however, only one of the many lava monuments described by Major Powell in his Report.

Some four or five miles below where we first entered between the basalt walls, we came to Rapid No. 364—the "Lava Falls"— formed at the foot of the volcano from which the lava came, and by the fault which here crosses the Canyon and on whose edge the volcano stands. This is the great "Hurricane Fault."

In the journey of 1869, the lava deposits, in this part of the Canyon, seem to have impressed Major Powell more than any one thing he saw. In his original diary, while but a few lines, and in some places only one or two, suffice to record his impressions of a whole day's run, on reaching the lava he writes two or more pages describing the basaltic deposits, their origin and effects, and in his first published Report he enlarges upon his original notes, in such a clear description that I take the liberty of copying it here, as far better than my own original notes:

August 25.—We make twelve miles this morning, when we come to monuments of lava, standing in the river; low rocks, mostly, but some of them shafts more than a hundred feet high. Going on down, three or four miles, we find them increasing in number. Great quantities of cooled lava and many cinder cones are seen on either side; and then we come to an abrupt cataract. Just over the fall, on the right wall, a cinder cone, or extinct volcano, with a well defined crater, stands on the very brink of the canyon. This, doubtless, is the one we saw two or three days ago. From this volcano vast floods of lava have been poured down into the river, and a stream of the molten rock has run up the canyon, three or four miles, and down, we know not how far. Just where it poured over the canyon wall is the fall. The whole north side, as far as we can see, is lined with the black basalt, and high up on the opposite wall are patches of the same material, resting on the benches, and filling old alcoves and caves, giving to the wall a spotted appearance.

The rocks are broken in two, along a line which here crosses the river, and the beds, which we have seen coming down the canyon for the last thirty miles, have dropped 800 feet, on the lower side of the line, forming what geologists call a fault. [This was the "Hurricane Fault."] The volcanic cone stands directly over the fissure thus formed. On the side of the river opposite, mammoth springs burst out of this crevice, one or two hundred feet above the river, pouring in a stream quite equal in volume to the Colorado Chiquito. . . .

We have no difficulty as we float along, and I am able to observe the wonderful phenomena connected with this flood of lava. The canyon was doubtless filled to a height of twelve or fifteen hundred feet, perhaps by more than one flood. This would dam the water back; and in cutting through this great lava bed, a new channel has been formed, sometimes on one side, sometimes on the other. The cooled lava, being of firmer texture than the rocks of which the walls are composed, remains in some places; in others a narrow channel has been cut, leaving a line of basalt on either side. It is possible that the lava cooled faster on the sides against the walls, and that the centre ran out; but of this we can only conjecture. There are other places, where almost the whole of the lava is gone, patches of it only being seen where it has caught on the walls. As we float down, we can see that it ran out into side canyons. In some places this basalt has a fine, columnar structure, often in concentric prisms, and masses of these concentric columns have coalesced. In some places, when the flow occurred, the canyon was probably at about the same depth as it is now, for we can see where the basalt has rolled out on the sands, and, what seems curious to me, the sands are not melted or metamorphosed to any appreciable extent. In places the bed of the river is of sandstone or limestone, in other places of lava, showing that it has all been cut out again where the sandstones and limestones appear; but there is a little yet left where the bed is of lava.

What a conflict of water and fire there must have been here! Just imagine a river of molten rock, running down into a river of melted snow. What a seething and boiling of the waters; what clouds of steam rolled into the heavens![4]

BELOW THE LAVA FALLS

The next morning, February 27th., we awoke to find the weather had cleared in the night and turned extremely cold. It was the coldest morning we had felt. As we were obliged to portage our supplies and boats over the Lava Falls, it was necessary to wait till the sun came up—or rather, down—into the Canyon to keep from freezing at the work. Hislop set fire to the dry reeds of the swamp on the bank, formed by the immense springs which flowed in from the fault on the left, and the whole Canyon was filled with smoke, as dense, if not as awful, as when the volcanoes first broke out. This smoke kept us till noon before we could take the photographs.

The Lava Falls had a drop of eighteen to twenty feet, and a length to the main rapid of some three hundred feet. . . . This Lava Falls, for three hundred feet, has a steeper grade than any

4 Powell, *Exploration of the Colorado River,* 94–95. Brackets by Stanton.

like distance on the whole River. It is at the rate of three hundred and fifty-two feet per mile.

We portaged our boats over the fall, and supplies to the foot of the rapid, and after lunch we pushed on as fast as we could, only stopping for notes and photographs, and ran seventeen more rapids that afternoon without a portage.

We had now been on our journey for three months, and our provisions were getting low. We had had no meat or sugar for two weeks, and—greatest privation of all—we had smoked up all our tobacco. We were all anxious to reach Diamond Creek, where we expected to get new supplies from the railroad at Peach Springs. We were up early and worked late. Rapids were thick and some of them heavy; but we dashed on and into the breakers without stopping, for the water was still high and the channels were clear, and all we could suffer was to get a wetting, and this we did at almost every run.

The weather, in this more open part of the Canyon, was colder than we had experienced during the winter. In the early morning, when covered completely by the spray of the breakers as we shot through them, we became encased in a thin sheet of ice. Surveying and photographing under such circumstances were a little out of the regular order, for the first operation before seting up a transit, or exposing a negative, was to build a fire and thaw the ice off the instruments. However, we made rapid progress, and during the last *two and a half days* from the Lava Falls on, we portaged over the head of one great rapid and ran *seventy-two others*.

Some of the scenes in this wider section are not surpassed in beauty by any on the River. The black, purple, and blue tints of the lava walls, next to the River as it flows in perfect stillness in the long, quiet stretches between the rapids, with the gentler slopes above covered with green grass and flowers, and the great barrel cactus, and the long wands of the ocotillo swaying in the breeze, with their beautiful blossoms of yellow, pink, and red, and above these the delicately tinted walls in soft reds, pinks, drabs and browns, with the little benches brightened with the green of the sage and greasewood in the distance, conical mountains carved into every imaginable fantastic form higher up still, and here and there the craters of extinct volcanoes, cinder cones and flows of lava, made pictures which it is to be regretted that the camera . . . could only catch their form, without recording the beauty of their perfect coloring.

WE REACH DIAMOND CREEK

Saturday, March 1st., we were up early, determined, if possible, to have our Sunday rest at Diamond Creek, for there we expected to go out to the railroad, at Peach Springs, for mail and supplies.

We were pretty well worn out and tired of living on graham mush and coffee three times a day. Graham mush is good, even without salt, and it is nourishing also, but it becomes rather monotonous, with only coffee added to mush for breakfast, fried mush for lunch, and more mush for supper, for a week at a time. Except for our survey notes and photographs, we would have put an end to this in a few hours—it took us, however, the whole day.

Early in the afternoon of that day, we stopped at what we supposed was Diamond Creek, from the form, description, and topography on the Geological Survey map we had, and spent some time trying to find the road to Peach Springs, but all in vain. Starting again, about five miles below I stopped to examine a rapid. On a sandy beach, in a part of the Canyon as much like the mouth of Diamond Creek shown on the map as a straight line is like a mule's hind leg,[5] I was surprised to see marked in the

[5] "Some years after, the Government Topographer told me the notes of the Geological survey of that portion of the River, made in 1873, were all lost, and this part of the map was evolved from his treacherous memory in the office at Washington."—Stanton.

sand "R.M.S.," in large letters. I called the men, they jumped ashore and ran up the creek with a cheer, tossing their hats in the air, for we had found the road—it was Diamond Creek at last. We soon found a more convincing proof—the footprint made by a dainty little *woman's boot*—and one of the men, I shall not give his name, fell down and kissed it, and we went into our camp No. 95.

Sunday morning came, and Kane and I walked to Peach Springs at the railroad, twenty-four and one-half miles distant, three thousand feet above the River, and found a great quantity of mail and one of Fred Harvey's eating houses. I left the rest of the men at the River, for, as we had been on short rations for a week, I feared for the men, as well as Fred Harvey's stock of provisions. By night I had sent, and the men had received at the River, a quarter of fresh beef, a case of eggs, a tub of butter, and all sorts of vegetables and other supplies, and by the time they did come up, they were all full (of grub) and in a good humor.

Kane and I did not leave camp at the River until late Sunday morning. We took a lunch of fried mush in our pockets, and, I suppose, we enjoyed it somewhere on the road. We reached the railroad station in the early part of the afternoon and satisfied ourselves with some good smoking tobacco—at least it was good to us, since we, except Hogue and I a week before, had had no tobacco for two weeks. We waited patiently, while we read our mail, for Fred Harvey's evening meal. When it came, I do not remember ever to have tasted anything quite so good. One dish in particular I recall. We had not tasted potatoes since leaving Lee's Ferry. After helping us numerous times, the waiter took in the situation, went out to the kitchen, and brought in a large granite iron dish, in which had been browned in the oven the mashed potatoes left from noon. This was being saved for the "help," but they resigned their claim and set it down before us. Each of had already ordered and eaten two good-sized dinners, but, when we got through, that two quart pan hardly needed washing, we had scraped it so clean.

During our long wait for supplies and photograph material, Hislop and his men, after a vacation at Peach Springs, continued the railroad survey on the River, above and below Diamond Creek, completely repaired the boats, and made everything ready for the continuing of our journey. And here it was that I received that cheering telegram from Denver, that my efforts at photography had not been a failure.

We were detained at Peach Springs for ten days, waiting for more photograph material, and the only bad news we received was the sad announcement of the death of Gibson's father, in New York, on February 20th., which was a most severe blow to Gibson, but, at the suggestion of his friends at home, he remained with the party and finished the journey to the end.

As their boat was lost, it was decided best to let Twining, Brown, and Hogue return to Denver. There were thus left only seven of the original party who completed the whole journey through the Grand Canyon and on to the Gulf of California. Besides myself, there were Hislop, Travers, Gibson, Edwards, Kane, and Ballard. A new cook was engaged at Peach Springs—George Melick—but his record on the River was only from Diamond Creek to the Gulf.

THE LOWER GRANITE GORGE

A few miles above Diamond Creek begins the second Granite Gorge. It extends for some thirty-five miles and is almost identical in form with that at the upper end of the Canyon, except that the buttresses on the sloping walls are higher and more bold, and the short, perpendicular granite cliffs are more frequent.

On the morning of March 12th., we were again on the River to complete the remaining fifty-three miles of the Grand Canyon. This granite section, like that above, proved the most difficult to navigate. The water, though not having so much force for miles at a time as that above, is in places confined between such narrow walls, is concentrated into such steep and powerful rapids and falls, its dashing current is torn up by so many more and more powerful whirlpools, sucks and eddies, that it seemed, although we had escaped the damages of the upper River, these few remaining rapids would vanquish our little fleet and our whole party. For there were rapids and falls where there was no choice left but to dash through them. It was physically impossible to portage around them with our heavy boats; they had to be run or the expedition stopped by abandoning the river.

On the first day's run, boat No. 2 narrowly escaped complete wreck against the cliff at the side of the rapid we were running. That day and the morning of the next were passed in running a succession of sharp and heavy rapids, with many lighter ones interspersed. All of these, though clear of rocks, were full of heavy waves, which seemed to take delight in dashing their foaming crests over us, keeping us wet from morning till night.

March 13th. brought one or two experiences that have impressed upon my mind the fact that in running the rapids of the Grand Canyon, at least one hundred times we rode at full speed into the head of a rapid, with no knowledge that we would come out alive at the foot, and with the chances largely against it.

The skill of the steersman and the faithfulness of the oarsmen were factors in the case, but there were other factors that no human mind could foresee, nor human skill avoid. Rapid No. 450 was exceedingly heavy and rough on account of the high water and the fact that there was a very large and high rock in the channel on the right, and one in the center, both of which must be avoided. *Around the larger* rock the whole of the current was drawn with terrific force. To miss them both, it was necessary to run close to the right hand rock so as not to let its rebounding wave dash the boat against the rock in the center, and then, just before passing the first, to swing *the stern* of the boat in towards the rock, so as to throw the boat out and keep

207

from being drawn around and into the whirlpool behind the rock, which always exists under such conditions. The steersman, Hislop, planned his work right, but he got a little too close to the first rock. At the critical moment, either under-estimating his strength or over-estimating the power of the wave, he forced the stern of the boat *against the rock* until it struck, which had the effect of turning the bow in exactly the wrong direction, and we started to plunge, bow down, into the vortex of the whirlpool, which looked from where I sat, on the bow seat, fully ten feet deep. But just as I expected to have the boat upended over me into that whirling pit, thanks to a kind Providence, or the total depravity of the raging River, a half-dozen waves came from as many different directions and, lashing each other and our boat, *filled the gaping vortex,* rose high in the air, and we went through in safety, though with a shaking-up that felt as if it would tear every timber in the boat to pieces.

THE DIFFICULT TASK OF THE OARSMEN

To sit, as I did, in the bow of the first boat, or to sit as the steersman did, and face such dangers was one thing, but to my mind the greater nerve belonged to the oarsmen—Gibson, Kane, Edwards, and Ballard—for it was their duty to row into every rapid without being able to see where they were going. Kane was the bow oarsman in my boat, and we sat back to back, and whenever he gave an extra-heavy stroke, or I suddenly dodged a wave that was about to hit me in the mouth (a favorite spot to them, it seemed), our backs bumped together, so that I was more familiar with his actions, under such circumstances, than any-one's else. From that day to this I have never heard a band play or a street urchin whistle that rag-time tune "McGinty"—the fellow who went to the bottom of the sea—unless I hear, *see, and feel* the sensations of running the rapids of the Grand Canyon; for all through that long winter, Kane never rowed into a rapid

without either whistling or singing that same "McGinty," changing the time and the pitch of his music (?) to suit the gentleness
or violence of the particular rapid we were running. Never once
in the whole journey did Kane turn his head to see into what
sort of terrors we were going, but kept up his rhythmic stroke,
only broken when a cross wave caught his oar, or a side wave
dashed the boat against a rock. On this 13th. day of March—a
memorable day for all of us—one rapid—No. 457—caused a
break, though it was but for a moment, in Kane's musical career!

This rapid was a peculiar one, in fact it was hardly a rapid at
all. The whole current of the River was running down a smooth,
straight rock channel, free from boulders, but forming long,
smooth rolling waves without breakers, which measured from
their crests to the "trough of the sea," were perhaps twelve or
fifteen feet high. The greater depth of the wave was not above
the normal level of the stream, but below it.

The conditions here described can be seen on a very small
scale in any steep, smooth gutter in a city after a heavy rain. A
string of little, smooth rolling waves go down the center, one-
third of their height rising above, and two-thirds of the depth
being below the strips of *unbroken level water on either side,*
which is *apparently* standing still. Multiply this hundreds of
times, and you will have our rapid No. 457 on the Colorado
River.

The strips of apparently *unmoved water* were thirty or forty
feet—they may have been more—wide on either side. The great,
rolling waves were some sixty or eighty feet wide across the
River—not very long, but steep in the direction they were rolling, and rose six or more feet above the still water on the sides
and sank below it so deep that when the boat was in the "trough
of the sea," the level water *stood* five to six feet above our heads
on either side.

The only way to run this chute was to go over the highest and
into the deepest waves in the center of the current. It was a charming and exhilarating ride, now to be carried up *above the level*

of the River, and then to be dropped *below it,* and see two great *walls of water* to the right and left far above our heads. In his usual way, Kane rowed into this rapid without looking round to see where he was going and began his accustomed song. He had for the third time bewailed the ruining of McGinty's best Sunday clothes when we rose on the highest wave and began the descent into the unknown depths. As we went down the incline and sank still farther down, with the stern of the boat high up before him, Kane saw the two walls of water rise above his head on either side and stopped for once his song, but only for a moment, and exclaimed: "My God, will we never get to the bottom of this?" He never lost the stroke of his oars, and, as we rose up on the next wave, he told us for the five thousandth time on the journey how McGinty went to the bottom of the sea, dressed in his best Sunday clothes. Is it surprising then, that hearing, even now, that rag-time tune brings back those memories, and that I *feel over again* the sensations of the dash through the rapids?

CHAPTER ELEVEN

I would not choose to have the stream of life
From first to last all calm and rippleless,
For broken waters sing a lovely song,
And valor grows on obstacles o'ercome.

—AUTHOR UNKNOWN

ABOUT three o'clock in the afternoon of this same 13th. of March—thirteen, as I have said, was my lucky number —we came to Rapid No. 465 in a part of the gorge where two streams enter directly opposite each other.[1] The boulders have washed into and down the River, forming three dams across it. These make three drops, or falls, in the one great rapid, that in all has a fall of perhaps thirty feet. On the right side is a Vertical cliff, fifty to eighty feet high, extending two-thirds of the length on the rapid. On the left side is a Vertical wall of 300 to 400 feet or more in height, and extending the whole length of the rapid. The current, turned from the right side by the large number of boulders from that creek, after passing over the first fall, dashes against the left cliff just at the head of the second fall, and is thrown back with awful force, and, as it meets the current from the right, hurls up in angry waves breaking into foam fifteen to twenty feet high, first from one side and then from the other. From this the whole current is thrown against the right wall, as it curves out into the stream, just at the head of the third fall.

We climbed up on the right or lower cliff and carefully looked it over. It took but a few moments to see that there was no way to get our boats or supplies around this rapid. It must be run. There was not a moment's hesitation. Every man went back to the boats and jumped in. We were soon ready for the plunge. For the first time on the expedition I took my notebook from

[1] "This is the famous rapid, where the three men—the Howlands and Dunn —left Major Powell's first party. It . . . is known as 'Separation Rapid.' "—Stanton.

212

my pocket and put it inside my inner shirt and buttoned it up tight and retied my cork jacket, for I seemed to feel that something unusual was going to happen.

In a moment we were at the head of the first fall, over or through a half dozen huge waves, and approaching the second fall. As I looked down into that pit of fury, I wondered if it were possible for our boats to go through it and come out whole and right side up. I had no time for a second thought. We were in the midst of the breakers. They lashed us first one side and then the other, breaking far above our heads, and half filled our boat. For a second we were blinded with the dashing, muddy waters. In another we were through and out, and right side up. I turned to look to see if all the men were safe. They were all in their places; but our boat, though right side up, had been turned quartering with the current, and we were being carried with fearful force toward the right cliff. Every instant I expected to be dashed against the cliff ahead, where the whole current of water was piled up in one boiling mass against the solid wall; but, just as I thought the last moment had come, our sturdy Scotch helmsman, Hislop, gave the boat a sudden turn, and, assisted by the rebounding wave, we went by the cliff, and I shouted to the men: "That's good! that's good! We are past!" But the words were hardly out of my mouth when, as we rounded the point into the third fall, our boat, thrown in by a huge side wave, and though checked in its speed, crashed into a rock that projected from the shore, and she stopped. We were all thrown forward. The boat filled with water, sank upon the rock, and stuck fast. Wave after wave in quick succession rolled over us. I tried to straighten myself up, when a great wave struck me in the back, and I was washed clean out of the boat into the whirlpool below the rock. For an instant I knew nothing; but, as I was drawn down, my consciousness returned, as I felt a cold streak around my head—the waters closing over me—and as I was carried by that whirlpool, down, down, down, I wondered if I should ever reach the bottom of the River. The time seemed an age. The

River seemed bottomless. In a few moments I was caught as by two forces—one around my legs, and another around my back—and, twisting in opposite directions; they sent me whirling away, and I was shot to the surface fifty feet (I am told) down the rapid from where I went in.

I caught my breath just in time to be carried under the next big wave—coming out again in the lighter waves at the lower end of the rapid. Thanks to my cork jacket, I floated high above the water, but was carried along through the swiftest of the current.

The second boat fared better than ours. She came over the falls much in the same way, but not being turned round in the second fall, she kept her course better, and, although she only missed our stranded boat about two feet as she passed, came through without a scratch. She was caught in the eddy at the foot of the third fall, but finally came down, stern foremost, and soon overtook me at the end of the rapid; and Edwards and the cook jerked me into the second boat as mercilessly as I had been dashed from the first.

When the "Bonnie Jean" stuck fast on the rock, Hislop jumped across about ten feet of water on to the broken down foot of the cliff and ran down the shore to try to give us some assistance. But the broken rocks were so rough he could make only slow progress. The second boat had overtaken me, and we had landed before he caught up with us. Kane and Gibson remained in the first boat, and, in a very few minutes, an extra-heavy swell lifted it off the rock into the current, and although full of water, with only the gunwales exposed, she could not sink. The two men sat up to their waists in the water, paddled her safely through the lower part of the rapid and to shore where the rest of us were waiting for them. We pulled the damaged boat out and found she had a hole in her side, eighteen by ten inches, the sharp rock having cut out the ribs, as well as the planking, as clean as if done with a broad axe. In about an hour's time we had put on a temporary copper patch with copper nails and pitch, and starting again in search of wood, ran another roaring, tumbling rapid and went into camp late, with plenty of wood and a pile of granite boulders to sleep upon. Every man was wet from head to foot, and almost every blanket soaked. We had a hot supper and sat around a glorious campfire and smoked many pipes of tobacco—they were comforting—and at last, wrapping ourselves in our wet blankets, lay down for the night.

This rapid, our No. 465, ... was the one where Major Powell's men, the Howland Brothers and Dunn, left him in 1869. ... I was exceedingly sorry that I did not then take a number of photographs of this noted and historic place, but the incidents and accidents of the day put all such thoughts for the time out of my mind. ...

A LAST GREAT RAPID

It was late the next morning, March 14th., when we were ready to leave our camp. Sleeping in well soaked blankets made us all a little weary at first, but we soon got used to such comforts, and it was well we did, for, as it turned out, we were doomed to this same luxury every night, save Sunday, to the end of the Canyon part of our trip. The River was still high, and it was impossible to keep the waves in many of the rapids from filling our boats and soaking everything that was not in the rubber sacks.

Shortly before ten o'clock we plunged into a heavy rapid—No. 467—whose waves swept over us many times, and by noon we had passed nine more without stopping except for notes and photographs. Since leaving Diamond Creek, we had run thirty-nine rapids without a single portage, and a number of them the most powerful on the river, not excepting the "Sockdologer."

At noon we stopped for lunch. I find in my note book the following record: "at 12:05 [P.M.] land on left bank at head of rapid No. 477/ This to me is the most dreadful [looking] rapid we have met/ it does *look* like destruction to attempt to run it and it is two days work to get round it any other way—[We]

215

will cross river and look at it after lunch. . . . On left . . . is real perp[endicular] cliff 1,000 ft hi[gh] but on right good sloping granite/"[2]

After lunch we crossed the River. It seemed almost impossible to line the boats down on that side on account of the rocks in the channel, although there was good walking all the way past the rapid. It was decided to let them over the fall, at the mouth of the creek on the left, portage the supplies that far, and then run the rest. In the channel were many rocks exposed even at the high stage of water, and one great angular rock in the left center of the River, and between it and the vertical wall on the left was a narrow but straight channel, in which all the force of the water was concentrated, and through this the boats must go. As the cook and I could be of no service in handling the boats, I decided to remain on the right bank and complete my notes and photographs while the crews lined the boats over the fall and ran the lower part of the rapid. It was not till near four o'clock that the boats started. The skill of the steersmen had grown with experience, and it was a grand sight to see them shoot by the great rock and, with one sweep of the long oar, turn down the shifting, lashing current so close to the high wall that it seemed impossible not to strike it, and as they rose and fell over wave after wave, and shot through their foaming crests, part of the time out of sight in the muddy waters, I saw what I had so often *felt*—that the boats were veritable "water ponies," as the Indians called them, as they reared and *bucked,* truly as things of life in a mad race, literally touching only the high places, till they reached the quiet waters below.

The boats being reloaded, all hands once more embarked.

Three more rapids brought us, by five o'clock, to the most difficult point to construct a railroad on the whole route, considering the short distance of the perpendicular wall on the right side—the railroad side of our survey. It was a real perpendicular wall—400 feet long and 300 feet high, in a very narrow part of

2 Entry for March 14, 1890, Field Notes, Book D.

the gorge, and on a gentle curve to the right, composed of solid, compact rock. To pass it with a tunnel on a cord of the circle would require a long and very expensive work. Hence, the only way would seem to be to use a halftunnel or gallery cut in the solid wall. This was the first instance of such a necessity that we had found, except a few short points in the sandstone in Glen Canyon. After photographing this difficult cliff, we skipped through Rapid No. 481 and camped for the night—to again enjoy our good, wet blankets.

During the night of the 14th., the River fell somewhere between four and six feet, but it was still high, and the remaining thirty-nine rapids were easily run without a single portage. Thus, from Diamond Creek to the end of the Grand Canyon, we portaged over *the head of one rapid* and ran eighty-two others in a little over four days. Late Saturday afternoon we made our Sunday camp only a few miles above the Grand Wash cliffs.

HOW SUCH A JOURNEY AFFECTS DIFFERENT MEN

While we take our well earned Sunday's rest, it may be interesting to note the effect that such a journey has upon different men, surrounded by so many dangers and cut off from the outside world. Wild explorations and journeys through the wilderness usually develop a reckless, devil-may-care spirit that is not true bravery. It requires a different kind of courage to continue, day after day, the facing of death in the rapids of the River, in the bowels of the earth, and at the same time the possibility of starvation, *without being able to retreat.* Such conditions affect different men in different ways. I have already related in my story the true bravery of the men of our first party who would not desert their posts, even though they had nothing to eat except crumbs of bread, while there was plenty a little distance down the River, and the nerve of the boatmen, who rowed so often into the worst of the rapids without seeing where they were going.

The one man who seemed never to be affected by anything that happened was John Hislop. Whether it was his Scotch nature that looked upon everything as "not half bad," or whether he was incapable of any anxiety or fear, I know not—that is, anxiety or fear for himself. For others he had a kindly care and thoughtfulness, shown in a hundred ways. In Rapid No. 465, when he saw me dashed from the stranded boat and sink in the whirlpool below, he went wild with excitement, screamed to the other men: "Look at Mr. Stanton," and seizing Gibson by the wrist, nearly broke his arm as he raised it and stood for a moment paralyzed in fear, when he suddenly leaped from the boat, over the waves, to the ragged shore in the hope of being able to help me. With this exception, on the whole journey he was as joyous and light-hearted as a child, thoroughly enjoying the wildness, the danger, and privations of the trip.

As for myself, I have already recorded where twice in Cataract Canyon and once in the Grand Canyon—the latter when I expected the boat to topple over on top of me from the rock on which it was caught—I am free to acknowledge I keenly feared the consequences I thought would surely follow. During the whole time, I felt the responsibility for the safety of my men, when directing them in any dangerous work, and it often comes back to me, how I, with my own hands, pushed the boat from shore that carried Hansbrough and Richards to their sudden death. On the other hand, the dash into the great rapids, particularly the one where I came near losing my life, was made with a joy of anticipation that it is a pleasure, even to this day, to remember. That part of the work never affected me, and when I lay down at night I had hardly pulled the blankets over me till I was sound asleep, and I slept peacefully until the morning.

To others it was different. Reginald Travers showed perhaps the greatest pluck and daring of any one of the men, in the face of every danger or misfortune he encountered; and yet he told me that, when he lay down at night, the realization of the whole situation came over him in such a way that he trembled with fear, sometimes for a half hour, before he could go to sleep. When morning came, he was again himself—a mass of nerve, bravery, and pluck—and ready, with a light heart, to face all the Cataracts and Devils that a dozen Grand Canyons could produce.

Another kind of real bravery was that of young L. G. Brown, who died a few months after leaving the River. A more willing, ready, conscientious young fellow I never knew. But he told me that from the first rapid he ran, in Glen Canyon, to the last one above Diamond Creek, at which place he left the party, he never got into the boat at the head of a rapid but what he was completely frightened—and yet he never shirked or drew back from a danger, and did his whole duty in every way with a determination and true grit that deserve unstinted praise.

TO THE END OF THE GRAND CANYON

From the end of the granite to the Grand Wash Cliffs, the Canyon is but a repetition of the lower end of Marble Canyon. The granite and sandstone have sunk below the River, and the great talus slopes, below the limestones and marbles, stretch down to the water's edge with large flats covered with bushes and trees.

In one section, for about ten miles, it differs. Numerous springs gush out at every possible position and height above the River, some dropping over cliffs and precipices in pure white foaming cascades, others trickling down in little streams through acres of green moss and ferns and a hundred varieties of wild flowers; while others, gushing out near the River's edge in torrents of boiling water, form pictures of beauty and life, in marked contrast with the barren and frowning granite walls only a short distance up the River. These springs coming from the limestone cliffs have deposited their carbonate of lime over the whole face of the exposed rock walls, and small pieces of rock, falling down, have been embedded in and covered with the lime coating, thus forming a covering like a rough, white stucco on both sides of the Canyon, through which the streams from the springs run in polished channels down the sloping cliffs, giving the impression of solid white (sloping) walls, different from anything in the whole five hundred and more miles of canyons on the Colorado.

From the great volcano on down the Canyon for many miles, the bright, flaming colors of the upper sandstones and marbles are gone, and the whole coloring is of a duller red and brown; but, in this lowest section, some little of the scarlet and flashing beauty has returned. The noble marble cliffs, rising from the top of the talus slopes, are cut by many side canyons and streams, so that they stand up in mountains almost overhanging the River.

One would think, after traveling through five hundred miles of these canyons, one would be satiated with beauty and grandeur, but in this fact lies the charm—of the five hundred miles no two miles are alike. The picture is ever-changing from grandeur to beauty, from beauty to sublimity, from the dark and frowning greatness of its granite walls to the dazzling colors of its upper cliffs, and from the roaring, tumbling waters of its cataracts to the peaceful stillness of its great lakes. I stood, in the last few miles of the Grand Canyon, spellbound in wonder and admiration, as firmly as I was fixed in the first few miles, in surprise and astonishment.

Our last Sunday in the Canyon was truly a day of rest. After a week of the hardest and most exciting work, wet from morning till night, with nothing but well-soaked blankets every night for a bed, it certainly was a pleasure to spread our beds, our clothes, and ourselves out in the sun and do nothing.

At 9:15 A. M., March 17th., 1890, we emerged from the Grand Canyon into an open country and onto a peaceful, quiet River. What a change! What a relief! What a joy! Our task virtually accomplished, our dangers all left behind, and now (humanly speaking) a certainty, which we never felt before, of once more seeing our families and dear ones at home! With our camp that night beside a quiet and gently flowing River, with not a sound to disturb, it is no wonder that we went to sleep with thankful hearts and overslept ourselves in the morning.

THE JOURNEY TO THE GULF

I had looked forward to the journey from the Grand Wash to the Gulf, a distance of some five hundred miles, as of quiet and uninteresting monotony. How I was mistaken! The broad and fertile valleys and sloping hillsides, only awaiting the hand of man, the irrigating ditch and a market, to turn them into lovely homes, and rich-producing farms; the Boulder, the Black and Mojave, and other short Canyons, rivaling in beauty some of the larger canyons above; the great Cottonwood, Mojave, and Colorado Valleys, with their miles upon miles of rich level plains and gently sloping hills, bounded on every side by the curious and intricate fringe of the Opal, the Black, the Dead, and the Needle Mountains, formed a panorama of beauty and surprise that was charming and instructive in the extreme.[3]

We stopped for our Sunday camp at Fort Mojave, then occupied by Company A, 9th. U.S. Infantry, and were royally entertained by Captain A. H. Bowman, the commandant, and Lieutenants M. L. Hersey and A. I. Moriarty. I regret exceedingly that it has not been my fortune, since that day, to meet Captain Bowman (I hope when I do I may be able to call him General) and thank him for a courtesy that I did not know of for some time after. On arrival, I asked Captain Bowman if we could get a piece of fresh beef for our Sunday dinner. He promised to find us a roast, if possible. When he sent us next morning, with his compliments by a messenger, a perfect tenderloin roast, we were, of

---

[3] "For a most delightful and fascinating description of the lower Colorado, from the Gulf to the Black Canyon, see Ives, *Report upon the Colorado River*."— Stanton.

course, thankful, but did not know till afterwards that he had taken his own Sunday dinner from his storeroom and gone without himself, because there was no more fresh beef in camp.

Postscript: My hope and wish have been realized. On the evening of January 26th, 1917, I had the honor and pleasure of calling on General A. H. Bowman at his home in Washington City. After twenty-seven years, to see his kind face once more was a joy; but to hear, from his good wife, that, only a few days before, he had been inquiring about me, was a compliment that I did not expect, but certainly did appreciate. After his long service, since I first met him, in caring for the Mojave Indians, of Arizona—with brotherly kindness, yet firm discipline; his military service in the Spanish War in Cuba and in the Philippines, and, as Governor of one of the Islands, helping to build up the manhood of the Philippinos [*sic*], may the Good General's last years be many, and each one as bright and joyous as he made my first visit to him at Fort Mojave, in March, 1890.

We remained some days at the Needles and celebrated our successful journey by a special banquet, furnished by Fred Harvey, in his inimitable style. With a clearance in official form for our little fleet from the Custom House at Yuma, we entered the Republic of Mexico, and on the 26th. day of April reached tide water, with our two little boats, at the head of the Gulf of California, where, three hundred and fifty years before, Alarcón had ordered Nicholas Zamorano and Domingo del Castillo to row their two little shallops—the first white men to enter the mouth of the River.

Here we left our boats, and to me it was a sad parting. Noble little craft, the "Bonnie Jean" and the "Lilly"! They had carried us and our stores a thousand miles and more, had gracefully danced over the waves, the torrents, and the cataracts of this, the wildest River of the world, *and never once been upset.*

And their gallant crews! It is enough to say that they never met a danger or difficulty, but what they were as ready to enter it, as they were quick to conquer.

We rested a day, and then, accepting the courtesy and four mule teams of Senor Andrades, returned overland to Yuma, and on April 30th., the party was disbanded.

THE RESULTS OF THE SURVEY

It has already been explained that for 355 miles a continuous, regular, preliminary survey was made, and that the balance of the work was an instrumental reconnaissance, with a total actual survey of six hundred miles. In addition to the tabulated figures given in [Table 1, page 226] . . . only a short statement will be required to show clearly the final results of our work.

The Grand Canyon has been pronounced "by far the most sublime of earthly spectacles," and at the same time it has been declared impracticable, and almost impossible, to build a railroad through it, unless the roadbed was hung on brackets on the side of the perpendicular cliffs. I think it has already been shown that neither of these statements has any direct bearing upon the question of a railroad route or upon the facts of the case as related thereto. The immensity of the chasm has no (railroad) connection with the lower two hundred feet of its walls, and the perpendicular cliffs for "much of the way" do not exist.

The two hundred or more miles of survey, from the Little Colorado to the Grand Wash, are divided into seven distinct sections,—[4]

First: The fourteen or fifteen miles above the first narrow gorge, taken as a whole, is quite a wide valley in which all classes of work exist, from earth to cliff bench work.

Second: The 35½ miles of granite (mostly black gneiss) following, is the first real canyon portion of the great gorge. Unlike other well known canyons in the Rocky Mountains through

[4] "It must be remembered that no final *location* survey was made, and that the general results given here are only intended as approximations for the purpose of comparison."—Stanton.

which railways have been built—the Royal Gorge or the Arkansas and Clear Creek Canyon—here the walls generally slope back in ragged, irregular slopes, 300 to 1,200 feet in height, at an angle of from a few degrees to forty-five degrees from vertical, with small patches jutting out into the River, forming buttresses and towers along the general slope of the walls. Above the Bright Angel the rock is massive and hard, while below it is softer and much broken up. In this distance were noted four short tunnels, aggregating one-half mile.

In the third section of 35½ miles, from the granite to Kanab Canyon, the softer strata of sandstones and limestones have come down to the River, and from great talus slopes and inclined benches of stratified rock, rising 300 to 600 feet, at a general angle of about forty degrees from vertical. There are points of cliff that come near the River, but the whole distance is easy construction as mountain railroads go.

Fourth: For twenty-one miles below Kanab Canyon is found the narrowest and deepest part of the *inner* gorge. At the bottom it is generally only 150 to 200 feet wide, and the River runs between vertical walls, but vertical only for from 80 to 100 feet up. Above this the walls are benched, and for nineteen miles there is a continuous bench some twenty or thirty feet above high water and running almost parallel with the river grade, . . . thirty to eighty feet wide, and well adapted for a railroad grade by tunneling some short, sharp points.

Fifth: In the next section, of 54½ miles, which reaches to the second granite, a number of points must be noted. In that distance there are thirty-seven miles of "hillside slopes" and nearly fifteen miles of heavy "talus slopes." In fact—from a railroad standpoint—it is a misnomer to call this section a canyon at all; it is a valley, broad, in places flat, with gently sloping hillsides. In places are found bold points of basalt, from the old volcanoes, which in a few points would require very heavy work.

Sixth: The lower granite—about thirty-nine miles—is almost a repetition of the upper granite gorge. In its first half the buttresses that jut out over the slopes are bolder and more numerous, and the granite is more compact and solid. The second half is shattered and broken, and has much flatter slopes. . . . One of the most formidable points of granite encountered by the railroad line . . . is on a slight curve and a long bend of the River, and there seemed no other economical way of passing this point except by half tunneling—this would be about one-half mile in length.

Seventh: From the lower granite to the end of the Grand Canyon "the walls" consist almost altogether of softer limestone covered with loose debris, practically a repetition of the lower end of Marble Canyon.

[Table 1 page 226] . . . [shows] more in detail the classification of the work. To sum the whole subject up in percentages, our preliminary survey and reconnaissance showed that in the Canyon Division of 630 miles from Grand Junction, Colorado, to the end of the Grand Canyon, there was

62½ per cent of comparatively light work earth, loose rock, and talus slopes of loose and stratified solid rock.

35½ per cent of heavy, solid rock and cliff bench work, and sloping granite walls.

2 per cent of tunneling and half tunneling; or, if the shorter line is used in Glen Canyon, this tunneling increases to 3 per cent.

100 Total

In the Lower or Valley Division of 408 miles to the Gulf there was
75 per cent of earth and gravel work.

24½ per cent of tunneling.

0½ per cent of tunneling.

100 Total

To anyone who has a knowledge of railroad construction through the mountain region of our western country, these figures, together with the facts and illustration given of operated railways through other canyons, tell the whole story. The line as proposed is neither impossible or impracticable, and as com-

TABLE 1*

GENERAL TABLE OF CLASSIFICATION IN MILES†

Divisions	Level bottoms—earth and gravel slopes—"earthwork"	Hillside slopes, E. and L.R.	Rough talus slopes of L.R. and S.R., and boulders	Smooth, solid rock slopes	Cliff bench work—sandstone and marble	High cliff work—not vertical	Sloping and heavy granite walls	Heavy through rock cuts	Heavy embankment in river	Rock bluffs in lower canyons	Tunnels	High vertical cliffs and half tunnels	Totals
Grand River	36.323	19.273	61.035	6.206			13.040				4.110		139.987
Cataract and Narrow Canyons	11.543	5.436	14.545	2.557	19.110				.739		.284		54.214
Glen Canyon	57.270	10.928	55.926	21.284				.501	6.553		4.118		156.580
Marble Canyon	.500		26.510		32.250			.125	.750		2.375		62.510
Grand Canyon	51.050		43.750	1.250	30.600	3.000	85.925		.200		.875	.500	217.150
To Rio Virgin	26.500								.250	10.750			37.500
To Las Vegas Wash	16.500									11.500	.500		28.500
To Needles	67.750									27.750	1.000		96.500
To end of Survey, near Gulf	197.255									47.500			244.755
Totals	413.641	86.687	201.766	31.297	81.960	3.000	98.965	.626	8.492	97.500	13.262	.500	1 037.696
If the long tunnel line in Glen Canyon is used—Totals	403.947	86.232	191.359	27.825	81.960	3.000	98.965	.570	7.356	97.500	20.002	.500	1 019.216

* The table is taken from Stanton, "The River and the Canyon," II, Appendix B, 823. Stanton employs these abbreviations: "E." for earth; "L.R." for loose rock; and "S.R." for solid rock.

† "In critically examining these figures, the reader, and especially engineers, must bear in mind that a final *location* survey was not made, and the results given here are only close approximations, and comparisons of possible alternative lines and are not intended, or claimed, as absolutely correct in detail."—Stanton.

pared with some other transcontinental railroads, could be built for a reasonable cost. From an operating standpoint, it would have many advantages in grades, distance, and permanency of its roadbed, and, through the driest section of the western country, have an unlimited supply of water, and it would be possible to operate 1,000 miles of its line, yes, the whole of it, by electricity generated by the power of the river tumbling down beside its tracks.

One point must not be forgotten. The objection raised, of great cost of crossing the large number of side canyons, is answered by the fact that they would be crossed almost always at an elevation of from 50 to 100 feet above their beds, where, at their mouths, they cut through solid rock; so that side canyons, which are from three to six miles wide on top in many instances, would be crossed with a single span bridge of 100 feet in length.

The final questions—Would it pay?— and would there be any business other than passenger traffic?—are outside the scope of this volume. They were somewhat discussed in my paper already referred to before the American Society of Civil Engineers, with, I think, a fairly good showing for the road. But again, as already stated, conditions and the business of the transcontinental railroads have changed since that time, for and against such a project, and I shall not enter into a discussion of this phase of the subject at all.

The examination was for the purpose of deciding the *practicability* of the River line; our actual survey was confined to that, ending our examination at the Gulf. But that was not intended to be the terminus of the road. Its immediate terminus, if ever built, was to be San Diego, California, with connections, of course, farther north.

Accidents: 46, 49–50, 51, 52–53, 54, 55–
56, 59, 144, 154–56, 161–62; *see also*
Frank M. Brown, George W. Gibson,
Peter M. Hansbrough, F. A. Nims,
Henry C. Richards, Robert Brewster
Stanton
Alarcón, Hernando de: *xi*, 222
Alpha Delta Phi: 76, 99
Amador Canal and Mining Company:
34
Andrades, Señor: 223
Arizona Territory: *xiii*, *xvi*, 20n., 23, 73,
74, 104
Ashley, William H.: *xi–xii*
Atcheson, Topeka and Santa Fe Rail-
road: 23–24
Atlantic and Pacific Railroad: *xiv–xv*,
21, 22, 23
Aubrey Valley: 20n.

Badger Creek: 76, 112
Ballard, H. G.: 96, 119, 125, 154, 173,
206, 208
Barnabee, Henry Clay: 133, 133n.
Beardsley, Mrs. M. H.: 37
Beaumont and Fletcher, quoted: 110
Best, James S.: 48, 48n.
Big Sandy Creek: *xii*
Black Canyon: 220n., 221
Black Canyon of the Gunnison: 18–19
Black Mountains: 221
Blaine, James G.: 27
Blake, Utah: *see* Green River Station,
Utah

Blickensderfer, Jacob: 21–23, 34
Boats: 30, 33, 35–38, 48, 52, 67–68, 72,
95, 95n., 99, 129–30, 154–56; *see also
individual names of boats*
Bonnie Jean (boat): 96, 161, 162, 172–
73, 177, 182, 192, 214, 222
Boulder Canyon: 221
Bow Knot Bend: 40, 41, 41n.
Bowdoin College, Brunswick, Maine: 34
Bowman, A. H.: 221, 222
Brahma Temple: 169–70
Bright Angel Creek: 5, 158–60, 224
British Columbia: 22
Brown, Frank M.: *xiii*, *xv*, *xvi*, 7–8, 11,
14n., 26–28, 30, 33, 34, 36, 37, 38, 45,
49, 50–51, 54, 57, 59, 60, 62, 69, 71,
72, 75, 84, 85, 87, 92, 94, 96–97n., 112;
biography, 34–35; fatal accident, 76–
81, 89
Brown, L. G.: *xvii*, 96, 96–97n., 125,
128, 173, 206, 219
Brown, Mary (Mrs. Frank M. Brown):
34, 37, 59, 76
Brown, Mason (son of Frank M.
Brown): 34, 37, 76
Brown, Ward (son of Frank M.
Brown): 34, 37, 76
Brown Betty (boat): 38, 39, 50
Bush, William H.: 36, 49, 50, 53, 59, 71,
75, 107

California: *xiii*, 20n., 27; legislature, 34
Canadian Pacific Railroad: 18–19
Cárdenas, García López de: *xi*

Cataract Canyon: *xvi*, 12, 38, 45, 46, 47–55, 56, 62, 63, 65, 67, 67n., 69, 71, 72, 96, 98, 102, 148, 218, 226

Cataract Creek: 199

Cattle and cattlemen: *xiii*, 25–26

Cedar City, Utah: *xi*

Chamberlin, H. B.: *xiv*, 94n.

Chillicothe, Ohio: *xiv*

Cisco Pump House, Colorado: 31, 33n.

Clear Creek Canyon: 18–19, 224

Coal: *xiii*

Coe, Edward: 36, 47, 49, 57, 68

Colorado: *xiii*, 26, 27

Colorado (boat): 37, 49, 50, 54

Colorado Chiquito: *see* Little Colorado River

Colorado Grand Canyon Mining and Improvement Company: 48n.; *see also* James S. Best

Colorado River: *xv*, 23, 24–25, 26, 37, 38, 61, 72–74, 98, 103, 116, 124; exploration, *xi–xii*, 18, 67, 67n.; history, *xvii*; sea waves, 194–96, 195n.; valley, 221

Cook, Joseph: 155

Coronado, Francisco: *xi*

Cottonwood Valley: 221

Crescent Creek: 98; Canyon, 98, 99

Crossing of the Fathers: *xi*, 74, 74n.

Dandy Crossing, Utah: 50–51, 57, 60, 62, 68, 69, 71, 72, 74n., 75, 98, 104

Danville Theological Seminary, Kentucky: *xiv*

Dead Mountains: 221

Del Castillo, Domingo: 222

Dellenbaugh, Frederick S., quoted: 11, 102

Denver (boat): 37, 39

Denver, Colorado: *xvi*, 8, 26, 27, 30, 32, 34, 36, 71, 92, 94, 95, 98, 122, 129, 146, 206

Denver, Colorado Canyon and Pacific Railroad: 48, 123, 138–39; history of, *xii–xiv*, *xv–xvii*, *xviii*, 7–8, 23–28; engineering feasibility of, 14–19; commercial value of, 19; route of, 30; start of survey expedition for, 36–37; retreat from survey for, 90–92; start of second survey expedition for, 94ff., 98–101; results of survey for, 223–227

Denver and Rio Grande Railroad: *xvi*, 18, 30, 31, 33

Deva Temple: 169–70

Devil's Anger: 39

Devil's Gate Viaduct: *see* Georgetown Loop

Diamond Creek: 10, 100, 115, 203, 204, 205, 206, 215, 216, 219

Díaz, Melchior: *xi*

Dirty Devil River: 72, 98; valley, 43

Domínguez, Francisco: *xi*

Duchesne River: *xii*

Dunn, Bill: 102, 211n., 215

Dutton, Clarence E., quoted: 5, 183

Echo Canyon: 82

Edwards, W. H.: 96, 119, 125, 155–56, 173, 206, 208, 214

El Vado de los Padres: see Crossing of the Fathers

Emma Dean (boat): 34

Equipment and supplies: 38–39, 46, 50–51, 54, 68–69, 72, 95–96, 95n., 99–101, 131, 162, 206; *see also* boats, photography, food

Escalante, Francisco de: *xi*, 74

Escalante Creek: 74–75, 74n.

Farwell Consolidated Mining Company: 34

Flagstaff, Arizona: 146

Food: 40, 51, 54–55, 57–58, 60, 66–67, 68–69, 75, 108–109, 204, 205, 221

Fort Mojave: 221, 222

Fraser River: 18–19

Fred Harvey restaurants: 205, 222

Fur trappers: *xi–xii*

Garcés, Padre: 199

Geology and geological formations: 41–42, 73, 90, 134, 135, 138, 141–42, 147n., 148, 152, 158–59, 171, 184–85, 190, 200–202, 203, 219–20, 223–27

Georgetown, Colorado: *xv*

Georgetown Loop: *xv*, 22

Gibson, Charles Dana: 96–97n.

Gibson, Charles De Wolf, letter to Langdon Gibson: 123–24

Gibson, George W.: 36, 40, 54, 59, 60, 61, 65, 66, 67, 72, 80, 81, 84, 86, 87, 96, 96–97n.; accident, 46

Gibson, Langdon: 96–97n., 118, 122, 173, 193, 206, 208, 214, 218; quoted, 123–28

Ginty, John, and son: 104

Glen Canyon: *xvi, xvii,* 15, 52, 71, 72–75, 74n., 75, 76, 93, 98, 101–107, 104n., 217, 219, 225, 226

Glenwood Springs, Colorado: 18

Grand Canyon: *xi, xiv, xvi,* 4, 5–6, 7, 8, 10, 14–15, 18, 19, 20n., 45n., 48, 71, 97, 102, 103, 104, 134, 137, 140–217, 218, 220, 223, 225, 226; described, 141–43, 144

Grand Canyon National Park: *xii*

Grand Junction, Colorado: *xv,* 30, 31, 69, 225

Grand River (Colorado River): *xv, xvi,* 18–19, 30–32, 37, 40, 41–42, 226

Grand Wash: 217, 219, 221, 223

Granite Gorge: 147–48, 158–59, 206

Graves Valley: 98; description, 43

Great Volcano: 199

Green River: *xi, xii, xv, xvi,* 30, 31, 32, 37, 38, 39, 40, 41–42, 48, 62

Green River Station, Utah: *xvi,* 32, 36, 40, 41, 98

Green River Station, Wyoming: *xii*

Gulf of California: *xi, xiii, xvii,* 11, 30, 69, 87, 94, 106, 116, 123, 206, 220n., 221, 222, 225, 226, 227

Hance Creek: 150

Hance Rapid: 150–51

Hance's Trail: 150; *see also* Hance Creek

Hanksville, Utah: 98

Hansbrough, Peter M.: *xvi,* 36, 53, 57, 61, 68, 72, 77–78, 79, 81, 92, 132, 218; fatal accident, 85–87; *see also* Point Hansbrough

Harper, S. S.: *xiii,* 7, 23–27, 35–36, 94n.

Harriman, Edward H., quoted: 4

Henry, T. C.: 94n.

Hersey, M. L.: 221

Hislop, John: 36, 47, 49, 50, 53, 56, 57, 60, 61, 64, 65, 67, 69, 72, 80, 81, 83, 89, 90, 96, 97, 112, 119, 120, 125, 152, 166–72, 173, 175, 177, 178, 182–83, 186, 188, 194, 202, 206, 208, 213, 214, 218; tribute to, 9

Hite, Cass: 62

Hogue, James S.: *xvii,* 10n., 96, 106, 114, 115, 154, 175, 196–97, 205, 206

Hoskaninni, gold mining: 104n.

Hotel El Tovar: 152

House Rock Valley: 89, 91

Howard, G. E.: 36, 40, 47, 54, 59, 68

Howland, Oramel: 102, 211n., 215

Howland, Seneca: 102, 211n., 215

Hughes, J. N.: 34, 36, 45, 49, 50–51, 53, 54, 57, 59, 72, 76

Huntington, Al.: 108

Hurlbert, John: *xiv*

Hurricane Fault: 200, 201

Idaho Territory: *xv*

Indian Territory: *xiv–xv*

Irrigation: *xiii,* 27

Ives, Joseph C.: *xii,* 20n., 25, 27

Jackson, W. H.: 117

Jensen, Utah: *xi*

Johnson, Utah: 91

Johnson, W. D.: 92

Johnson, Warren M.: 75, 76, 108, 111, 121, 125

Julien, Denis: *xii,* 67, 67n.

Kaibab Plateau: 5, 169, 170

Kanab, Utah: 75, 92, 102, 162
Kanab Canyon: 102, 103, 149, 181, 184, 188,, 190–91, 198, 199, 224
Kanab Wash: *xii*
Kane, Elmer: 96, 118, 119, 161, 166–72, 173, 177, 179, 193, 194, 205, 206, 208–10, 214
Kansas City, Missouri: 24
Kendrick, Frank C.: *xv, xvi;* survey, 30–33, 33n., 37, 45
Kentucky Central Railroad: *xv*
Kingman, Louis, quoted: 8
Kolb, Ellsworth L.: 176n
Kolb, Emory C.: *xii,* 176n.
Kwangunt Valley: 134

Labyrinth Canyon: 40, 41–43
Lake Mead: *xii*
Land of the Standing Rock: 42, 43n.
Lantier, Felix: 146
Las Vegas Wash: 226
Lava Falls: 200, 202–203
Leadville, Colorado: 26
Lee, John D.: 108, 199
Lees Ferry, Arizona: *xvi,* 24, 45n., 71, 72, 74n., 75, 90, 105, 107–109, 112, 120, 121, 122, 125, 129, 131, 138, 205
Lily (Lilly) (boat): 130, 147, 162, 173, 176, 177, 183, 222
Little Colorado River: 103, 131, 132, 134, 137, 138, 139, 195n., 201, 223
Little Grand River Valley: 31
Lodore Canyon: 48, 148
Lumbering: *xiii*

McDonald, Harry: *xvi,* 10, 72, 77, 78, 80, 81, 83, 86, 87, 89, 95, 96, 115, 118, 120, 125, 126, 152, 155–56, 162–63, 173; quoted, 78–79
Manitou Springs, Colorado: 123
Marble Canyon: *xvi,* 8, 61, 71, 72, 76–89, 91, 94, 103, 110, 111–39, 141, 219, 225, 226
Marble Pier: 129
Marie (boat): 129, 154–56, 161–62

Marriger, Bishop Lawrence C.: 92
Mary (boat): 37, 47, 51, 54, 59
Mason (boat): 37
Melick, George: 206, 214
Mesken, Edward: 107
Mexico: 22, 222
Miami University, Oxford, Ohio: *xiv,* 19–20
Milford, Utah: 92
Millecrag Bend: 69
Mining and prospecting: *xiii,* 23, 104n.
Moab, Utah: 31
Mojave Canyon: 221
Mojave Valley: 221
Monterey, California: *xi*
Montgomery, J. C.: *xiv*
Moriarty, A. I.: 221
Mormon Crossing: 74n.
Mormons: 25, 31, 74, 92, 122
Mountain Meadows Massacre: 108, 199
Mountain men: *xi*

Nan-co-weap River: 133, 134
Narrow Canyon: *xvi,* 52, 68, 69, 72, 226
Narrow Gorge: 144
Needle Mountains: 221
Needles, California: 71, 222, 226
New Mexico: 23
New Orleans, Louisiana: *xiv*
Newspapers: 10, 10n., 129, 129n.; see also *Republican, Rocky Mountain News,* and *Times*
Nims, F. A.: *xvi,* 36, 49, 66, 72, 80, 81, 85, 96; accident, 114–29

Oakland College, Mississippi: *xiv*
Opal Mountains: 221
Osiris Temple: 169, 170, 170n.

Pacific Coast: *viii,* 24, 26, 28
Palmer William J.: 20n.
Paria Creek: 75, 111
Patch, Sam: 116, 116n.
Peach Springs, Arizona: 117, 146, 203, 205, 206

Photography: 11, 101, 114, 116–17, 146, 174–75, 176n., 194, 203, 206
Pierce, John: 26, 27
Pierce City, Missouri: 21
Pikes Peak: 123
Plutarch, quoted: 29
Point Hansbrough: 132, 133, 134, 138
Point Retreat: 90, 130–31, 132, 133, 138
Point Sublime: 184
Potter, C. W.: 36, 49, 54, 57, 61, 65, 66, 67
Powell, John Wesley: 25, 33, 35, 39, 40, 41, 43n., 88, 104, 111, 141, 144, 149, 153, 161, 200, 211n., 215; expedition of, xii, xiii, xiv, xv, xviii, 11, 16, 20, 26, 28, 40–41, 48, 48n., 102; quoted, 6, 13, 42, 63, 67–68, 141–43, 143–44, 200–202, 150, 150n., 161n.
Powell's Plateau: 184
Prehistoric sites: 73–74, 74–75, 90, 106–107

Raymond Rossiter W.: 141n.; quoted, 140
Red Canyon: 150
Republican (Denver): 10, 10n., 129n.
Reynolds, Ethan A.: xiv, 34, 36, 45n., 49, 50–51, 54, 57, 72, 76; quoted, 45, 53
Richards, Henry C.: xvi, 36, 61, 65, 66, 72, 77, 78, 79, 80, 81, 92, 218; accident, 46; fatal accident, 85–87
Rigney, T. P.: 30, 36, 49, 50, 57, 71
Río Virgin: xii, 226
Rocky Mountain News (Denver): 10, 10n., 129n.
Rocky Mountain region: 16–18, 24, 28, 32, 88, 123, 147, 223
Royal Gorge of the Arkansas: 18–19, 224

St. Louis, Missouri: xi, 21, 23
San Diego, California: xiii, xvii, 21, 30, 227
San Francisco, California: 21
San Francisco Mountains: 23, 180
San Juan River: 106

San Rafael River: 32, 40, 41, 98
Santa Fe, New Mexico: xi
Sears, Alfred F.: 97
Shinumo Creek: 182
Shirley, James, quoted: 70
Shiva Temple: 169
Silver Plume, Colorado: xv
Soap Creek: 76
Soap Creek Rapid: 76, 77, 112
Sockdologer Rapid: 102, 153–56, 153n., 160, 215
Stanton, Jean Moore (Mrs. Robert Brewster Stanton): 9, 92, 129, 129n.
Stanton, Robert Brewster: 56–57, 104n., 196–97; expedition, xii, xvi, 45; biography of, xiv–xv, 19–20, 22–23, 36; "The River and the Canyon," xvii–xix; purpose and method of survey of, 3–4, 11–12, 39, 52–53, 68, 82–83, 112, 112n., 132n., 136–37n., 148–49, 223n.; effect of the river upon, 4–7; becomes expedition leader, 8–9; pays tribute to colleagues, 9–10, 20–21, 65–66, 217–19; Field Notes quoted, 12, 46, 49–51, 57–59, 77–81, 90, 99, 150, 177–78, 184, 215–16; survey preparations of, 33–34; running rapids, 47–48, 134–37, 151–52, 153–54, 157–58, 160–62, 173–75, 174n., 176–78, 181, 186–87, 191–94, 197–98, 206–208, 212–15; accident of, 55–56; canyon storm, 88–89, 90–91, 179–81; organizes second expedition, 94–96; qualifications of personnel, 97–98; becomes official photographer, 116–17, 120; side trip in Grand Canyon, 165–72
Stillwater Canyon: 40, 41–43
Stimpson, Mr.: 123
Sumner, Jack: 105, 105n.
Sutherland, George A.: 36, 50, 57
Sweet Marie (boat): 96

Taylor, S. W.: 91
Tehachapa Pass: 20n.
Terry, E. W.: 36, 49, 50, 51, 71

Texas: *xv*
Tickaboo mines: 62, 72
Times (Denver): 129, 129n.
Tourists: *xiii*, 5, 18–19
Tower of Ra: 168n.
Trachyte Creek: 69
Travers, Reginald: 96, 97–98, 119, 125, 128, 154, 155–56, 173, 178, 186–87, 192, 194, 206, 218–19
Trin-Alcove Bend: 40, 40n.
Twining, A. B.: *xvii*, 10n., 96, 119, 125, 144, 173, 183, 206

Ulloa, Francisco de: *xi*
Una, Colorado: *xi*
Union Pacific Railroad: *xv*, 20
Utah: *xvi*, 33, 62, 104
Utah Lake, Utah: *xi*

Vasey's Paradise: 88, 89, 130–31, 132

VT Cattle Ranch: 91

Ward (boat): 37, 49–50, 54, 59
Ward, Judge and Mrs. W. S.: 34
Water Lily (boat): 96
Waukegan, Illinois, boat builders: 33, 95, 99
Wellington, Arthur M.: 94–95; quoted, 2, 13, 15
Wheeler Brothers Cattle Ranch: 32
Whirlpool: *see* Devil's Anger
Williams, Jesse L.: 20
Winslow, Arizona: 129
Woodville, Mississippi: *xiv*
Wordsworth, William, quoted: 93, 189

Yuma, Arizona: *xvii*, 222–23

Zamorano, Nicholas: 222
Zoroaster Temple: 169–70

of which *Down the Colorado* is Number 45, was started in 1939 by the University of Oklahoma Press. It follows rather logically the Press's program of regional exploration. Behind the story of the gradual and inevitable recession of the American frontier lie the accounts of explorers, traders, and travelers, which individually and in the aggregate present one of the most romantic and fascinating chapters in the development of the American domain. The following list is complete as of the date of publication of this volume.

1. Captain Randolph B. Marcy and Captain George B. McClellan. *Adventure on Red River:* Report on the Exploration of the Headwaters of the Red River. Edited by Grant Foreman. Out of print.
2. Grant Foreman. *Marcy and the Gold Seekers:* The Journal of Captain R. B. Marcy, with an Account of the Gold Rush over the Southern Route. Out of print.
3. Pierre-Antoine Tabeau. *Tabeau's Narrative of Loisel's Expedition to the Upper Missouri.* Edited by Annie Heloise Abel. Translated from the French by Rose Abel Wright. Out of print.
4. Victor Tixier. *Tixier's Travels on the Osage Prairies.* Edited by John Francis McDermott. Translated from the French by Albert J. Salvan. Out of print.
5. Teodoro de Croix. *Teodoro de Croix and the Northern Frontier of New Spain, 1776–1783.* Translated from the Spanish and edited by Alfred Barnaby Thomas. Out of print.
6. A. W. Whipple. *A Pathfinder in the Southwest:* The Itinerary of Lieutenant A. W. Whipple During His Explorations for a Railway Route from Fort Smith to Los Angeles in the Years 1853 & 1854. Edited and annotated by Grant Foreman. Out of print.
7. Josiah Gregg. *Diary & Letters.* Two volumes. Edited by Maurice Garland Fulton. Introductions by Paul Horgan.
8. Washington Irving. *The Western Journals of Washington Irving.* Edited and annotated by John Francis McDermott. Out of print.
9. Edward Dumbauld. *Thomas Jefferson, American Tourist:* Being an Account of His Journeys in the United States of America, England, France, Italy, the Low Countries, and Germany.
10. Victor Wolfgang von Hagen. *Maya Explorer:* John Lloyd Stephens and the Lost Cities of Central America and Yucatán.

11. E. Merton Coulter. *Travels in the Confederate States:* A Bibliography.

12. W. Eugene Hollon. *The Lost Pathfinder:* Zebulon Montgomery Pike.

13. George Frederick Ruxton. *Ruxton of the Rockies.* Collected by Clyde and Mae Reed Porter. Edited by LeRoy R. Hafen. Out of print.

14. George Frederick Ruxton. *Life in the Far West.* Edited by LeRoy R. Hafen. Foreword by Mae Reed Porter.

15. Edward Harris. *Up the Missouri with Audubon:* The Journal of Edward Harris. Edited by John Francis McDermott.

16. Robert Stuart. *On the Oregon Trail:* Robert Stuart's Journey of Discovery (1812–1813). Edited by Kenneth A. Spaulding.

17. Josiah Gregg. *Commerce of the Prairies.* Edited by Max L. Moorhead.

18. John Treat Irving, Jr. *Indian Sketches.* Taken During an Expedition to the Pawnee Tribes (1833). Edited and annotated by John Francis McDermott.

19. Thomas D. Clark (ed.). *Travels in the Old South, 1527–1860:* A Bibliography. Three volumes. Volumes One and Two issued as a set (1956); Volume Three (1959).

20. Alexander Ross. *The Fur Hunters of the Far West.* Edited by Kenneth A. Spaulding.

21. William Bollaert. *William Bollaert's Texas.* Edited by W. Eugene Hollon and Ruth Lapham Butler. Out of print.

22. Daniel Ellis Conner. *Joseph Reddeford Walker and the Arizona Adventure.* Edited by Donald J. Berthrong and Odessa Davenport.

23. Matthew C. Field. *Prairie and Mountain Sketches.* Collected by Clyde and Mae Reed Porter. Edited by Kate L. Gregg and John Francis McDermott.

24. Ross Cox. *The Columbia River:* Scenes and Adventures During a Residence of Six Years on the Western Side of the Rocky Mountains Among Various Tribes of Indians Hitherto Unknown; Together with a Journey Across the American Continent. Edited by Edgar I. and Jane R. Stewart.

25. Noel M. Loomis. *The Texan—Santa Fé Pioneers.*

26. Charles Preuss. *Exploring with Frémont:* The Private Diaries of Charles Preuss, Cartographer for John C. Frémont on His First, Second, and Fourth Expeditions to the Far West. Translated and edited by Erwin G. and Elisabeth K. Gudde.
27. Jacob H. Schiel. *Journey Through the Rocky Mountains and the Humboldt Mountains to the Pacific Ocean.* Translated from the German and edited by Thomas N. Bonner.
28. Zenas Leonard. *Adventures of Zenas Leonard, Fur Trader.* Edited by John C. Ewers.
29. Matthew C. Field. *Matt Field on the Santa Fe Trail.* Collected by Clyde and Mae Reed Porter. Edited and with an introduction and notes by John E. Sunder.
30. James Knox Polk Miller. *The Road to Virginia City:* The Diary of James Knox Polk Miller. Edited by Andrew F. Rolle.
31. Benjamin Butler Harris. *The Gila Trail:* The Texas Argonauts and the California Gold Rush. Edited and annotated by Richard H. Dillon.
32. Lieutenant James H. Bradley. *The March of the Montana Column:* A prelude to the Custer Disaster. Edited by Edgar I. Stewart.
33. Heinrich Lienhard. *From St. Louis to Sutter's Fort, 1846.* Translated and edited by Erwin G. and Elisabeth K. Gudde.
34. Washington Irving. *The Adventures of Captain Bonneville.* Edited and with an introduction by Edgeley W. Todd.
35. Jean-Bernard Bossu. *Jean-Bernard Bossu's Travels in the Interior of North America, 1751–1762.* Translated and edited by Seymour Feiler.
36. Thomas D. Clark (ed.). *Travels in the New South, 1865–1955:* A Bibliography. Two volumes.
37. John Lloyd Stephens. *Incidents of Travel in Yucatán.* Edited and with an introduction by Victor Wolfgang von Hagen. Two volumes.
38. Richard A. Bartlett. *Great Surveys of the American West.*
39. Gloria Griffen Cline. *Exploring the Great Basin.*
40. Francisco de Miranda. *The New Democracy in America:* Travels of Francisco de Miranda in the United States, 1783–84. Translated by Judson P. Wood. Edited by John S. Ezell.

41. Col. Joseph K. F. Mansfield. *Mansfield on the Condition of the Western Forts, 1853–54*. Edited by Robert W. Frazer.
42. Louis Antoine de Bougainville. *Adventure in the Wilderness:* The American Journals of Louis Antoine de Bougainville, 1756–1760. Translated and edited by Edward P. Hamilton.
43. James H. Simpson. *Navaho Expedition:* Journal of a Military Reconnaissance from Santa Fe, New Mexico, to the Navaho Country Made in 1849. Edited by Frank McNitt.
44. Washington Irving. *Astoria; or, Anecdotes of an Enterprise Beyond the Rocky Mountains*. Edited and with an introduction by Edgeley W. Todd.
45. Robert Brewster Stanton. *Down the Colorado*. Edited and with an introduction by Dwight L. Smith.

Down the Colorado has been printed on paper bearing the water-mark of the University of Oklahoma Press, with an expected life of three hundred years. The type chosen for the text is machine-set Baskerville, with display letters in Eric Gill's distinguished Perpetua face.

UNIVERSITY OF OKLAHOMA PRESS

NORMAN